THE FOR KIDS ALMANAC 2008

with

FACT MONSTER™

D0462174

Beth Rowen

EDITOR

TIME FOR KIDS ALMANAC 2008 with FACT MONSTER™

PRODUCED BY DOWNTOWN BOOKWORKS
PRESIDENT: Julie Merberg
EDITOR AND PHOTO RESEARCHER: Sarah Parvis
ASSISTANT EDITOR AND PHOTO RESEARCHER: Kate Gibson
SPECIAL THANKS: Sara Newberry, Kerry Acker, Dinah Dunn

DESIGNED BY
Georgia Rucker Design

TIME INC. HOME ENTERTAINMENT
PUBLISHER: Richard Fraiman
GENERAL MANAGER: Steven Sandonato
EXECUTIVE DIRECTOR, MARKETING SERVICES:
Carol Pittard
DIRECTOR, RETAIL & SPECIAL SALES: Tom Mifsud
DIRECTOR, NEW PRODUCT DEVELOPMENT: Peter Harper
ASSISTANT DIRECTOR, BRAND MARKETING: Laura Adam
BOOK PRODUCTION MANAGER: Jonathan Polsky
DESIGN & PREPRESS MANAGER: Anne-Michelle Gallero
RETAIL MANAGER: Bozena Bannett
SPECIAL SALES MANAGER: Ilene Schreider
MARKETING MANAGER: Alexandra Bliss
SPECIAL THANKS: Glenn Buonocore, Suzanne Janso, Robert Marasco, Brooke McGuire, Mary Sarro-Waite, Adriana Tierno Alex Voznesenskiy
SPECIAL THANKS TO IMAGING: Patrick Dugan, Eddie Matros, Neal Clayton

FACT MONSTER
EDITOR: Beth Rowen
CONTRIBUTORS: Christine Frantz, Shmuel Ross
FACT-CHECKING AND PROOFREADING:
Amy Fletcher, Shmuel Ross
INDEXING: Marilyn Rowland

TIME FOR KIDS
PUBLISHER, TIME FOR KIDS MEDIA GROUP:
John Stevenson
MANAGING EDITOR, TIME FOR KIDS MAGAZINE:
Martha Pickerill
EDITOR-IN-CHIEF, TIME LEARNING VENTURES:
Jonathan Rosenbloom
SENIOR EDITOR, TIME LEARNING VENTURES: Curtis Slepian
MAPS: Joe Lertola

ISSN: 1534-5718
ISBN 10: 1-933821-84-1
ISBN 13: 978-1-933821-84-9

We welcome your comments and suggestions about TIME For Kids Books. Please write to us at:
TIME For Kids Books
Attention: Book Editors
PO Box 11016
Des Moines, IA 50336-1016

If you would like to order any of our hardcover Collector's Edition books, please call us at 1-800-327-6388. (Monday through Friday, 7:00 a.m.– 8:00 p.m. or Saturday, 7:00 a.m.– 6:00 p.m. Central Time).

3

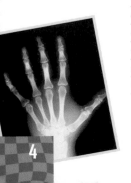

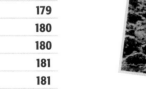

Contents

7

FROM
TFK
MAGAZINE

FOLLOW THE HERD

A new study of elephants' hair and travels
could help save the species

Lewis, a wild elephant in Kenya's Samburu National Reserve, spent his days as any elephant would—eating, roaming and hanging out with his friends and family. But by doing what comes naturally, Lewis could help save his species.

This tranquilized elephant has just been fitted with a GPS tracking collar.

Lewis was part of a study published in 2006 about efforts to help save elephants, which are endangered. Nature reserves in Africa and Asia aim to protect the animals by giving them a secure place to roam. But because elephants are large and eat so much, it's hard to find spaces that are big enough to hold them. Sometimes, they roam away into areas that are not safe.

"The conservation of elephants requires understanding how much space they need and why they need it," scientist Thure Cerling told TFK. Cerling teamed up with the Save the Elephants Foundation to study elephants, including Lewis, for two years on the Samburu reserve.

Collecting the Clues

A two-part method was used to find out what tempts elephants to wander out of their sanctuary. Save the Elephants fitted the animals with radio collars equipped with global positioning system (GPS) tracking devices. Researchers collected hair samples from the tails of 35 elephants. Analysis of the chemicals in the hair shows what each elephant ate over time. The team matched up the information

about movement and diet to reveal the story of the animals' daily life.

Of seven elephants tested, six had similar diets. But a foot-long hair from Lewis told a different tale. It showed that during the dry season, when grass in the sanctuary turned brown, Lewis ventured out of Samburu to eat tasty crops at a farm. To find this food, he walked for 15 hours. If Lewis had what he wanted inside of the sanctuary, he might not have left his protected habitat. Leaving was a risky move.

Scientists are now taking more hair samples and doing more studies. They hope to paint a more complete picture of elephant behavior and needs. Conservationists can then use this information to plan sanctuaries where elephants can feel at home.

–BY ANDREA DELBANCO

Did You Know?

A newborn elephant stands over 3 feet tall and weighs about 220 pounds.

Elephants are endangered. There are only 35,000 to 50,000 Asian and 300,000 to 600,000 African elephants left in the wild.

An elephant can use its trunk as a snorkel. The trunk stays above the water's surface, allowing the elephant to cross rivers and lakes.

Pet Ownership

Pet ownership reached its highest point in 2004, with 63% of U.S. households owning a furry—or scaly—friend. Here are some of the most popular pets in America.

ANIMAL	% OF U.S. HOUSEHOLDS OWNING A PET	NUMBER OF PETS IN THE U.S.
DOG	39%	74 million
CAT	34	91 million
FRESHWATER FISH	13	139 million
BIRD	6	17 million
SMALL ANIMAL	5	18 million
REPTILE	4	11 million

Source: American Pet Products Manufacturers Association

Animal Longevity

Here's a look at the longevity (life span) of certain animals.

ANIMAL	LONGEVITY (YEARS)
CAT	10–12
COW	9–12
DOG	10–12
HAMSTER	2
HORSE	20–25
KANGAROO	4–6
LION	10
PIG	10
PIGEON	10–12
RABBIT	6–8
WOLF	10–12

Source: James G. Doherty, general curator, Wildlife Conservation Society

Parakeet

Iguana

Top Pet Names

Did you know your furry friend was destined to be a "Smokey" the moment you looked at her? You're not alone. The American Society for the Prevention of Cruelty to Animals (ASPCA) conducted a survey to find out which pet names are most popular in the U.S. Here are the top ten.

1. Max
2. Sam
3. Lady
4. Bear
5. Smokey
6. Shadow
7. Kitty
8. Molly
9. Buddy
10. Brandy

TOP TEN DOG BREEDS

1. Labrador retriever
2. Golden retriever
3. German shepherd
4. Beagle
5. Dachshund
6. Yorkshire terrier
7. Boxer
8. Poodle
9. Chihuahua
10. Shih tzu

Source: The American Kennel Club

TOP TEN CAT BREEDS

1. Persian
2. Maine coon
3. Exotic
4. Siamese
5. Abyssinian
6. Oriental
7. Birman
8. American shorthair
9. Tonkinese
10. Burmese

Source: Cat Fanciers' Association

Animals

HYBRID ANIMALS

Ligers—the result of crossbreeding lions and tigers—have roamed animal preserves and sanctuaries for years. It wasn't until recently, however, that these intriguing animals gained wide fame—thanks in part to the film *Napoleon Dynamite*.

In one of his many memorable lines, Napoleon declared the liger "pretty much my favorite animal." He didn't mention the zorse, however, which is produced when a zebra and a horse mate.

LIGERS AND ZORSES, BUT NO PONKEY

Not all animals can be crossbred. You'll never see a ponkey (pig and monkey). In general, the two animals that are to be crossbred must belong to the same genus and share the same number of chromosomes. Chromosomes are threadlike strands that carry genetic information. The offspring of crossbred animals share traits from both parents. For example, the liger inherits a full mane from the lion and stripes from the tiger. Hybrid animals are usually born sterile; they cannot produce offspring.

Hybrid animals are definitely interesting to look at, but some scientists think cross-breeding species is a bad idea. Not all of these animals survive to adulthood, and they can be born with genetic defects. In addition, crossbreeding typically does not occur in nature, only in captivity. Here are some examples of crossbred animals:

Beefalo or cattalo: American bison and cow

Cama: camel and llama

Grolar or pizzly: grizzly bear and polar bear

Leopon: leopard and lion

Liger: male lion and female tiger

Mule: male donkey and female horse

Tigon: male tiger and female lion

Wolphin: false killer whale and dolphin

Yakalo: yak and buffalo

Zeedonk: zebra and donkey

LIGER

CAMA

BEEFALO

Did You Know?

Warm-blooded animals regulate their own body temperature; their bodies use energy to maintain a constant temperature. Mammals and birds are warm-blooded animals. Cold-blooded animals depend on their surroundings to establish their body temperature. Reptiles and amphibians are cold-blooded.

Animal Names

ANIMAL	MALE	FEMALE	YOUNG	GROUP NAME
bear	boar	sow	cub	sleuth, sloth
cat	tom	queen	kitten	clutter, clowder
cattle	bull	cow	calf	drove
chicken	rooster	hen	chick	brood, clutch
deer	buck	doe	fawn	herd, leash
dog	dog	bitch	pup	litter, pack
duck	drake	duck	duckling	brace, team
elephant	bull	cow	calf	herd
fox	dog	vixen	cub	leash, skulk
goose	gander	goose	gosling	flock, gaggle, skein
horse	stallion	mare	foal	pair, team
lion	lion	lioness	cub	pride
pig	boar	sow	piglet	litter
sheep	ram	ewe	lamb	drove, flock
swan	cob	pen	cygnet	bevy, wedge

EXTINCT, ENDANGERED AND THREATENED SPECIES

Many animal species are disappearing from our planet. In fact, more than 5,600 species of animals are in danger of extinction.

Humans are largely responsible for animals becoming extinct, endangered or threatened. Here are some of the things that can put animals at risk.

Brown bear

EXTINCT means the entire species has died out.

DESTRUCTION OF HABITAT

Humans destroy precious habitat—the natural environment of a living thing—when they fill swamps and marshes, dam rivers and cut down trees to build homes, roads and other structures or developments.

ENDANGERED animals are in immediate danger of becoming extinct.

THREATENED species are likely to become endangered in the future.

POLLUTION

Oil spills, acid rain and water pollution have been devastating for many species of fish and birds.

Success Stories

In 1973, the U.S. government passed the Endangered Species Act to save endangered species of animals and plants. Efforts have paid off, and several species of animals have been removed from the endangered list. They include the peregrine falcon, the red kangaroo, the Palau owl and the gray whale.

Peregrine falcon

Here is a list of some endangered animals.
Mammals: brown bear, jaguar, red wolf, snow leopard
Birds: golden parakeet, bald eagle, northern spotted owl
Fish: desert pupfish, chinook salmon, white sturgeon
Reptiles: Nile crocodile, Galápagos tortoise, Jamaican boa
Amphibians: Houston toad, Goliath toad

Chinook salmon

HUNTING AND FISHING

Many animals are overhunted because their meat, fur and other parts are very valuable.

INTRODUCTION OF EXOTIC SPECIES

When foreign animals or plants are introduced into a new habitat, they sometimes bring diseases that the native species can't fight. Exotic species, although able to prey on native species, often have no natural enemies.

Did You Know?

The Basilisk lizard of South and Central America is nicknamed the "Jesus Christ lizard" because when escaping predators, it runs so fast that it can run on top of water.

ANIMAL GROUPS

Crocodiles

Almost all animals belong to one of two groups, vertebrates or invertebrates.

VERTEBRATES

Adult vertebrates have a spinal column, or backbone, running the length of their body.

Reptiles breathe with lungs, have scaly skin and most lay eggs. Examples: turtles, crocodiles, snakes

Fish breathe through gills and most lay eggs (sharks give birth to live young, however). Examples: tuna, cod, halibut, salmon

Mammals breathe with lungs, nourish their young with mother's milk, most live on land (whales and dolphins are exceptions) and most give birth to live young (exceptions are the echidna and platypus, which are hatched from eggs). Examples: dogs, squirrels, tigers, humans

Birds have feathers, wings, lightweight bodies, lay eggs and most can fly (except the ostrich and penguin). Examples: owls, parrots, turkeys

Amphibians live on both land (breathing with lungs) and in water (breathing with gills) at different times of their lives. Examples: salamanders, frogs, caecilians

Northern spotted owl

INVERTEBRATES

Invertebrates do not have a backbone. There are many more invertebrates than vertebrates.

Sponges, the most primitive of all animal groups, live in water, are sessile (they stay in one place) and filter tiny organisms out of the water for food.

Sea urchin

Echinoderms live in seawater and have external skeletons. Examples: starfish, sea urchins, sea cucumbers

Worms live in many habitats, from the bottom of the ocean to the insides of other animals.

Mollusks are soft-bodied animals and some live in hard shells. Examples: snails, slugs, octopuses, oysters, clams, scallops

Arthropods have segmented bodies supported by a hard external skeleton (or exoskeleton). Examples: insects, arachnids (spiders and their relatives), crustaceans (shrimps and crabs)

Coelenterates take in food and get rid of waste through their mouths, which are surrounded by stinging tentacles. Examples: jellyfish, corals, sea anemones

Jellyfish

Tiger

ANIMAL HALL OF FAME

BIGGEST → → → →

Land mammal: **African elephants** weigh up to 16,500 pounds and can eat as much as 600 pounds of food a day!

Bird: The **ostrich** can grow to 9 feet tall and weigh as much as 350 pounds.

Fish: The **whale shark,** which is not a whale, reaches 46 feet in length and weighs up to 15 tons.

Reptile: The **saltwater crocodile** can grow to 23 feet long.

Insect: Giant **walking sticks** can grow to about 20 inches in length.

SMALLEST → → → →

Land mammal: The **bumblebee bat** tips the scales at about 2 grams and measures between 30 and 40 millimeters as an adult.

Bird: The **hummingbird** grows only to 2.5 inches long and weighs only 0.06 of an ounce.

Hummingbird

Fish: The *Paedocypris progenetica* measures just over 1/3 of an inch long.

Reptile: The **British Virgin Islands gecko** is about 3/4 of an inch long when fully grown.

Insect: **Fairyflies** are only about 1/5 of a millimeter long.

Anopheles mosquito

FASTEST → → → →

Land mammal: The **cheetah** can run as fast as 70 m.p.h.

Bird: The **peregrine falcon** dives at speeds of up to 200 m.p.h. and can fly at a rate of 90 m.p.h., making it not only the fastest bird but also the fastest animal. **Ostriches** can run as fast as 43 m.p.h.

Fish: The **Indo-Pacific sailfish** can swim at speeds of up to 68 m.p.h.

Reptile: The **spiny-tailed iguana** has clocked in at 21 m.p.h.

Insect: **Hawk moths** can reach a speed of about 33 m.p.h.

MEANEST → → → →

Land mammal: The **ratel,** or honey badger, is one of the fiercest, most predatory animals on the planet. It preys upon many animals, including scorpions, porcupines, tortoises, crocodiles and snakes. Attracted to honey, it also ravages beehives. Healthy ratels have no predators.

Bird: The **peregrine falcon,** an extremely aggressive hunter, preys on small mammals and other birds. It descends on its victims from the air at speeds of up to 200 m.p.h.

Fish: The **stonefish,** which lives at the bottom of the ocean, is the most poisonous fish in the world. Its 13 dorsal spines release deadly venom, making it dangerous to both humans and marine life.

Reptile: One bite from the **inland taipan** contains enough toxin to kill about 100 people.

Insect: The **anopheles mosquito** is the deadliest creature on Earth. It's responsible for more than 300 million cases of malaria each year and causes between one million and three million deaths.

Cheetahs

Fascinating Animal Facts

Albatross

→ Each zebra has its own stripe pattern, just as each person has his or her own fingerprint.

→ Some **dolphins**, **whales** and **bats** navigate and track prey using echolocation. This is a very advanced form of hearing that allows them to "see" their surroundings by listening to and analyzing the way sound reflects off objects in their environment.

→ **Starfish** that lose arms can grow new ones; sometimes an entire animal can grow from a single lost arm.

→ The **sea cucumber** squirts its insides out to defend itself from predators. (It then grows a new stomach.)

Starfish

→ **Amazon ants** steal the larvae of other ants to keep as slaves. The slave ants build homes for and feed the Amazon ants, who cannot do anything but fight. They depend completely on their slaves for survival.

→ Only female **mosquitoes** bite. Females need the protein from blood to produce their eggs.

→ The **giant tortoise** can live up to about 175 years. In fact, Harriet, a Galápagos tortoise and likely the world's oldest creature, died in Australia in June 2006. She was 176 years old!

→ **Horned lizards** can shoot blood from their eyes.

→ An **albatross** can sleep while it flies—even while cruising at 25 m.p.h.

→ **Hippopotamuses** are quick-footed giants. They can weigh up to 9,000 pounds and run up to 20 m.p.h.

→ **Kangaroos** can jump as far as 30 feet in one leap.

→ A **chameleon** can move its eyes in two directions at the same time.

Hippopotamus

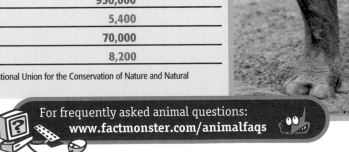

Big Numbers

No one knows for sure how many species of animals exist on Earth. In fact, some 10,000 species of animals are discovered each year. Most scientists agree, however, that there are more than one million species of animals. Here's a look at how that number breaks down.

ANIMAL GROUP	APPROXIMATE NUMBER OF SPECIES
Amphibians	6,000
Birds	10,000
Fish	29,000
Insects	950,000
Mammals	5,400
Mollusks	70,000
Reptiles	8,200

Source: The International Union for the Conservation of Nature and Natural

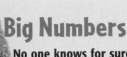

For frequently asked animal questions:
www.factmonster.com/animalfaqs

EXTREME DINOS

Dinosaur exhibit, Shanghai, China

LARGEST

Seismosaurus "quake lizard"
→ Cretaceous Period
→ It measured about 120 feet from head to tail and stood about 18 feet tall.

SMALLEST

Compsognathus "delicate jaw"
→ Jurassic Period
→ This tiny creature was about the size of a chicken and weighed about 6.5 pounds.

Compsognathus fossil

FASTEST

Ornithomimus "bird mimic"
→ Cretaceous Period
→ This dinosaur, which looked like an ostrich, could run about 40 to 50 m.p.h.

SMARTEST

Troödon "wounding tooth"
→ Cretaceous Period
→ *Troödon* had the largest brain-size-to-body-size ratio of all known dinosaurs. It's believed to have been as smart as modern-day birds.

MOST FAMOUS

Tyrannosaurus rex "tyrant lizard"
→ Cretaceous Period
→ T. rex ran the show during the Cretaceous Period and still dominates the popular imagination.

T. rex

Stegosaurus model, Calgary Zoo

DUMBEST

Stegosaurus "plated lizard"
→ Jurassic Period
→ This giant's brain was the size of a walnut. If the ratio of brain size to body size indicated intelligence (or lack of it!), then this 3-ton herbivore was definitely not a mental giant.

OLDEST

Eoraptor lunensis "dawn plunderer"
→ Triassic Period
→ *Eoraptor lunensis* lived about 227 million years ago.

MOST TEETH

Hadrosaurs "duck-billed lizards"
→ Cretaceous Period
→ Several of these plant eaters had about 960 cheek teeth.

LONGEST NECK

Mamenchisaurus "Mamenchi lizard"
→ Jurassic Period
→ The *Mamenchisaurus*'s neck was 33 feet long.

T. rex teeth were often the size of bananas.

BEST DEFENSE

Ankylosaurus "bent" or "crooked lizard"
→ Cretaceous Period
→ The *Ankylosaurus* was the most heavily armored dinosaur, with bony plates, studs and spikes lining its entire back—even its eyelids had spikes. In addition, its tail had a thick knob of bone at the end of it, which was probably used as a club against its enemies.

Did You Know?

Dinosaurs lived throughout the Mesozoic Era, which began 245 million years ago and lasted for 180 million years. It is sometimes called the Age of the Reptiles. The era is divided into three periods: Triassic (245 million to 208 million years ago), Jurassic (208 million to 146 million years ago) and the Cretaceous (146 million to 65 million years ago).

Animals

Art Movements

Two Sisters on the Terrace, Renoir

Palace of Versailles

Baroque

A form of art and architecture that was popular in Europe in the 17th and early 18th centuries, Baroque art was very ornate and dramatic. The Palace of Versailles near Paris is considered to be the greatest example of Baroque architecture. Peter Paul Rubens and Rembrandt were Baroque painters.

Romanticism

Romanticism was popular in the early 19th century. Romantic artists produced dreamlike, passionate works that portrayed an idealized world and nostalgia for the past. William Blake and Eugène Delacroix were members of the Romantic school of painters.

Impressionism

Impressionism developed in France during the late 19th century. The Impressionists tried to capture fleeting moments and moods with unmixed colors and broken brushstrokes in natural light. Claude Monet and Pierre-Auguste Renoir were Impressionist painters.

Post-impressionism

Popular in the late 19th century and early 20th century, Post-impressionist painters rebelled against the naturalistic quality of Impressionism and created emotional, personal works. Vincent Van Gogh and Paul Gauguin were Post-impressionist painters.

Did You Know?

In 1903 the company Binney & Smith introduced the first Crayola Crayons. There were eight colors in a box: black, blue, brown, green, orange, red, violet and yellow. Now, there are 120 colors. The five most popular colors in 2006 were: blue, cerulean, purple heart, midnight blue and aquamarine.

Expressionism

One of many art movements evolving in the late 19th and early 20th century, Expressionism began in Germany. Expressionist painters interpreted things around them in exaggerated, distorted ways as they tried to paint what they were feeling inside, rather than portraying what they were actually seeing. Edvard Munch and James Ensor were among the best-known Expressionist painters.

Surrealism

Surrealist artists came from all over the world. The movement, popular in the 1920s, drew on images from artists' eerie imaginations and dreams. Spanish painters Salvador Dalí and Joan Miró were Surrealists.

Abstract Expressionism

Developed in the mid-20th century, this style emphasizes form and color rather than an actual subject. Jackson Pollock and Willem de Kooning were Abstract Expressionists.

Pop Art

Pop Art emerged in England and the United States after 1950. Pop artists use materials and inspiration from the everyday world, such as tin cans and comic strips. Andy Warhol and Roy Lichtenstein were Pop artists.

The Three Musicians, Picasso

Cubism

Cubism was a radical art movement that started in Paris around 1907 and lasted for less than 20 years. The first truly modern style of art, it stressed basic abstract geometric forms and usually presented the subject from many angles at the same time. Many consider Pablo Picasso and Georges Braque to be the founders of Cubism.

Liz, **Andy Warhol**

Minimalism

This style was popular from the 1950s through the 1970s. Minimalist paintings and sculpture were very simple, both in how they were presented and what they represented. Richard Serra is a Minimalist artist, and Frank Stella devoted part of his career to Minimalism.

Skokomish basketmaker

The World of Art

There are as many uses for baskets as there are ways to make them. Archaeologists have found 7,000-year-old farming baskets in Egypt.

Drawing is everywhere—in newspapers, books, posters and more. It is the starting point for other arts, such as painting and sculpture.

In prehistoric times, people wore jewelry even before they wore clothing. Jewelry has been made from countless objects, from berries to gold.

For thousands of years, people all over the world have made masks to use in rituals, work, theater and just for fun.

A mosaic is a picture or design made by gluing together small stones, pieces of glass or other hard materials. In ancient times, exquisite homes sometimes had mosaic floors.

Mayan mask

As technology changes, the tools artists use change too. New Media include video, performance, computer imagery and installation (where an entire room may be made into a work of art).

From prehistoric cave paintings to graffiti art today, painting has always been a part of human life. Some of the best-known artists, such as Michelangelo and Picasso, were painters.

Photography was invented about 200 years ago. We see photographs every day in newspapers and magazines, on billboards and buses and in museums and galleries. Ansel Adams and Mathew Brady were famous photographers.

Mathew Brady photograph

Pottery is probably the most ancient art and one of the most common. Prehistoric clay bowls, beautifully glazed tiles and other works are not only useful but also decorative.

People have made sculpture from materials such as clay, marble, ice, wood and bronze. Some artists today create sculptures that move with the wind. Alberto Giacometti, Auguste Rodin and Louise Nevelson were important sculptors.

People have been weaving since the Stone Age. Tapestries and rugs in every color have brought warmth and beauty to walls and floors.

Mosaic doorway in Morocco

13th-century pottery

The Thinker, Rodin

Great Artists and Their works

Leonardo Da Vinci (1452-1519) Italian Renaissance artist who was most famous as a painter but also excelled at drawing (particularly the human anatomy), architecture and sculpture. More than 500 years after it was painted, his *Mona Lisa* remains perhaps the best-known painting in the world. Art fans have long debated the symbolism of the subject's sly smile.

Rembrandt (1606-1669) Dutch Baroque artist whose hundreds of richly ornate paintings depict historical and biblical scenes. He also painted many portraits. One of his most famous is *The Night Watch*. Enormous in size, it shows a military company moving forward. His use of light draws the eye to the main figures in the painting.

Vincent Van Gogh (1853-1890) Dutch Post-impressionist artist who painted nearly all of his most famous works over a period of 29 months, while suffering from mental illness. Many of his paintings reveal his emotional distress. Van Gogh painted *Starry Night* when he

Vincent Van Gogh

was in a French hospital. In the painting, probably his most famous, bright yellow stars and planets burst forth from a swirling night sky.

Louise Nevelson (1900-1988) American sculptor who created huge, abstract arrangements of stacked objects that were usually painted black, white or gold. She often used items that she found, including pieces of wood, broken mirrors and glass, metal and electric lights.

Salvador Dalí (1904-1989) Spanish Surrealist painter known for his wild imagination. His paintings are eerily nightmarish and realistic. One of his most famous paintings, *Persistence of*

Memory, features droopy watches that seem to be melting.

Jackson Pollock (1912-1956) American Abstract artist famous for his drip-and-pour style of painting. He dripped paint onto huge canvasses, creating complicated works with a splattered effect. In 2006, his painting *No. 5* sold for $140 million, becoming the highest price ever paid for a painting.

Annie Liebovitz (b. 1949) American portrait photographer who often takes pictures of celebrities for magazines. At age 23, Liebovitz became chief photographer for *Rolling Stone* magazine. She worked there from 1973 to 1983, earning celebrity status herself.

Jean-Michel Basquiat (1960-1988) American painter who was a graffiti artist before being accepted into the art establishment. He often incorporated graffiti and text into his paintings, which are powerful yet angry.

$135 Million!!

Most Expensive Paintings Ever Sold

	PRICE	PAINTING	ARTIST	YEAR SOLD
1.	$140 million	*No. 5*	Jackson Pollock	2006
2.	$135 million	*Adele Bloch-Bauer I*	Gustav Klimt	2006
3.	$104 million	*Boy with a Pipe*	Pablo Picasso	2004
4.	$95.2 million	*Dora Maar with Cat*	Pablo Picasso	2006
5.	$82.5 million	*Portrait du Dr. Gachet*	Vincent Van Gogh	1990
6.	$78.1 million	*Au Moulin de la Galette*	Pierre-Auguste Renoir	1990
7.	$76.7 million	*The Massacre of the Innocents*	Peter Paul Rubens	2002
8.	$71.5 million	*Portrait de L'Artiste sans Barbe*	Vincent Van Gogh	1998
9.	$60.5 million	*Rideau, Cruchon et Compotier*	Paul Cézanne	1999
10.	$55 million	*Femme aux Bras Croises*	Pablo Picasso	2000

BOOKS

COMIC BOOK TIMELINE

1961 Marvel presents **The Fantastic Four.** Unlike other characters, the team doesn't hide their real identities.

1962 Marvel adds **Spider-Man** and **The Hulk.**

1963 Marvel Comics starts its first series of mutants, the *X-Men*. **Angel, Beast, Cyclops, Marvel Girl** and **Iceman** are led by **Professor X.**

1937 The first issue of *Detective Comics* is released by the company that becomes DC Comics.

1938 *Action Comics* features the first superhero: **Superman.**

1939 "The Bat-Man" debuts in *Detective Comics.*

Timely Comics (later renamed Marvel) releases *Marvel Comics*, which includes **Prince Namor the Sub-Mariner** and other heroes.

DC introduces **The Flash,** a superhero who can run faster than the speed of light, and the first **Green Lantern.**

1941 Marvel creates **Captain America,** a soldier with a mighty shield.

DC introduces **Wonder Woman,** designed to embody female ideals of heroism.

Archie Andrews debuts in Pep Comics.

1964 DC introduces *Teen Titans:* **Aqualad, Kid Flash, Robin** and **Wonder Girl.**

1974 **Wolverine** appears as a Canadian superhero fighting the Hulk. He later joins the X-Men.

1977 Dave Sim's *Cerebus* is released. It's notable for being a successful independent comic, and for being a self-contained 300-issue story. It ends as planned in 2004.

1984 Cowabunga! **The Teenage Mutant Ninja Turtles** appear (in black-and-white).

1985 DC begins *Crisis on Infinite Earths*, a year-long crossover affecting all its superhero comics. It does the same again in 1994 (*Zero Hour*) and in 2005 (*Infinite Crisis*).

1986 Art Spiegelman publishes *Maus: A Survivor's Tale,* a graphic novel based on his father's Holocaust experiences. In 1991, Volume Two is published. The combined work wins a Pulitzer Prize.

Frank Miller's *The Dark Knight Returns* presents a darker, more adult **Batman.**

1988 Fans vote by phone to kill the then **Robin,** Jason Todd. He's murdered by the **Joker.**

1992 Todd McFarlane begins *Spawn* at his newly founded Image Comics.

1996 Marvel and DC join forces for *Amalgam Comics*, mingling their superheroes.

2000 Marvel begins the *Ultimate Marvel* line featuring updated versions of older characters.

2002 The first American edition of *Shonen Jump*, a digest of Japanese comic books (manga) is released. It includes installments of *Yu-Gi-Oh!* and *One Piece.*

Yu-Gi-Oh cards

2004 DC Comics establishes the DMX imprint to publish manga translations.

2005 The publishers of *Shonen Jump* introduce *Shojo Beat*, manga for teenage girls.

2007 **Captain America** is shot and killed by his nemesis, **Red Skull.**

20

BOOK AWARDS

→ The **CALDECOTT MEDAL** honors an outstanding American picture book. **2007 winner:** *Flotsam,* **by David Wiesner**

→ The **NEWBERY MEDAL** honors an outstanding example of children's literature. The Newbery winner is not a picture book. **2007 winner:** *The Higher Power of Lucky,* **Susan Patron**

→ **NATIONAL BOOK AWARD FOR YOUNG PEOPLE'S LITERATURE** **2006 winner:** *The Astonishing Life of Octavian Nothing, Traitor to the Nation, Vol. 1: The Pox Party,* **M. T. Anderson**

→ The **CORETTA SCOTT KING AWARDS** recognize black authors and illustrators whose works have promoted an understanding and appreciation of all cultures. **2007 winners: Writer:** *Copper Sun,* **by Sharon Draper; Illustrator:** *Moses: When Harriet Tubman Led Her People to Freedom,* **by Kadir Nelson; written by Carole Boston Weatherford**

→ *BOSTON GLOBE* **HORN BOOK AWARD 2006 winners:** Nonfiction: *If You Decide to Go to the Moon,* **Faith McNulty** Picture Book: *Leaf Man,* **Lois Ehlert** Fiction and Poetry: *The Miraculous Journey of Edward Tulane,* **Kate DiCamillo**

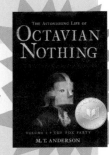

SPELLBINDING MYSTERY SERIES

WARNING: Don't crack open these books if you're eager for a good night's sleep. These page-turners are impossible to put down!

Bernie Magruder series
by Phyllis Reynolds Naylor
Bernie Magruder, who lives at the Besseldorf Hotel with his eccentric family, often solves the mysteries that plague Middleburg, Indiana, faster than the local police.

Chet Gecko series
by Bruce Hale
Chet Gecko, a wisecracking 4th-grade lizard detective with an enormous appetite for such sumptuous snacks as Lice Krispie Treats, partners with Natalie Attired, a mockingbird, to solve some of Emerson Hickey Elementary School's most baffling mysteries.

Herculeah Jones series
by Betsy Byars
Herculeah Jones uses the sleuthing skills she has picked up from her parents (a private detective mother and police officer father) to solve every crime that comes her way. She is as strong and courageous as her name suggests.

Lady Grace Mysteries
by Lady Patricia Finney
Set in 1569, Lady Grace Cavendish, a spirited 13-year-old maid of honor to Queen Elizabeth I, solves intriguing mysteries that perplex the queen's court.

Lewis Barnavelt series
by John Bellairs
After his parents die, Lewis Barnavelt moves into his uncle's mansion. He is thrilled to learn that Uncle Jonathan is a wizard. Together with Mrs. Zimmerman (their neighbor, who is a witch) and Lewis's friend Rose Rita, they outwit forces of evil.

Nancy Drew series
by Carolyn Keene
In this classic series, Nancy Drew, a plucky amateur detective, tackles her own cases and helps her father, an attorney, with his.

Sammy Keyes series
By Wendelin Van Draanen
Sammy Keyes deals with many problems common to seventh graders: cliques, detention, an archenemy. But unlike most middle schoolers, Sammy lives with her grandmother in a retirement community and has a knack for solving crimes.

MUST-READ BOOKS

Anne of Green Gables by Lucy Maud Montgomery
The Cuthberts of Prince Edward Island planned to adopt a boy orphan, but Anne Shirley arrived instead. Redheaded, imaginative and mischievous, Anne provides the family with a dose of daily adventure. The first installment in a series of eight books.

The BFG by Roald Dahl
Although most children are terrified of giants and their wicked ways, Sophie has nothing to worry about when she's abducted by the BFG. The Big Friendly Giant blows happy dreams through children's windows.

Chasing Vermeer by Blue Balliet
Sixth graders Petra and Calder, who share a love of art and blue M&Ms, put their heads together to track down the culprit who has stolen a Vermeer painting.

Coraline by Neil Gaiman
A girl unlocks a door in her home and finds herself in a creepy alternate universe that eerily parallels her own.

Double Act by Jacqueline Wilson
Twins cope with the death of their mother, their father's new girlfriend, a new town and a new school. As they deal with their stress, the twins begin to form their own identities.

The Egypt Game by Zilpha Keatley Snyder
Six kids from different backgrounds and cultures share one thing in common: a love of ancient Egypt. They gather in a vacant lot and create an elaborate role-playing game that soon becomes all too real.

Eragon by Christopher Paolini
Paolini started writing this book, the first of three in his Inheritance series, when he was only 15! Eragon, a 15-year-old farm boy, finds what he thinks is a beautiful stone. When a blue dragon hatches from it, Eragon decides to raise the creature, which he names Saphira. Using magic and fighting techniques, they try to avoid becoming servants to the evil emperor Galbatorix. They encounter elves, dwarves and evil beasts on their epic adventure.

From the Mixed-Up Files of Mrs. Basil E. Frankweiler by E. L. Konigsburg
Feeling unappreciated by her parents, spunky Claudia Kincaid runs away to the Metropolitan Museum of Art in New York City. Her brother Jamie joins her, and they become enthralled by a statue of an angel. Determined to discover the identity of the statue's maker, Claudia and Jamie embark on an adventure that leads them to the home of Mrs. Basil E. Frankweiler.

Holes by Louis Sachar
Stanley Yelnats, accused of a crime he didn't commit, is sentenced to Camp Green Lake, a detention center where boys dig holes to build character.

The Princess Diaries by Meg Cabot
Mia Thermopolis is like any normal ninth grader in New York until her father tells her that he's the Prince of Genovia, and she's the crown princess. (Other books in the series include Princess in the Spotlight, Princess in Love and Princess in Waiting.)

The Thief Lord by Cornelia Funke
Two trouble-prone boys flee their unpleasant aunt and uncle and escape to Venice, Italy, where they become entangled with the Thief Lord, a boy who steals from the rich to help his poor friends. They end up on a dangerous mission to recover a wooden wing that was once part of a magical merry-go-round.

The Westing Game by Ellen Raskin
Millionaire Sam Westing met an untimely death at his mansion. At the reading of his will, Westing's quirky heirs are invited to participate in a game to help unravel the mysterious circumstances of his death. They have plenty of incentive: whoever solves the puzzling crime will inherit Westing's $200 million fortune.

Types of Literature

Here are some of the different styles of fiction (made-up stories) and nonfiction (books about real-life events and people). Examples follow each description.

NONFICTION

An **autobiography** or **memoir** is the story of a person's life written by that person.
26 Fairmount Avenue by Tomie dePaola

A **biography** is the story of a person's life written by another person.
Traitor: The Case of Benedict Arnold by Jean Fritz

FICTION

A **fable** is a story that teaches a moral or a lesson, often with animal characters.
The Tortoise and the Hare

Fantasy novels are often set in worlds much different from our own, and they usually include magic, sorcery and mythical creatures.
The Lion, the Witch and the Wardrobe by C. S. Lewis

A **folktale** is a story that has been passed down over generations, usually orally, within a culture. It may be based on superstition and feature supernatural characters. Folktales include fairy tales, tall tales, trickster tales and other stories.
Hansel and Gretel

A **legend** is a story that has been handed down over generations and is believed to be based on history, though it typically mixes fact and fiction. The hero of a legend is usually a human.
King Arthur and the Round Table

In **mysteries**, the plot focuses on a character trying to solve a crime or puzzle.
The Encyclopedia Brown series by Donald Sobol

A **myth** is a traditional story that a particular culture once accepted as sacred and true. It may center on a god or supernatural being and often explains how something came to be.
The Greek story of the Titan Prometheus bringing fire to humankind

Science fiction examines how science and technology affect the world. Stories often involve fantasy inventions.
The Left Hand of Darkness by Ursula K. Le Guin

URSULA K. LE GUIN

THE LEFT HAND OF DARKNESS

"[A] serious fiction masterpiece" —*Newsweek*

TFK MYSTERY PERSON

CLUE 1: I was born on April 4, 1928, in Saint Louis, Missouri.

CLUE 2: I have written 12 best-sellers, including *I Know Why the Caged Bird Sings*.

CLUE 3: I read my poem "On the Pulse of Morning" at the inauguration of President Bill Clinton in 1993.

WHO AM I? (See Answer Key on page 242.)

Did You Know?

R. L. Stine, the author of the Goosebumps series, has sold more children's books than any other author—including J. K. Rowling. More than 220 million of the Goosebumps books have been sold since 1992, when the first book, *Welcome to the Dead House*, was published. It's not surprising since Stine produces about two books every month.

Standing Tall

Taj Mahal

For thousands of years, buildings have been used to show off power and wealth, to honor leaders or religions, to stretch architectural limits and even to impress the competition. Some of the most dramatic buildings of the past include the **Great Pyramids at Giza** in Egypt (built around 2680 B.C.), the **Taj Mahal** in India (built in the 1600s) and the **Pharos of Alexandria** in Egypt (built during the third century B.C.). While these buildings look different, they have one thing in common: They were built with load-bearing walls made of stone or bricks and mortar. Load-bearing walls support the weight of the building and its contents.

Reaching New Heights

In the 19th century, engineering developments paved the way for a whole new type of building: the skyscraper. Steam-operated elevators had been used to move materials in factories, mines and warehouses. But these elevators were not considered safe for people. A safe steam-powered elevator was devised in 1853. Later, the

Taipei 101

switch to an electric motor made the elevator an even more practical way to get up and down tall buildings.

By the 1880s, there was little space for new buildings in major cities. The only way to expand was to build up. But in order to achieve new heights, construction techniques had to change. A new method of construction used a grid of steel beams and columns that was strong enough to support the weight of the building and any force caused by wind or even earthquakes. And with this new building method, the skyscraper was born.

The Forces of Nature

Wind posed a serious problem to early skyscrapers. Strong winds could cause the buildings to sway—as much as two feet in any direction! Engineers solved the problem by first installing diagonally braced steel trusses between central elevator shafts to create a stronger core. Later designs moved most of the beams and columns to the outside edge of the walls, making a stiff tube.

The tuned mass damper was developed in the 1970s. Located near the top of the building, it is designed like a pendulum to move in one direction when a computer senses the structure has begun to move in the other.

Empire State Building

Tallest Buildings Timeline

These dates indicate when the building was completed, becoming the tallest in the world.

1890 New York World Building, New York City (309 feet. The number of stories is disputed, but figures range from 16 to 26.)

1894 Manhattan Life Insurance Building, New York City (348 feet, 18 stories)

1913 Woolworth Building, New York City (792 feet, 60 stories)

Petronas Towers

1930 Chrysler Building, New York City (1,046 feet, 77 stories)

1931 Empire State Building, New York City (1,250 feet, 102 stories)

1972 World Trade Center, New York City (1,368 feet, 110 stories)

1974 Sears Tower, Chicago (1,450 feet, 110 stories)

1998 Petronas Towers, Kuala Lumpur, Malaysia (1,483 feet, 88 stories)

2004 Taipei 101, Taiwan (1,670 feet, 101 stories)

Notable Skyscrapers

Eiffel Tower Completed in 1889, the Eiffel Tower was briefly the tallest building in the world. It was built for the World's Fair to prove that iron could be as strong as stone while being much lighter. The wrought-iron tower is twice as tall as the stone Washington Monument, yet it weighs 70,000 tons less! The Eiffel Tower is repainted every seven years with 50 tons of dark brown paint.

Eiffel Tower

Chrysler Building Auto tycoon Walter Chrysler took part in an intense race with the Bank of Manhattan Trust Company to build the world's tallest skyscraper. Just when it looked as if the bank had captured the coveted title, workers at the Chrysler Building jacked a thin spire hidden inside the building through the top of the roof to win the contest. Chrysler decorated his building, finished in 1930, with hubcaps, mudguards and hood ornaments.

Chrysler Building

John Hancock Center In order to strengthen the John Hancock Center against Chicago's famous winds, engineers included five enormous diagonal braces on the exterior walls of the building. These diagonals block the view from two windows on each floor. Clever marketing, however, has made these viewless windows a status symbol and it actually costs more money to rent these rooms!

Sears Tower On a clear day, you can see four states from the top of Chicago's Sears Tower: Illinois, Indiana, Wisconsin and Michigan. To make sure your view is clear, the building features six robotic window-washing machines mounted on the roof.

Sears Tower

World's Tallest Towers

TOP 5 TFK

These structures are mainly telecommunications towers, and while they may have observation decks or restaurants, they do not have floors all the way to the top. Unlike buildings, towers are not designed for businesses or as residences.

Oriental Pearl Tower

Ostankino Tower

TOWER	LOCATION	HEIGHT
1. Canadian National (CN) Tower	Toronto, Canada	1,815 feet
2. Ostankino Tower	Moscow, Russia	1,762 feet
3. Oriental Pearl Tower	Shanghai, China	1,535 feet
4. Milad Tower	Tehran, Iran	1,427 feet
5. Menara Kuala Lumpur	Kuala Lumpur, Malaysia	1,403 feet

For a list of the world's 100 tallest buildings:
www.factmonster.com/tallestbuildings

Buildings & Landmarks

Seven wonders of the modern world

1. EMPIRE STATE BUILDING Finished in 1931, it towers 1,250 feet over New York City. Until the first tower of the World Trade Center was finished in 1972, it was the world's tallest building.

2. ITAIPÚ DAM Built by Brazil and Paraguay on the Paraná River, it is the world's largest hydro-electric power plant. Completed in 1991, it took 16 years to build this series of dams whose length totals 25,406 feet.

Golden Gate Bridge

3. CN TOWER In 1976, it became the world's tallest freestanding structure. It soars about one-third of a mile (1,815 feet) above Toronto, Canada.

Panama Canal

4. PANAMA CANAL It took 34 years to create this 50-mile-long canal across the Isthmus of Panama. Its huge locks connect the Atlantic and Pacific Oceans.

5. CHANNEL TUNNEL Known as the Chunnel, it links France and England. It is 31 miles long, and 23 of those miles are 150 feet below the seabed of the English Channel. High-speed trains whiz through its side-by-side tubes.

6. NORTH SEA PROTECTION WORKS The Netherlands is below sea level, so a series of dams, floodgates and surge barriers have been built to keep the sea from flooding the country during storms. The biggest part of the project, which some compare in scale to the Great Wall of China, was a 2-mile-long surge barrier across an estuary.

7. GOLDEN GATE BRIDGE For many years, this suspension bridge that connects San Francisco and Marin County was the longest in the world. Begun in 1933, it took about four years—and 80,000 miles of steel wire—to complete the graceful and beloved 1.2-mile-long bridge.

Capital Landmarks

In addition to the White House, several architectural masterpieces and symbolic landmarks are found in Washington, D.C. Here are some of them.

Capitol Building This is where Congress meets and conducts business.

Jefferson Memorial This memorial to Thomas Jefferson is modeled on the Roman Pantheon.

Lincoln Memorial Lincoln's Gettysburg Address is carved into the walls of the south chamber, and his famous Second Inaugural Address is on the north-chamber wall.

National Archives The records of the three branches of government, including the Declaration of Independence, are kept here.

Smithsonian Institution The Smithsonian is a network of 14 museums, art galleries and research centers.

Vietnam Veterans Memorial This V-shaped monument lists the names of the 58,000 veterans who died during the Vietnam War.

Washington Monument This monument to our first President stands just over 555 feet high. Stones from the 50 states and several foreign countries line the inside walls.

Amazing Architects and Their Stunning Structures

An architect designs homes, libraries, museums and other structures or environments. Here are some famous modern architects and their signature creations.

→ **R. Buckminster Fuller (1895–1983)** Fuller's revolutionary designs were both innovative and efficient. He developed the Dymaxion principle, which called for using the least possible amount of material and energy in construction and manufacturing. His most famous creation was the geodesic dome.

→ **Frank Gehry (b. 1929)** Many of Gehry's designs are curvy in shape and are made from novel materials, such as corrugated metal and chain-link fencing. His best-known project is the Guggenheim Museum in Bilbao, Spain.

→ **Maya Lin (b. 1959)** Lin earned fame when, as a student at Yale, she won a contest to design the Vietnam Veterans Memorial in Washington,

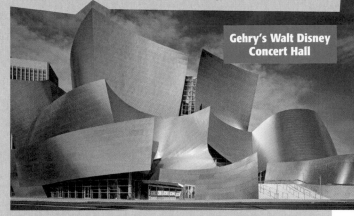

Gehry's Walt Disney Concert Hall

D.C. She also designed the Civil Rights Memorial in Montgomery, Alabama.

→ **I. M. Pei (b. 1917)** Born in China and educated in the United States, Pei has designed landmarks all over the world. He frequently incorporates marble, concrete and glass into his geometric designs. Among his famous designs are the Rock and Roll Hall of Fame and Museum in Cleveland, Ohio, the expansion of the Louvre in Paris and the John F. Kennedy Library in Boston, Massachusetts.

→ **Frank Lloyd Wright (1869–1959)** Wright is widely considered the greatest American

architect. He developed the Prairie style of architecture, which features low horizontal lines, earth-tone colors and protruding overhangs. Although he mostly designed homes and furniture, Wright also designed the Oak Park Unity Temple near Chicago and the Larkin Office Building in Buffalo, New York.

Lin's Vietnam Veterans Memorial

Wright's Falling Water

? TFK MYSTERY PERSON

CLUE 1: A Jewish-American poet, I was born in New York City in 1849.

CLUE 2: One of my poems, "The New Colossus," appears on the pedestal of the Statue of Liberty.

CLUE 3: The poem, in part, says "'Give me your tired, your poor,/Your huddled masses yearning to breathe free...'"

WHO AM I? (See Answer Key on page 242.)

CALENDAR & HOLIDAYS

2003

JANUARY
S	M	T	W	T	F	S
			1	2	3	4	5
6	7	8	9	10	11	12
13	14	15	16	17	18	19
20	21	22	23	24	25	26
27	28	29	30	31		

FEBRUARY
S	M	T	W	T	F	S
					1	2
3	4	5	6	7	8	9
10	11	12	13	14	15	16
17	18	19	20	21	22	23
24	25	26	27	28	29	

MARCH
S	M	T	W	T	F	S
						1
2	3	4	5	6	7	8
9	10	11	12	13	14	15
16	17	18	19	20	21	22
23	24	25	26	27	28	29
30	31					

APRIL
S	M	T	W	T	F	S
		1	2	3	4	5
6	7	8	9	10	11	12
13	14	15	16	17	18	19
20	21	22	23	24	25	26
27	28	29	30			

1 New Year's Day
21 Martin Luther King Jr. Day

7 Chinese New Year
14 Valentine's Day
18 Washington's Birthday

9 Daylight Saving Time begins
17 St. Patrick's Day
20 Spring begins
23 Easter

1 April Fools' Day
22 Earth Day

MAY
S	M	T	W	T	F	S
				1	2	3
4	5	6	7	8	9	10
11	12	13	14	15	16	17
18	19	20	21	22	23	24
25	26	27	28	29	30	31

JUNE
S	M	T	W	T	F	S
1	2	3	4	5	6	7
8	9	10	11	12	13	14
15	16	17	18	19	20	21
22	23	24	25	26	27	28
29	30					

JULY
S	M	T	W	T	F	S
		1	2	3	4	5
6	7	8	9	10	11	12
13	14	15	16	17	18	19
20	21	22	23	24	25	26
27	28	29	30	31		

AUGUST
S	M	T	W	T	F	S
					1	2
3	4	5	6	7	8	9
10	11	12	13	14	15	16
17	18	19	20	21	22	23
24	25	26	27	28	29	30
31						

11 Mother's Day
26 Memorial Day

15 Father's Day
20 Summer begins

4 Independence Day

SEPTEMBER
S	M	T	W	T	F	S
	1	2	3	4	5	6
7	8	9	10	11	12	13
14	15	16	17	18	19	20
21	22	23	24	25	26	27
28	29	30				

OCTOBER
S	M	T	W	T	F	S
			1	2	3	4
5	6	7	8	9	10	11
12	13	14	15	16	17	18
19	20	21	22	23	24	25
26	27	28	29	30	31	

NOVEMBER
S	M	T	W	T	F	S
						1
2	3	4	5	6	7	8
9	10	11	12	13	14	15
16	17	18	19	20	21	22
23	24	25	26	27	28	29
30						

DECEMBER
S	M	T	W	T	F	S
	1	2	3	4	5	6
7	8	9	10	11	12	13
14	15	16	17	18	19	20
21	22	23	24	25	26	27
28	29	30	31			

For a description of the religious holidays, see page 172.

1 Labor Day
22 Fall begins

13 Columbus Day
31 Halloween

2 Daylight Saving Time ends
11 Veterans Day
27 Thanksgiving

21 Winter begins
25 Christmas
26 Kwanzaa begins

FEDERAL HOLIDAYS

NEW YEAR'S DAY
January 1
New Year's Day has its origin in ancient Roman times, when sacrifices were offered to Janus. This two-faced Roman god looked back on the past and forward to the future.

MARTIN LUTHER KING JR. DAY
Third Monday in January
Honors the civil rights leader

MARTIN LUTHER KING JR.

WASHINGTON'S BIRTHDAY
Third Monday in February
Sometimes called President's Day to honor both George Washington and Abraham Lincoln, it is officially called Washington's Birthday.

MEMORIAL DAY
Last Monday in May
A holiday dedicated to the memory of all war dead

INDEPENDENCE DAY
July 4
It celebrates the Declaration of Independence, which was adopted on July 4, 1776. The Declaration stated that the 13 colonies were independent from Britain.

INDEPENDENCE DAY

For national holidays around the world:
www.factmonster.com/holidays

LABOR DAY
First Monday in September
A day set aside in honor of workers, it was first celebrated in New York City in 1882.

COLUMBUS DAY
Second Monday in October
This holiday honors Christopher Columbus's landing in the New World in 1492.

COLUMBUS

VETERANS DAY
November 11
Honors all men and women who have served America in its armed forces

THANKSGIVING
Fourth Thursday in November
First took place in 1621 to celebrate the harvest reaped by the Plymouth Colony after it survived a harsh winter

CHRISTMAS DAY
December 25
Celebrates the birth of Jesus

Calendar & Holidays

Other Fun Holidays

GROUNDHOG DAY
➔ February 2
Legend has it that if a groundhog sees its shadow on this morning, there will be six more weeks of winter.

VALENTINE'S DAY
➔ February 14
Named for the third-century martyr St. Valentine, this day is celebrated with candy, cards and other tokens of love.

APRIL FOOLS' DAY
➔ April 1
April Fools' Day, sometimes called All Fools' Day, is one of the most lighthearted days of the year. On this day, people sometimes play pranks on each other and tell tall tales.

MOTHER'S DAY
➔ Second Sunday in May
Having a day to honor mothers goes back at least as far as 17th-century England, when Mothering Sunday began.

FLAG DAY
➔ June 14
Americans celebrate the adoption of the first national flag on this day. The first American flag was approved by the Continental Congress on June 14, 1777. In 1818, Congress passed legislation setting the number of stripes at 13 and requiring that the number of stars equal the number of states.

FATHER'S DAY
➔ Third Sunday in June
This U.S. holiday honoring fathers began in 1910 in Spokane, Washington.

HALLOWEEN
➔ October 31
Halloween is celebrated with jack-o'-lanterns, costumes, trick-or-treating and the sharing of spooky stories.

KWANZAA
➔ December 26 through January 1
Kwanzaa, an African American holiday, honors the values of ancient African culture.

BIRTHSTONES

MONTH	STONE	MONTH	STONE
January	Garnet	July	Ruby or star ruby
February	Amethyst	August	Peridot or sardonyx
March	Aquamarine or bloodstone	September	Sapphire or star sapphire
April	Diamond	October	Opal or tourmaline
May	Emerald	November	Topaz or citrine
June	Pearl, alexandrite or moonstone	December	Turquoise, lapis lazuli, blue zircon or blue topaz

A WORLD OF FUN

MARDI GRAS

Mardi Gras means "Fat Tuesday." Traditionally, it is the last day for Catholics to celebrate and indulge before Ash Wednesday starts the weeks of fasting that come with Lent.

In the United States, Mardi Gras has been celebrated in New Orleans with masked balls and colorful parades since French settlers arrived in the early 1700s. Feather-covered dancers, painted clowns, masked lions—you can find them all (and countless others) in the streets of New Orleans at Mardi Gras.

Marching bands, some of them founded more than 100 years ago, also take to the streets. They begin the day by spreading jazz music through the city before the more than 350 floats and 15,000 costumed paraders take over the scene. Mardi Gras has long combined wild street activities open to everyone with events organized by private clubs known as krewes.

The millions of colorful beaded necklaces thrown from floats are the most visible symbols and souvenirs of Mardi Gras. In addition, millions of cups and toy coins known as "doubloons" are decorated with krewe logos and thrown to parade-watchers.

Hurricane Katrina slammed into New Orleans at the end of August 2005. Within a few months the city decided that Mardi Gras would go on, preserving a special tradition.

A Mardi Gras float

PURIM

Purim celebrates the salvation of the Jews from the wicked Haman. Through the leadership of Queen Esther and her cousin Mordecai, a decree against the Jews in the Persian Empire was suddenly overturned.

Purim takes place on the 14th day of Adar, the 12th month of the Jewish calendar. It usually falls in March. The traditional observances of Purim include public readings of the Book of Esther (during which noisemakers are used to drown out any mention of Haman's name), feasting, the giving of gifts to the poor and the exchanging of food among friends.

A plate of *hamantaschen*

Purim has a food of its own: *hamantaschen*. Literally "Haman's pockets," these triangular cookies are said to resemble Haman's three-cornered hat. These traditionally contain poppy-seed or prune fillings, but other fruit fillings are also popular.

ESALA PERAHERA

Every July or August, thousands of Sri Lankans travel to the hill city of Kandy to watch dancers, acrobats, drummers, whip-crackers, flame-throwers and more than 100 decorated elephants parade through the streets during Esala Perahera. This 10-day festival honors the country's prized possession, the Tooth Relic of Lord Buddha.

Esala Perahera, first celebrated in the third century B.C., kicks off with the cutting of a ceremonial jack tree. Pieces of the tree are then planted near the shrines of the four Buddhist gods that protect Sri Lanka: Natha, Vishnu, Kataragama and Pattini. Festivities take place outside each of the temples. Later, processions begin from each shrine and parade toward the Temple of the Tooth (*Dalada Maligawa*). The processions grow longer and more spectacular each night, until the last night of the pageant, when an enormous elephant carries the Tooth Relic in a gold casket on its back. The ceremony ends at dawn after the full moon with a water-cutting ceremony.

A man celebrating the end of Esala Perahera

COMPUTERS & THE INTERNET

Computer and Internet Timeline

1945 → The computer age begins with the debut of ENIAC (Electronic Numerical Integrator and Calculator). It's the first multipurpose computer.

ENIAC

1969 → The Internet era is launched when four universities in the U.S. are connected in a communications network called ARPANET.

1972 → Email is introduced.

1975 → Bill Gates and Paul Allen establish Microsoft.

1976 → Steve Jobs and Steve Wozniak start Apple Computer. → Queen Elizabeth is the first state leader to send an email.

Apple II

1977 → The Apple II computer hits shelves.

1978 → Floppy disks are introduced.

1981 → IBM debuts a complete desktop PC.

1982 → The word "Internet" is used for the first time.

Steve Jobs

Floppy disk

1984 → The Apple Macintosh goes on sale.

1985 → Microsoft launches Windows. → Quantum Computer Services (later called America Online) offers email, electronic bulletin boards, news and other information.

1988 → A virus called the Internet Worm temporarily shuts down about 10% of the world's Internet servers.

Bill Gates

1989 → The World debuts as the first dial-up Internet service.

Steve Wozniak

1991 → The World Wide Web is introduced as a text-only interface.

1992 → Laptop computers go on sale.

Laptop

1993 → Mosaic, the first graphics-based browser, is launched. → The White House creates a website: www.whitehouse.gov. → The first online shopping sites are established.

1995 → CompuServe, America Online and Prodigy start providing dial-up Internet access. → Amazon.com launches as a virtual bookstore. → eBay is founded. → Craigslist.org is started in San Francisco.

1996 → Napster, the music-swapping site, goes live. → Hotmail is launched.

1997 → The term "web log" is coined. It's later shortened to "blog."

1998 → Google opens its first office, in California.

Google office

1999 → MySpace.com is launched.

2000 → America Online buys Time Warner for $16 billion. It's the biggest merger of all time.

2001 → Wikipedia is created. → Apple introduces the iPod.

2003 → Spam, unsolicited email, becomes a server-clogging menace. It accounts for about half of all emails. → Apple Computer introduces the iTunes Music Store, which allows people to download songs for 99 cents each.

iPod

2005 → YouTube.com is launched.

2006 → There are more than 92 million websites online.

MySpace.com founders Tom Anderson and Chris DeWolfe

INTERNET STATS AND FACTS

Cyberkids

This table shows the percentage of U.S. kids who spend time online.

AGE	% OF U.S. KIDS WHO SURF THE WEB
3–4	20%
5–9	42
10–13	67
14–17	79

Source: U.S. Department of Commerce

China

Wired World

These are the countries with the most Internet users.

	COUNTRY	NUMBER OF INTERNET USERS
1.	U.S.	197,800,000
2.	China	119,500,000
3.	Japan	86,300,000
4.	India	50,600,000
5.	Germany	46,300,000
6.	United Kingdom	35,800,000
7.	South Korea	33,900,000
8.	Italy	28,800,000
9.	France	28,800,000
10.	Brazil	25,900,000

Brazil

Source: Computer Industry Almanac

What Kids Do Online

Many kids age 6 to 11 spend hours each week surfing the Internet, for both fun and schoolwork. Here's a look at the most popular things kids do online.

ACTIVITY	% OF ALL KIDS
Play online games	42.6%
Do stuff for school	23.1
Use email	10.5
Use instant messenger	6.5
Go to chat rooms	2.6

Source: Mediamark Research, Inc.

Phone Tunes

These are the most popular songs that people downloaded onto their cell phones in 2006.

RANK	SONG	ARTIST
1.	"Super Mario Bros."	Game theme
2.	"My Humps"	Black Eyed Peas
3.	"Grillz"	Nelly
4.	"Ms. New Booty"	Bubba Sparxxx
5.	"Laffy Taffy"	D4L
6.	"Pink Panther"	Movie theme
7.	"Gold Digger"	Kanye West
8.	"Halloween"	Movie theme
9.	"Mission Impossible"	Movie theme
10.	"Candy Shop"	50 Cent

Source: Nielsen SoundScan

TOP 5 TFK Top Sites*

These are the most popular websites on the Internet.

1. Yahoo! sites
2. MSN-Microsoft sites
3. Time Warner Network
4. Google sites
5. eBay

*This list is a snapshot of Internet traffic for November 2006.
Source: comScore Media Metrix.

Computers & the Internet

33

FacTMonSteR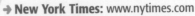

INTERNET RESOURCE GUIDE

The Internet is a convenient tool for finding information on just about anything. Here's a list of especially useful and informative sites.

ANIMALS

→ **Association of Zoos and Aquariums:** www.aza.org

→ **Animals A-Z:** www.oaklandzoo.org/atoz/atoz.html

→ **Kids' Planet:** www.kidsplanet.org

→ **National Wildlife Federation:** www.nwf.org/kids/

ART

→ **The @rt Room:** www.arts.ufl.edu/art/rt_room/index.html

→ **Metropolitan Museum of Art, New York:** www.metmuseum.org/explore/museumkids.htm

→ **Worldwide Art Gallery:** www.theartgallery.com.au/kidsart.html

→ **National Gallery of Art for Kids:** www.nga.gov/kids

→ **Smithsonian Institution, Washington, D.C.:** www.smithsonianeducation.org/students

ENTERTAINMENT AND GAMES

→ **Cartoonster:** cartoonster.kidzdom.com

→ **Fact Monster Sudoku:** www.factmonster.com/games/sudoku.html

→ **Fun Brain:** www.funbrain.com

→ **A Game a Day:** www.agameaday.com

→ **Nickelodeon:** www.nick.com

→ **Official Harry Potter Website:** harrypotter.warnerbros.com

→ **Yahoo! Kids:** kids.yahoo.com/music/index

GEOGRAPHY

→ **National Geographic for Kids:** www.nationalgeographic.com/ngforkids/

→ **CIA World Factbook:** www.cia.gov/cia/publications/factbook/index.html

→ **50 States.com:** www.50states.com

GOVERNMENT AND POLITICS

→ **White House:** www.whitehouse.gov/kids/

→ **Congress for Kids:** www.congressforkids.net

→ **Kids.gov:** www.kids.gov/

→ **State and Local Governments:** www.loc.gov/rr/news/stategov/stategov.html

NEWS

→ **Yahooligans! News:** www.kids.yahoo.com/news/

→ **The Internet Public Library:** www.ipl.org/div/news/

→ **New York Times:** www.nytimes.com

→ **Time for Kids:** www.timeforkids.com/TFK

REFERENCE

→ **Fact Monster:** www.factmonster.com

→ **Internet Public Library:** www.ipl.org

→ **Kids Zone:** www.lycoszone.lycos.com/

→ **Refdesk:** www.refdesk.com

SCIENCE AND MATH

→ **Ask Dr. Math:** mathforum.org/dr.math

→ **Astronomy for Kids:** www.kidsastronomy.com

→ **BAM! Body and Mind:** www.bam.gov

→ **Bill Nye the Science Guy:** www.billnye.com

→ **Cool Science for Curious Kids:** www.hhmi.org/coolscience/

→ **How Stuff Works:** express.howstuffworks.com/

→ **KidsHealth:** www.kidshealth.org/index2.html

→ **NASA Kids:** www.nasa.gov/audience/forkids

→ **Space:** www.space.com

→ **WebMath:** www.webmath.com

SPORTS

→ **Major League Baseball:** www.mlb.com

→ **Major League Soccer:** www.mlsnet.com

→ **National Basketball Association:** www.nba.com

→ **National Football League:** www.nfl.com

→ **National Hockey League:** www.nhl.com

→ **Sports Illustrated Kids:** www.sikids.com

→ **Women's National Basketball Association:** www.wnba.com

Did You Know?

Blogging is the hottest new Internet trend since instant messaging. A blog, a contraction of the words "web" and "log," is an online diary that people post for others to read. About 32 million Americans read blogs.

Tips for Safe Surfing

Here are some things to remember to make sure you have a safe, enjoyable online experience.

DO

✔ Treat everyone that you meet online as a stranger, and use the same rules for dealing with strangers online as you would for strangers you see on the street.

✔ Tell your parents or a teacher if you get an email that makes you feel uncomfortable. Don't respond to it.

✔ Let your parents or a teacher know if you see or read something on the Internet that makes you feel uncomfortable.

✔ Treat others online the way you would like to be treated.

DON'T

✗ Give out your real last name, address, phone number, password or school name to any website unless you check with your parents.

✗ Agree to meet face-to-face with a person you've met online unless you first get permission from your parents.

✗ Send people pictures of yourself unless you have permission from your parents.

✗ Download any software or pictures without asking a parent or teacher first.

2006 Webby Awards

Here's a selection of winners of the 2006 Webby Awards for the best Web sites.

ACTIVISM➔ Youthink!: youthink.worldbank.org/

ARTS➔ MoMA: Contemporary Voices: www.moma.org/exhibitions/2005/ contemporaryvoices/flash.html

CELEBRITY/FAN➔ NPG Music Club: www.npgmusicclub.com

FASHION➔ Style.com: www.style.com

GAMES➔ Stackopolis: www.stackopolis.com

MAGAZINE➔ National Geographic Magazine Online: ngm.com

MOVIE AND FILM➔ 2006 Sundance Film Festival: festival.sundance.org/2006/

MUSIC➔ Fabchannel.com–Concerts Online: www.fabchannel.com

NEWS➔ BBC News: news.bbc.co.uk

NEWSPAPER➔ Guardian Unlimited: www.guardian.co.uk

SCIENCE➔ The Genographic Project: www3.nationalgeographic.com/ genographic/

SPORTS➔ ESPN.com: www.espn.com

YOUTH➔ Above the Influence: www.abovetheinfluence.com

Top-Selling Video Games of 2006

RANK	TITLE	PUBLISHER
1.	Madden NFL 07	Electronic Arts
2.	*Cars*	THQ
3.	Lego *Star Wars* II: The Original Trilogy	LucasArts
4.	NCAA Football 07	Electronic Arts
5.	New Super Mario Brothers	Nintendo
6.	Need for Speed: Most Wanted	Electronic Arts
7.	Gears of War	Microsoft
8.	Call of Duty 3	Activision
9.	Lego *Star Wars*	LucasArts
10.	Fight Night Round 3	Electronic Arts

Source: The NPD Group/Retail Tracking Service

MYSTERY PERSON

CLUE 1: I was born in Waterville, New York, in 1854. In 1889, I invented roll film and a handheld box camera. It was the very first Kodak camera.

CLUE 2: In 1900, I introduced a camera for kids, called the Brownie. It sold for $1.

CLUE 3: My inventions helped make photography easier. Taking digital pictures has now become a popular hobby.

WHO AM I? (See Answer Key on page 242.)

Computers & the Internet

35

SEEDS OF HOPE

A program aims to help Africa's farmers at the grassroots level

Walk through countless small villages in Sub-Saharan Africa and you will see the same scene: women and kids bent over, tending to scrawny plants. Every year, Africa's farms yield fewer and fewer crops. Many Africans are living on the edge of starvation.

Philanthropists Bill and Melinda Gates say it is time for a revolution. The Gates Foundation recently announced it was teaming up with the Rockefeller Foundation to fight hunger in Africa. The two groups will spend $150 million to boost farming methods on the continent. "Together, we share a vision for creating lasting change that will help millions of people in Africa lift themselves out of extreme poverty," says Melinda Gates.

SEEDS OF CHANGE

The new program is called the Alliance for a Green Revolution in Africa (AGRA). It is a back-to-basics plan that will start with the seeds farmers plant and end with the markets where they sell crops. AGRA wants to help scientists breed crops that flourish in Africa, then get seeds for those crops into the hands of farmers. In time, better harvests will result in surpluses that farmers can sell. AGRA also hopes to help farmers get and use chemical fertilizers, which will improve soil quality.

A WOMAN'S PLACE

Sub-Saharan Africa contains 16 of the world's 18 most undernourished countries. It is the only region on Earth where people have less food each year. The continent's farmers are mainly women.

For years, the Rockefeller Foundation has funded smaller programs to improve crop varieties in Africa. Most women scientists older than 40 "come from the land," Kenyan scientist Margaret Karembu told TIME. "We know what it means to have to harvest all day," she says. "When you have more women being exposed to technology, it helps, because they are more likely to work on ways to help their sisters back in the village."

African women scientists have developed more than 100 new crop varieties. New rice plants, called NERICA (New Rice for Africa), are adapted to growing conditions in the area. They have a shorter growing cycle and are resistant to weeds. The effects of planting hardier plants can already be felt. Children are spending less time in the field. School attendance is up in the areas where the new rice is grown.

Between 1960 and 1984, a green revolution more than doubled total food production in developing countries in Asia and Latin America. But experts agree that Africa is more complex, because growing conditions vary across the continent. "You're not going to develop a single crop that revolutionizes African agriculture," says Paula Bramel, a researcher in Tanzania. "This is a much more diverse place."

No one expects success to come easily. Even if governments and farmers do everything right, it will take years to see the fruits of their labor. But the Gates and Rockefeller Foundations envision a new Africa, where farmers aren't doomed to a life of hunger. They have started by planting a small seed of hope.

–BY NELLIE GONZALEZ CUTLER
REPORTED BY CHRISTINE GORMAN/NEW YORK; SIMON ROBINSON/JOHANNESBURG

NERICA seeds in Guinea

The World's Nations from A to Z

On the following pages you will find information about the world's nations. Here's an example.

If you divide the population by the area, you can find out the population density—how many people there are per square mile.

This tells the main languages and the official languages (if any) spoken in a nation. In this case, most people speak Icelandic.

This is the type of money used in the nation.

This tells an interesting fact about the country.

Iceland

WHERE? Europe
CAPITAL: Reykjavik
AREA: 39,768 sq mi (103,000 sq km)
POPULATION ESTIMATE (2007): 301,931
GOVERNMENT: Constitutional republic
LANGUAGE: Icelandic
MONETARY UNIT: Icelandic króna
LIFE EXPECTANCY: 80.2
LITERACY RATE: 100%
DID YOU KNOW? Iceland boasts the world's oldest constitution, drafted around 930.

Life expectancy is the number of years a person can expect to live. It's affected by heredity, a person's health and nutrition, the health care and wealth of a nation and a person's occupation.

This tells the percentage of people who can read and write.

Afghanistan

WHERE? Asia
CAPITAL: Kabul
AREA: 251,737 sq mi (647,500 sq km)
POPULATION ESTIMATE (2007): 31,889,923
GOVERNMENT: Multiparty republic
LANGUAGES: Pushtu, Dari Persian, other Turkic and minor languages
MONETARY UNIT: Afghani
LIFE EXPECTANCY: 42.5
LITERACY RATE: 36%
DID YOU KNOW? Afghanistan is the world's largest producer of opium.

Albania

WHERE? Europe
CAPITAL: Tirana
AREA: 11,100 sq mi (28,750 sq km)
POPULATION ESTIMATE (2007): 3,600,523
GOVERNMENT: Emerging democracy
LANGUAGES: Albanian (Tosk is the official dialect), Greek
MONETARY UNIT: Lek
LIFE EXPECTANCY: 77.1
LITERACY RATE: 87%
DID YOU KNOW? This former communist country is now a struggling democracy.

Algeria

WHERE? Africa
CAPITAL: Algiers
AREA: 919,590 sq mi (2,381,740 sq km)
POPULATION ESTIMATE (2007): 33,333,216
GOVERNMENT: Republic
LANGUAGES: Arabic (official), French, Berber dialects
MONETARY UNIT: Dinar
LIFE EXPECTANCY: 72.7
LITERACY RATE: 70%
DID YOU KNOW? The Sahara is a desert that covers about 85% of Algeria.

Andorra

WHERE? Europe
CAPITAL: Andorra la Vella
AREA: 181 sq mi (468 sq km)
POPULATION ESTIMATE (2007): 71,822
GOVERNMENT: Parliamentary democracy
LANGUAGES: Catalán (official), French, Spanish
MONETARY UNIT: Euro (formerly French franc and Spanish peseta)
LIFE EXPECTANCY: 83.5
LITERACY RATE: 100%
DID YOU KNOW? This country has the world's highest life expectancy.

For tons of world statistics, go to:
www.factmonster.com/worldstats

Countries of the World

Angola

WHERE? **Africa**
CAPITAL: **Luanda**
AREA: **481,350 sq mi
(1,246,700 sq km)**
POPULATION ESTIMATE (2007): **11,190,786**
GOVERNMENT: **Republic**
LANGUAGES: **Bantu, Portuguese (official)**
MONETARY UNIT: **Kwanza**
LIFE EXPECTANCY: **36.8**
LITERACY RATE: **42%**
DID YOU KNOW? **Angola is a major oil producer, but one of the world's poorest countries.**

Antigua and Barbuda

WHERE? **North America**
CAPITAL: **St. John's**
AREA: **171 sq mi
(443 sq km)**
POPULATION ESTIMATE (2007): **69,481**
GOVERNMENT: **Constitutional monarchy**
LANGUAGE: **English**
MONETARY UNIT: **East Caribbean dollar**
LIFE EXPECTANCY: **71.6**
LITERACY RATE: **89%**
DID YOU KNOW? **Barbuda's Frigate Bird Sanctuary is home to more than 170 bird species.**

Argentina

WHERE? **South America**
CAPITAL: **Buenos Aires**
AREA: **1,068,296 sq mi
(2,766,890 sq km)**
POPULATION ESTIMATE (2007): **40,301,927**
GOVERNMENT: **Republic**
LANGUAGES: **Spanish (official), English, Italian, German, French**
MONETARY UNIT: **Peso**
LIFE EXPECTANCY: **75.7**
LITERACY RATE: **96%**
DID YOU KNOW? **Most Argentineans are of Spanish or Italian descent.**

Armenia

WHERE? **Asia**
CAPITAL: **Yerevan**
AREA: **11,500 sq mi
(29,800 sq km)**
POPULATION ESTIMATE (2007): **2,971,650**
GOVERNMENT: **Republic**
LANGUAGE: **Armenian**
MONETARY UNIT: **Dram**
LIFE EXPECTANCY: **71.2**
LITERACY RATE: **99%**
DID YOU KNOW? **About 60% of the world's 8 million Armenians live outside Armenia.**

Australia

WHERE? **Pacific Islands**
CAPITAL: **Canberra**
AREA: **2,967,893 sq mi
(7,686,850 sq km)**
POPULATION ESTIMATE (2007): **20,434,176**
GOVERNMENT: **Democracy**
LANGUAGE: **English**
MONETARY UNIT: **Australian dollar**
LIFE EXPECTANCY: **80.3**
LITERACY RATE: **100%**
DID YOU KNOW? **Australia's Great Barrier Reef is the largest coral reef in the world.**

Austria

WHERE? **Europe**
CAPITAL: **Vienna**
AREA: **32,375 sq mi
(83,850 sq km)**
POPULATION ESTIMATE (2007): **8,199,783**
GOVERNMENT: **Federal Republic**
LANGUAGE: **German**
MONETARY UNIT: **Euro (formerly schilling)**
LIFE EXPECTANCY: **78.9**
LITERACY RATE: **98%**
DID YOU KNOW? **Three-quarters of Austria is covered by the Alps.**

Azerbaijan

WHERE? **Asia**

CAPITAL: **Baku**

AREA: **33,400 sq mi
(86,600 sq km)**

POPULATION ESTIMATE (2007): **8,120,247**

GOVERNMENT: **Republic**

LANGUAGES: **Azerbaijani Turkic, Russian, Armenian**

MONETARY UNIT: **Manat**

LIFE EXPECTANCY: **63.2**

LITERACY RATE: **97%**

DID YOU KNOW? **Oil recently discovered in Azerbaijan may improve its economy.**

Bahamas

WHERE? **North America**

CAPITAL: **Nassau**

AREA: **5,380 sq mi
(13,940 sq km)**

POPULATION ESTIMATE (2007): **305,655**

GOVERNMENT: **Parliamentary democracy**

LANGUAGE: **English**

MONETARY UNIT: **Bahamian dollar**

LIFE EXPECTANCY: **65.6**

LITERACY RATE: **96%**

DID YOU KNOW? **The Bahamas is made up of more than 700 islands.**

Bahrain

WHERE? **Asia**

CAPITAL: **Manamah**

AREA: **257 sq mi
(665 sq km)**

POPULATION ESTIMATE (2007): **708,573**

GOVERNMENT: **Constitutional monarchy**

LANGUAGES: **Arablc (official), English, Farsi, Urdu**

MONETARY UNIT: **Bahrain dinar**

LIFE EXPECTANCY: **74**

LITERACY RATE: **89%**

DID YOU KNOW? **Bahrain means "two seas."**

Bangladesh

WHERE? **Asia**

CAPITAL: **Dhaka**

AREA: **55,598 sq mi
(144,000 sq km)**

POPULATION ESTIMATE (2007):
150,448,339

GOVERNMENT: **Parliamentary democracy**

LANGUAGES: **Bangla (official), English**

MONETARY UNIT: **Taka**

LIFE EXPECTANCY: **61.7**

LITERACY RATE: **43%**

DID YOU KNOW? **Until 1971, Bangladesh was part of Pakistan.**

Barbados

WHERE? **North America**

CAPITAL: **Bridgetown**

AREA: **166 sq mi
(431 sq km)**

POPULATION ESTIMATE (2007): **280,946**

GOVERNMENT: **Parliamentary democracy**

LANGUAGE: **English**

MONETARY UNIT: **Barbados dollar**

LIFE EXPECTANCY: **71.6**

LITERACY RATE: **97%**

DID YOU KNOW? **Barbados was a British colony before its independence in 1966.**

Belarus

WHERE? **Europe**

CAPITAL: **Minsk**

AREA: **80,154 sq mi
(207,600 sq km)**

POPULATION ESTIMATE (2007): **9,724,723**

GOVERNMENT: **Republic**

LANGUAGE: **Belarussian**

MONETARY UNIT: **Belarussian ruble**

LIFE EXPECTANCY: **68.6**

LITERACY RATE: **100%**

DID YOU KNOW? **Belarus was part of the Soviet Union until becoming independent in 1991.**

Belgium

WHERE? Europe

CAPITAL: Brussels

AREA: 11,781 sq mi (30,510 sq km)

POPULATION ESTIMATE (2007): 10,392,226

GOVERNMENT: Constitutional monarchy

LANGUAGES: Dutch (Flemish), French, German (all official)

MONETARY UNIT: Euro (formerly Belgian franc)

LIFE EXPECTANCY: 78.4

LITERACY RATE: 98%

DID YOU KNOW? Nuclear power generates more than 75% of Belgium's electricity.

Belize

WHERE? Central America

CAPITAL: Belmopan

AREA: 8,865 sq mi (22,960 sq km)

POPULATION ESTIMATE (2007): 294,385

GOVERNMENT: Parliamentary democracy

LANGUAGES: English (official), Creole, Spanish, Garifuna, Mayan

MONETARY UNIT: Belize dollar

LIFE EXPECTANCY: 67.4

LITERACY RATE: 94%

DID YOU KNOW? Belize is the only English-speaking country in Central America.

Benin

WHERE? Africa

CAPITAL: Porto-Novo

AREA: 43,483 sq mi (112,620 sq km)

POPULATION ESTIMATE (2007): 8,078,314

GOVERNMENT: Multiparty democracy

LANGUAGES: French (official), African languages

MONETARY UNIT: CFA franc

LIFE EXPECTANCY: 50.8

LITERACY RATE: 41%

DID YOU KNOW? Benin's pottery, masks and bronze statues are world renowned.

Bhutan

WHERE? Asia

CAPITAL: Thimphu

AREA: 18,147 sq mi (47,000 sq km)

POPULATION ESTIMATE (2007): 2,327,849

GOVERNMENT: Monarchy

LANGUAGE: Dzongkha

MONETARY UNIT: Ngultrum

LIFE EXPECTANCY: 54

LITERACY RATE: 42%

DID YOU KNOW? About 75% of Bhutanese are Buddhists.

Bolivia

WHERE? South America

CAPITAL: La Paz (seat of government), Sucre (legal capital)

AREA: 424,162 sq mi (1,098,580 sq km)

POPULATION ESTIMATE (2007): 9,119,152

GOVERNMENT: Republic

LANGUAGES: Spanish (official), Quechua, Aymara, Guarani

MONETARY UNIT: Boliviano

LIFE EXPECTANCY: 65.1

LITERACY RATE: 87%

DID YOU KNOW? Bolivia has had more than 190 revolutions and coups since 1825.

Bosnia and Herzegovina

WHERE? Europe

CAPITAL: Sarajevo

AREA: 19,741 sq mi (51,129 sq km)

POPULATION ESTIMATE (2007): 4,552,198

GOVERNMENT: Emerging democracy

LANGUAGES: The language is called Serbian, Croatian or Bosnian depending on the speaker.

MONETARY UNIT: Dinar

LIFE EXPECTANCY: 72.6

LITERACY RATE: 94.6%

DID YOU KNOW? This country was a part of Yugoslavia until 1992.

Botswana

WHERE? **Africa**
CAPITAL: **Gaborone**
AREA: **231,800 sq mi (600,370 sq km)**
POPULATION ESTIMATE (2007): **1,639,131**
GOVERNMENT: **Parliamentary republic**
LANGUAGES: **English (official), Setswana**
MONETARY UNIT: **Pula**
LIFE EXPECTANCY: **34.2**
LITERACY RATE: **80%**
DID YOU KNOW? **The Kalahari is a desert located in this southern African country.**

Brazil

WHERE? **South America**
CAPITAL: **Brasília**
AREA: **3,286,470 sq mi (8,511,965 sq km)**
POPULATION ESTIMATE (2007): **190,010,647**
GOVERNMENT: **Federative republic**
LANGUAGE: **Portuguese**
MONETARY UNIT: **Real**
LIFE EXPECTANCY: **71.4**
LITERACY RATE: **86%**
DID YOU KNOW? **Brazil is the largest country in South America.**

Brunei

WHERE? **Asia**
CAPITAL: **Bandar Seri Begawan**
AREA: **2,228 sq mi (5,770 sq km)**
POPULATION ESTIMATE (2007): **386,511**
GOVERNMENT: **Constitutional sultanate**
LANGUAGES: **Malay (official), Chinese, English**
MONETARY UNIT: **Brunei dollar**
LIFE EXPECTANCY: **74.5**
LITERACY RATE: **92%**
DID YOU KNOW? **Brunei Darussalam, the country's full name, means "Brunei, the abode of peace."**

Bulgaria

WHERE? **Europe**
CAPITAL: **Sofia**
AREA: **48,822 sq mi (110,910 sq km)**
POPULATION ESTIMATE (2007): **7,322,858**
GOVERNMENT: **Parliamentary democracy**
LANGUAGE: **Bulgarian**
MONETARY UNIT: **Lev**
LIFE EXPECTANCY: **71.8**
LITERACY RATE: **99%**
DID YOU KNOW? **Bulgaria was a communist country until 1991.**

Burkina Faso

WHERE? **Africa**
CAPITAL: **Ouagadougou**
AREA: **105,870 sq mi (274,200 sq km)**
POPULATION ESTIMATE (2007): **14,326,203**
GOVERNMENT: **Parliamentary republic**
LANGUAGES: **French (official), tribal languages**
MONETARY UNIT: **CFA franc**
LIFE EXPECTANCY: **44.2**
LITERACY RATE: **27%**
DID YOU KNOW? **Burkina Faso means "the land of upright men."**

Burundi

WHERE? **Africa**
CAPITAL: **Bujumbura**
AREA: **10,745 sq mi (27,830 sq km)**
POPULATION ESTIMATE (2007): **8,390,505**
GOVERNMENT: **Republic**
LANGUAGES: **Kirundi and French (both official), Swahili**
MONETARY UNIT: **Burundi franc**
LIFE EXPECTANCY: **43.4**
LITERACY RATE: **52%**
DID YOU KNOW? **Burundi was once a German colony.**

For a list of the rulers of the world:
www.factmonster.com/worldrulers

Countries of the World

Cambodia

WHERE? **Asia**
CAPITAL: **Phnom Penh**
AREA: **69,900 sq mi (181,040 sq km)**
POPULATION ESTIMATE (2007): **14,131,858**
GOVERNMENT: **Democracy under a constitutional monarchy**
LANGUAGES: **Khmer (official), French, English**
MONETARY UNIT: **Riel**
LIFE EXPECTANCY: **58.4**
LITERACY RATE: **70%**

DID YOU KNOW? **Cambodia's Angkor Wat temple is one of the world's wonders.**

Cameroon

WHERE? **Africa**
CAPITAL: **Yaoundé**
AREA: **183,567 sq mi (475,440 sq km)**
POPULATION ESTIMATE (2007): **18,060,382**
GOVERNMENT: **Unitary republic**
LANGUAGES: **French and English (both official), African languages**
MONETARY UNIT: **CFA franc**
LIFE EXPECTANCY: **48**
LITERACY RATE: **79%**

DID YOU KNOW? **Germany, France and Britain have controlled Cameroon in the past.**

Canada

WHERE? **North America**
CAPITAL: **Ottawa, Ontario**
AREA: **3,851,788 sq mi (9,976,140 sq km)**
POPULATION ESTIMATE (2007): **33,390,141**
GOVERNMENT: **Parliamentary democracy**
LANGUAGES: **English and French (both official)**
MONETARY UNIT: **Canadian dollar**
LIFE EXPECTANCY: **80**
LITERACY RATE: **97%**

DID YOU KNOW? **Canada is the world's second largest country.**

Cape Verde

WHERE? **Africa**
CAPITAL: **Praia**
AREA: **1,557 sq mi (4,033 sq km)**
POPULATION ESTIMATE (2007): **423,613**
GOVERNMENT: **Republic**
LANGUAGES: **Portuguese, Crioulo**
MONETARY UNIT: **Cape Verdean escudo**
LIFE EXPECTANCY: **70.1**
LITERACY RATE: **77%**

DID YOU KNOW? **Cape Verde is home to loggerhead turtles and humpback whales.**

Central African Republic

WHERE? **Africa**
CAPITAL: **Bangui**
AREA: **240,534 sq mi (622,984 sq km)**
POPULATION ESTIMATE (2007): **4,369,038**
GOVERNMENT: **Republic**
LANGUAGES: **French (official), Sangho, Arabic, Hansa, Swahili**
MONETARY UNIT: **CFA franc**
LIFE EXPECTANCY: **41.4**
LITERACY RATE: **51%**

DID YOU KNOW? **This country was called the Central African Empire from 1976 to 1979.**

Chad

WHERE? **Africa**
CAPITAL: **N'Djamena**
AREA: **495,752 sq mi (1,284,000 sq km)**
POPULATION ESTIMATE (2007): **10,238,807**
GOVERNMENT: **Republic**
LANGUAGES: **French and Arabic (both official), Sara, other languages**
MONETARY UNIT: **CFA franc**
LIFE EXPECTANCY: **48.2**
LITERACY RATE: **48%**

DID YOU KNOW? **The country is named for its largest lake, Lake Chad.**

Chile

WHERE? South America
CAPITAL: Santiago
AREA: 292,258 sq mi (756,950 sq km)
POPULATION ESTIMATE (2007): 16,284,741
GOVERNMENT: Republic
LANGUAGE: Spanish
MONETARY UNIT: Peso
LIFE EXPECTANCY: 76.4
LITERACY RATE: 96%
DID YOU KNOW? Chile's Atacama Desert is the driest place on Earth.

China

WHERE? Asia
CAPITAL: Beijing
AREA: 3,705,386 sq mi (9,596,960 sq km)
POPULATION ESTIMATE (2007): 1,321,851,888
GOVERNMENT: Communist state
LANGUAGES: Chinese (Mandarin), local dialects
MONETARY UNIT: Yuan
LIFE EXPECTANCY: 72
LITERACY RATE: 86%
DID YOU KNOW? China is the most populous country in the world.

Colombia

WHERE? South America
CAPITAL: Bogotá
AREA: 439,733 sq mi (1,138,910 sq km)
POPULATION ESTIMATE (2007): 44,227,550
GOVERNMENT: Republic
LANGUAGE: Spanish
MONETARY UNIT: Peso
LIFE EXPECTANCY: 71.4
LITERACY RATE: 93%
DID YOU KNOW? Coffee is Colombia's major crop.

Comoros

WHERE? Africa
CAPITAL: Moroni
AREA: 838 sq mi (2,170 sq km)
POPULATION ESTIMATE (2007): 710,960
GOVERNMENT: Republic
LANGUAGES: French and Arabic (both official), Shaafi Islam (Swahili dialect), Malagasu
MONETARY UNIT: CFA franc
LIFE EXPECTANCY: 61.6
LITERACY RATE: 57%
DID YOU KNOW? Comoros is made up of three tiny islands off the East African coast.

Congo, Democratic Republic of the

WHERE? Africa
CAPITAL: Kinshasa
AREA: 905,562 sq mi (2,345,410 sq km)
POPULATION ESTIMATE (2007): 64,606,759
GOVERNMENT: Dictatorship
LANGUAGES: French (official), Swahili, Lingala, Ishiluba, Kikongo, others
MONETARY UNIT: Congolese franc
LIFE EXPECTANCY: 49.1
LITERACY RATE: 66%
DID YOU KNOW? This country was formerly named Zaïre.

Congo, Republic of the

WHERE? Africa
CAPITAL: Brazzaville
AREA: 132,046 sq mi (342,000 sq km)
POPULATION ESTIMATE (2007): 3,800,610
GOVERNMENT: Dictatorship
LANGUAGES: French (official), Lingala, Kikongo, others
MONETARY UNIT: CFA franc
LIFE EXPECTANCY: 49.5
LITERACY RATE: 84%
DID YOU KNOW? Petroleum production provides 90% of the country's revenues and exports.

Costa Rica

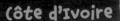

WHERE? Central America
CAPITAL: San José
AREA: 19,730 sq mi (51,100 sq km)
POPULATION ESTIMATE (2007): 4,133,884
GOVERNMENT: Republic
LANGUAGE: Spanish
MONETARY UNIT: Colón
LIFE EXPECTANCY: 76.6
LITERACY RATE: 96%
DID YOU KNOW? This country's name means "rich coast."

Côte d'Ivoire

WHERE? Africa
CAPITAL: Yamoussoukro
AREA: 124,502 sq mi (322,460 sq km)
POPULATION ESTIMATE (2007): 18,013,409
GOVERNMENT: Republic
LANGUAGES: French (official), African languages
MONETARY UNIT: CFA franc
LIFE EXPECTANCY: 48.4
LITERACY RATE: 51%
DID YOU KNOW? Côte d'Ivoire is the world's largest exporter of cocoa.

Croatia

WHERE? Europe
CAPITAL: Zagreb
AREA: 21,829 sq mi (56,538 sq km)
POPULATION ESTIMATE (2007): 4,493,312
GOVERNMENT: Parliamentary democracy
LANGUAGE: Croatian
MONETARY UNIT: Kuna
LIFE EXPECTANCY: 74.1
LITERACY RATE: 99%
DID YOU KNOW? Croatia was part of Yugoslavia until it declared independence in 1991.

Cuba

WHERE? North America
CAPITAL: Havana
AREA: 42,803 sq mi (110,860 sq km)
POPULATION ESTIMATE (2007): 11,416,987
GOVERNMENT: Communist state
LANGUAGE: Spanish
MONETARY UNIT: Peso
LIFE EXPECTANCY: 77
LITERACY RATE: 97%
DID YOU KNOW? Cuba is one of five Communist countries in the world.

Cyprus

WHERE? Middle East
CAPITAL: Nicosia
AREA: 3,572 sq mi (9,250 sq km)
POPULATION ESTIMATE (2007): 788,457
GOVERNMENT: Republic
LANGUAGES: Greek, Turkish
MONETARY UNITS: Cypriot pound, Turkish lira
LIFE EXPECTANCY: 77.5
LITERACY RATE: 98%
DID YOU KNOW? This nation is divided by a long-standing conflict between its Greek and Turkish populations.

Czech Republic

WHERE? Europe
CAPITAL: Prague
AREA: 30,450 sq mi (78,866 sq km)
POPULATION ESTIMATE (2007): 10,228,744
GOVERNMENT: Parliamentary democracy
LANGUAGE: Czech
MONETARY UNIT: Koruna
LIFE EXPECTANCY: 75.8
LITERACY RATE: 100%
DID YOU KNOW? Until 1993, the country was part of Czechoslovakia, which no longer exists.

Denmark

WHERE? **Europe**
CAPITAL: **Copenhagen**
AREA: **16,639 sq mi
(43,094 sq km)**
POPULATION ESTIMATE (2007): **5,468,120**
GOVERNMENT: **Constitutional monarchy**
LANGUAGES: **Danish, Faeroese,
Greenlandic, German**
MONETARY UNIT: **Krone**
LIFE EXPECTANCY: **77.4**
LITERACY RATE: **100%**
DID YOU KNOW? **One of Denmark's territories,
Greenland, is the world's largest island.**

Djibouti

WHERE? **Africa**
CAPITAL: **Djibouti**
AREA: **8,800 sq mi
(23,000 sq km)**
POPULATION ESTIMATE (2007): **496,374**
GOVERNMENT: **Republic**
LANGUAGES: **Arabic and French (both
official), Afar, Somali**
MONETARY UNIT: **Djibouti franc**
LIFE EXPECTANCY: **43.1**
LITERACY RATE: **68%**
DID YOU KNOW? **This country contains
the only U.S. military base in Africa.**

Dominica

WHERE? **North America**
CAPITAL: **Roseau**
AREA: **290 sq mi
(750 sq km)**
POPULATION ESTIMATE (2007): **68,925**
GOVERNMENT: **Parliamentary democracy**
LANGUAGES: **English (official), French patois**
MONETARY UNIT: **East Caribbean dollar**
LIFE EXPECTANCY: **74.4**
LITERACY RATE: **94%**
DID YOU KNOW? **This mountainous
Caribbean island nation was explored by
Columbus in 1493.**

Dominican Republic

WHERE? **North America**
CAPITAL: **Santo Domingo**
AREA: **18,815 sq mi
(48,730 sq km)**
POPULATION ESTIMATE (2007): **9,365,818**
GOVERNMENT: **Representative democracy**
LANGUAGE: **Spanish**
MONETARY UNIT: **Peso**
LIFE EXPECTANCY: **67.6**
LITERACY RATE: **85%**
DID YOU KNOW? **This country and Haiti
make up the island of Hispaniola in the
Caribbean.**

East Timor

WHERE? **Asia**
CAPITAL: **Dili**
AREA: **5,814 sq mi
(15,057 sq km)**
POPULATION ESTIMATE (2007): **1,084,971**
GOVERNMENT: **Republic**
LANGUAGES: **Tetum, Portuguese (official),
Bahasa Indonesia, English**
MONETARY UNIT: **U.S. dollar**
LIFE EXPECTANCY: **65.6**
LITERACY RATE: **48%**
DID YOU KNOW? **In 2002, East Timor gained
independence from Indonesia, becoming
the first new country of the millennium.**

Ecuador

WHERE? **South America**
CAPITAL: **Quito**
AREA: **109,483 sq mi
(283,560 sq km)**
POPULATION ESTIMATE (2007): **13,755,680**
GOVERNMENT: **Republic**
LANGUAGES: **Spanish (official), Quechua**
MONETARY UNIT: **U.S. dollar**
LIFE EXPECTANCY: **76**
LITERACY RATE: **93%**
DID YOU KNOW? **The country takes its
name from the equator, which runs
through it.**

Egypt

WHERE? **Africa**
CAPITAL: **Cairo**
AREA: **386,660 sq mi
(1,001,450 sq km)**
POPULATION ESTIMATE (2007): **80,264,543**
GOVERNMENT: **Republic**
LANGUAGE: **Arabic**
MONETARY UNIT: **Egyptian pound**
LIFE EXPECTANCY: **70.7**
LITERACY RATE: **58%**
DID YOU KNOW? Almost 95% of Egypt
is desert.

El Salvador

WHERE? **Central America**
CAPITAL: **San Salvador**
AREA: **8,124 sq mi
(21,040 sq km)**
POPULATION ESTIMATE (2007): **6,939,688**
GOVERNMENT: **Republic**
LANGUAGE: **Spanish**
MONETARY UNIT: **U.S. dollar**
LIFE EXPECTANCY: **70.9**
LITERACY RATE: **80%**
DID YOU KNOW? El Salvador is the
smallest country in Central America.

Equatorial Guinea

WHERE? **Africa**
CAPITAL: **Malabo**
AREA: **10,830 sq mi
(28,050 sq km)**
POPULATION ESTIMATE (2007): **551,201**
GOVERNMENT: **Republic**
LANGUAGES: **Spanish, French (both official),
pidgin English, Fang, Bubi, Creole**
MONETARY UNIT: **CFA franc**
LIFE EXPECTANCY: **55.1**
LITERACY RATE: **86%**
DID YOU KNOW? This is Africa's only
Spanish-speaking country.

Eritrea

WHERE? **Africa**
CAPITAL: **Asmara**
AREA: **46,842 sq mi
(121,320 sq km)**
POPULATION ESTIMATE (2007): **4,906,585**
GOVERNMENT: **Transitional**
LANGUAGES: **Afar, Bilen, Kunama, Nara,
Arabic, Tobedawi, Saho, Tigre, Tigrinya**
MONETARY UNIT: **Nakfa**
LIFE EXPECTANCY: **52.7**
LITERACY RATE: **59%**
DID YOU KNOW? Once a part of Ethiopia,
Eritrea became independent in 1993.

Estonia

WHERE? **Europe**
CAPITAL: **Tallinn**
AREA: **17,462 sq mi
(45,226 sq km)**
POPULATION ESTIMATE (2007): **1,315,912**
GOVERNMENT: **Parliamentary democracy**
LANGUAGES: **Estonian (official), Russian,
Finnish, English**
MONETARY UNIT: **Kroon**
LIFE EXPECTANCY: **71.4**
LITERACY RATE: **100%**
DID YOU KNOW? Estonia was once part of
the Soviet Union and gained its
independence in 1991.

Ethiopia

WHERE? **Africa**
CAPITAL: **Addis Ababa**
AREA: **485,184 sq mi
(1,127,127 sq km)**
POPULATION ESTIMATE (2007): **76,511,887**
GOVERNMENT: **Federal republic**
LANGUAGES: **Amharic (official), English,
Orominga, Tigrigna, others**
MONETARY UNIT: **Birr**
LIFE EXPECTANCY: **48.6**
LITERACY RATE: **43%**
DID YOU KNOW? Remains of the oldest-
known human ancestors have
been found in Ethiopia.

Fiji

WHERE? **Oceania**
CAPITAL: **Suva**
AREA: **7,054 sq mi (18,270 sq km)**
POPULATION ESTIMATE (2007): **918,675**
GOVERNMENT: **Republic**
LANGUAGES: **Fijian, Hindustani, English (official)**
MONETARY UNIT: **Fiji dollar**
LIFE EXPECTANCY: **69.2**
LITERACY RATE: **94%**
DID YOU KNOW? **Fiji is made up of 332 islands in the South Pacific.**

Finland

WHERE? **Europe**
CAPITAL: **Helsinki**
AREA: **130,127 sq mi (337,030 sq km)**
POPULATION ESTIMATE (2007): **5,238,460**
GOVERNMENT: **Republic**
LANGUAGES: **Finnish and Swedish (both official)**
MONETARY UNIT: **Euro (formerly markka)**
LIFE EXPECTANCY: **78.2**
LITERACY RATE: **100%**
DID YOU KNOW? **Laplanders live in the north of Finland, above the Arctic Circle.**

France

WHERE? **Europe**
CAPITAL: **Paris**
AREA: **211,208 sq mi (547,030 sq km)**
POPULATION ESTIMATE (2007): **61,083,916**
GOVERNMENT: **Republic**
LANGUAGE: **French**
MONETARY UNIT: **Euro (formerly French franc)**
LIFE EXPECTANCY: **79.4**
LITERACY RATE: **99%**
DID YOU KNOW? **France is the world's top travel destination.**

Gabon

WHERE? **Africa**
CAPITAL: **Libreville**
AREA: **103,347 sq mi (267,670 sq km)**
POPULATION ESTIMATE (2007): **1,454,867**
GOVERNMENT: **Republic**
LANGUAGES: **French (official), Fang, Myene, Bateke, Bapounou/Eschira, Bandjabi**
MONETARY UNIT: **CFA franc**
LIFE EXPECTANCY: **56.5**
LITERACY RATE: **63%**
DID YOU KNOW? **Gabon's president, Omar Bongo Ondimba, has been in office since 1967.**

The Gambia

WHERE? **Africa**
CAPITAL: **Banjul**
AREA: **4,363 sq mi (11,300 sq km)**
POPULATION ESTIMATE (2007): **1,688,359**
GOVERNMENT: **Republic**
LANGUAGES: **English (official), native languages**
MONETARY UNIT: **Dalasi**
LIFE EXPECTANCY: **54.8**
LITERACY RATE: **40%**
DID YOU KNOW? **Gambia is Africa's smallest country.**

Georgia

WHERE? **Asia**
CAPITAL: **T'bilisi**
AREA: **26,911 sq mi (69,700 sq km)**
POPULATION ESTIMATE (2007): **4,646,003**
GOVERNMENT: **Republic**
LANGUAGES: **Georgian (official), Russian, Armenian, Azerbaijani**
MONETARY UNIT: **Lari**
LIFE EXPECTANCY: **75.6**
LITERACY RATE: **99%**
DID YOU KNOW? **Georgia was part of the Soviet Union before its breakup in 1991.**

Germany

WHERE? Europe
CAPITAL: Berlin
AREA: 137,846 sq mi (357,021 sq km)
POPULATION ESTIMATE (2007): 82,400,996
GOVERNMENT: Federal republic
LANGUAGE: German
MONETARY UNIT: Euro (formerly deutsche mark)
LIFE EXPECTANCY: 78.5
LITERACY RATE: 99%
DID YOU KNOW? The country was divided into East and West Germany from 1949 to 1990.

Ghana

WHERE? Africa
CAPITAL: Accra
AREA: 92,456 sq mi (239,460 sq km)
POPULATION ESTIMATE (2007): 22,931,299
GOVERNMENT: Constitutional democracy
LANGUAGES: English (official), native languages
MONETARY UNIT: Cedi
LIFE EXPECTANCY: 56.3
LITERACY RATE: 75%
DID YOU KNOW? Ghana was formerly a British colony called the Gold Coast.

Greece

WHERE? Europe
CAPITAL: Athens
AREA: 50,942 sq mi (131,940 sq km)
POPULATION ESTIMATE (2007): 10,706,290
GOVERNMENT: Parliamentary republic
LANGUAGE: Greek
MONETARY UNIT: Euro (formerly drachma)
LIFE EXPECTANCY: 78.9
LITERACY RATE: 98%
DID YOU KNOW? Greece is known for its magnificent ancient temples, particularly the world-renowned Parthenon.

Grenada

WHERE? North America
CAPITAL: Saint George's
AREA: 133 sq mi (344 sq km)
POPULATION ESTIMATE (2007): 89,971
GOVERNMENT: Constitutional monarchy
LANGUAGE: English
MONETARY UNIT: East Caribbean dollar
LIFE EXPECTANCY: 64.5
LITERACY RATE: 90%
DID YOU KNOW? Grenada is an important producer of spices, including nutmeg, cinnamon and ginger.

Guatemala

WHERE? Central America
CAPITAL: Guatemala City
AREA: 42,042 sq mi (108,890 sq km)
POPULATION ESTIMATE (2007): 12,728,111
GOVERNMENT: Republic
LANGUAGES: Spanish (official), Indian languages
MONETARY UNIT: Quetzal
LIFE EXPECTANCY: 65.2
LITERACY RATE: 71%
DID YOU KNOW? Most Guatemalans are of Mayan or Spanish descent.

Guinea

WHERE? Africa
CAPITAL: Conakry
AREA: 94,925 sq mi (245,860 sq km)
POPULATION ESTIMATE (2007): 9,947,814
GOVERNMENT: Republic
LANGUAGES: French (official), native languages
MONETARY UNIT: Guinean franc
LIFE EXPECTANCY: 49.7
LITERACY RATE: 36%
DID YOU KNOW? Guinea's chief exports are agricultural products and minerals, especially bauxite.

Guinea-Bissau

WHERE? **Africa**
CAPITAL: **Bissau**
AREA: **13,946 sq mi (36,120 sq km)**
POPULATION ESTIMATE (2007): **1,472,041**
GOVERNMENT: **Republic**
LANGUAGES: **Portuguese (official), African languages**
MONETARY UNIT: **CFA franc**
LIFE EXPECTANCY: **47**
LITERACY RATE: **42%**
DID YOU KNOW? **This country was once a Portuguese colony.**

Guyana

WHERE? **South America**
CAPITAL: **Georgetown**
AREA: **83,000 sq mi (214,970 sq km)**
POPULATION ESTIMATE (2007): **769,095**
GOVERNMENT: **Republic**
LANGUAGES: **English (official), Amerindian dialects**
MONETARY UNIT: **Guyana dollar**
LIFE EXPECTANCY: **65.1**
LITERACY RATE: **99%**
DID YOU KNOW? **Guyana's people are primarily of East Indian and African descent.**

Haiti

WHERE? **North America**
CAPITAL: **Port-au-Prince**
AREA: **10,714 sq mi (27,750 sq km)**
POPULATION ESTIMATE (2007): **8,706,497**
GOVERNMENT: **Elected government**
LANGUAGES: **Creole and French (both official)**
MONETARY UNIT: **Gourde**
LIFE EXPECTANCY: **52.6**
LITERACY RATE: **53%**
DID YOU KNOW? **In 1804, Haiti became the world's first independent black republic.**

Honduras

WHERE? **Central America**
CAPITAL: **Tegucigalpa**
AREA: **43,278 sq mi (112,090 sq km)**
POPULATION ESTIMATE (2007): **7,483,763**
GOVERNMENT: **Republic**
LANGUAGES: **Spanish, Amerindian dialects**
MONETARY UNIT: **Lempira**
LIFE EXPECTANCY: **66.2**
LITERACY RATE: **76%**
DID YOU KNOW? **About 80% of Honduras is mountainous.**

Hungary

WHERE? **Europe**
CAPITAL: **Budapest**
AREA: **35,919 sq mi (93,030 sq km)**
POPULATION ESTIMATE (2007): **9,956,108**
GOVERNMENT: **Parliamentary democracy**
LANGUAGE: **Magyar (Hungarian)**
MONETARY UNIT: **Forint**
LIFE EXPECTANCY: **72.2**
LITERACY RATE: **99%**
DID YOU KNOW? *Magyar* **is the Hungarian name for Hungary's people.**

Iceland

WHERE? **Europe**
CAPITAL: **Reykjavik**
AREA: **39,768 sq mi (103,000 sq km)**
POPULATION ESTIMATE (2007): **301,931**
GOVERNMENT: **Constitutional republic**
LANGUAGE: **Icelandic**
MONETARY UNIT: **Icelandic krona**
LIFE EXPECTANCY: **80.2**
LITERACY RATE: **100%**
DID YOU KNOW? **Iceland boasts the world's oldest constitution, drafted around 930.**

India

WHERE? Asia
CAPITAL: New Delhi
AREA: 1,269,338 sq mi
(3,287,590 sq km)
POPULATION ESTIMATE (2007): 1,129,866,154
GOVERNMENT: Republic
LANGUAGES: Hindi (national), English;
24 major languages plus more than
1,600 dialects
MONETARY UNIT: Rupee
LIFE EXPECTANCY: 64
LITERACY RATE: 60%
DID YOU KNOW? The Indian film industry
makes more films than any other.

Indonesia

WHERE? Asia
CAPITAL: Jakarta
AREA: 741,096 sq mi
(1,919,440 sq km)
POPULATION ESTIMATE (2007): 234,693,997
GOVERNMENT: Republic
LANGUAGES: Bahasa Indonesia (official),
Dutch, English; more than 500 languages
and dialects
MONETARY UNIT: Rupiah
LIFE EXPECTANCY: 69.3
LITERACY RATE: 89%
DID YOU KNOW? Indonesia has the largest
number of active volcanoes in the world.

Iran

WHERE? Middle East
CAPITAL: Tehran
AREA: 636,293 sq mi
(1,648,000 sq km)
POPULATION ESTIMATE (2007): 65,397,521
GOVERNMENT: Theocratic republic
LANGUAGES: Farsi (Persian), Azari,
Kurdish, Arabic
MONETARY UNIT: Rial
LIFE EXPECTANCY: 69.7
LITERACY RATE: 79%
DID YOU KNOW? Iran was once known
as Persia.

Iraq

WHERE? Middle East
CAPITAL: Baghdad
AREA: 168,753 sq mi
(437,072 sq km)
POPULATION ESTIMATE (2007): 27,499,638
GOVERNMENT: Transitional
LANGUAGES: Arabic, Kurdish
MONETARY UNIT: Iraqi dinar
LIFE EXPECTANCY: 68.3
LITERACY RATE: 40%
DID YOU KNOW? The ancient civilization
of Mesopotamia was located in what is
today called Iraq.

Ireland

WHERE? Europe
CAPITAL: Dublin
AREA: 27,136 sq mi
(70,280 sq km)
POPULATION ESTIMATE (2007): 4,109,086
GOVERNMENT: Republic
LANGUAGES: English, Irish Gaelic
MONETARY UNIT: Euro (formerly Irish
pound, or punt)
LIFE EXPECTANCY: 77.4
LITERACY RATE: 98%
DID YOU KNOW? The name for Ireland in
Gaelic (the Irish language) is *Eire*.

Israel

WHERE? Middle East
CAPITAL: Jerusalem
AREA: 8,020 sq mi
(20,770 sq km)
POPULATION ESTIMATE (2007): 6,426,679
GOVERNMENT: Parliamentary democracy
LANGUAGES: Hebrew (official), Arabic,
English
MONETARY UNIT: Shekel
LIFE EXPECTANCY: 79.2
LITERACY RATE: 95%
DID YOU KNOW? Modern Israel became a
country in 1948.

Italy

WHERE? **Europe**
CAPITAL: **Rome**
AREA: **116,305 sq mi
(301,230 sq km)**
POPULATION ESTIMATE (2007): **2,780,132**
GOVERNMENT: **Republic**
LANGUAGE: **Italian**
MONETARY UNIT: **Euro (formerly lira)**
LIFE EXPECTANCY: **79.5**
LITERACY RATE: **99%**
DID YOU KNOW? **Italy is known for its magnificent art treasures and architecture.**

Jamaica

WHERE? **North America**
CAPITAL: **Kingston**
AREA: **4,244 sq mi
(10,991 sq km)**
POPULATION ESTIMATE (2007): **2,780,132**
GOVERNMENT: **Parliamentary democracy**
LANGUAGES: **English, patois English**
MONETARY UNIT: **Jamaican dollar**
LIFE EXPECTANCY: **76.1**
LITERACY RATE: **88%**
DID YOU KNOW? **Jamaica once had a large slave population that worked on sugarcane plantations.**

Japan

WHERE? **Asia**
CAPITAL: **Tokyo**
AREA: **145,882 sq mi
(377,835 sq km)**
POPULATION ESTIMATE (2007): **127,467,972**
GOVERNMENT: **Constitutional monarchy**
LANGUAGE: **Japanese**
MONETARY UNIT: **Yen**
LIFE EXPECTANCY: **81**
LITERACY RATE: **99%**
DID YOU KNOW? **Japan has the world's second largest economy.**

Jordan

WHERE? **Middle East**
CAPITAL: **Amman**
AREA: **34,445 sq mi
(89,213 sq km)**
POPULATION ESTIMATE (2007): **6,053,193**
GOVERNMENT: **Constitutional monarchy**
LANGUAGES: **Arabic (official), English**
MONETARY UNIT: **Jordanian dinar**
LIFE EXPECTANCY: **78.1**
LITERACY RATE: **91%**
DID YOU KNOW? **Jordan is a kingdom ruled by the Hashemite dynasty.**

Kazakhstan

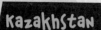

WHERE? **Asia**
CAPITAL: **Astana**
AREA: **1,049,150 sq mi
(2,717,300 sq km)**
POPULATION ESTIMATE (2007): **15,284,929**
GOVERNMENT: **Republic**
LANGUAGES: **Kazak (Qazaq) and Russian (both official)**
MONETARY UNIT: **Tenge**
LIFE EXPECTANCY: **66.1**
LITERACY RATE: **98%**
DID YOU KNOW? **Oil was discovered in Kazakhstan in 2000. It was the largest oil find in 30 years.**

Kenya

WHERE? **Africa**
CAPITAL: **Nairobi**
AREA: **224,960 sq mi
(582,650 sq km)**
POPULATION ESTIMATE (2007): **36,913,721**
GOVERNMENT: **Republic**
LANGUAGES: **English (official), Swahili, several others**
MONETARY UNIT: **Kenyan shilling**
LIFE EXPECTANCY: **47.2**
LITERACY RATE: **85%**
DID YOU KNOW? **About 40 different ethnic groups live in Kenya.**

Kiribati

WHERE? **Pacific Islands**
CAPITAL: **Tarawa**
AREA: **313 sq mi**
(811 sq km)
POPULATION ESTIMATE (2007): **107,817**
GOVERNMENT: **Republic**
LANGUAGES: **English (official), I-Kiribati (Gilbertese)**
MONETARY UNIT: **Australian dollar**
LIFE EXPECTANCY: **61.3**
LITERACY RATE: **Not available**
DID YOU KNOW? **This nation is made up of three widely separated island groups in the South Pacific.**

Korea, North

WHERE? **Asia**
CAPITAL: **Pyongyang**
AREA: **46,540 sq mi**
(120,540 sq km)
POPULATION ESTIMATE (2007): **23,301,725**
GOVERNMENT: **Communist dictatorship**
LANGUAGE: **Korean**
MONETARY UNIT: **Won**
LIFE EXPECTANCY: **71.1**
LITERACY RATE: **99%**
DID YOU KNOW? **North Korea is one of the world's few communist countries.**

Korea, South

WHERE? **Asia**
CAPITAL: **Seoul**
AREA: **38,023 sq mi**
(98,480 sq km)
POPULATION ESTIMATE (2007): **49,044,790**
GOVERNMENT: **Republic**
LANGUAGE: **Korean**
MONETARY UNIT: **Won**
LIFE EXPECTANCY: **75.6**
LITERACY RATE: **98%**
DID YOU KNOW? **About half of South Korea's religious people are Christian; the other half are Buddhist.**

Kuwait

WHERE? **Middle East**
CAPITAL: **Kuwait**
AREA: **6,880 sq mi**
(17,820 sq km)
POPULATION ESTIMATE (2007): **2,505,559**
GOVERNMENT: **Constitutional monarchy**
LANGUAGES: **Arabic (official), English**
MONETARY UNIT: **Kuwaiti dinar**
LIFE EXPECTANCY: **76.8**
LITERACY RATE: **84%**
DID YOU KNOW? **This small country has the fourth largest oil reserves in the world.**

Kyrgyzstan

WHERE? **Asia**
CAPITAL: **Bishkek**
AREA: **76,641 sq mi**
(198,500 sq km)
POPULATION ESTIMATE (2007): **5,284,149**
GOVERNMENT: **Republic**
LANGUAGES: **Kyrgyz (official), Russian**
MONETARY UNIT: **Som**
LIFE EXPECTANCY: **67.8**
LITERACY RATE: **97%**
DID YOU KNOW? **The Tien Shan mountain range covers about 95% of the country.**

Laos

WHERE? **Asia**
CAPITAL: **Vientiane**
AREA: **91,429 sq mi**
(236,800 sq km)
POPULATION ESTIMATE (2007): **6,521,998**
GOVERNMENT: **Communist state**
LANGUAGES: **Lao (official), French, English**
MONETARY UNIT: **Kip**
LIFE EXPECTANCY: **54.7**
LITERACY RATE: **53%**
DID YOU KNOW? **Subsistence farmers make up more than 80% of Laos's population.**

Latvia

WHERE? **Europe**
CAPITAL: **Riga**
AREA: **24,938 sq mi (64,589 sq km)**
POPULATION ESTIMATE (2007): **2,259,810**
GOVERNMENT: **Parliamentary democracy**
LANGUAGE: **Latvian**
MONETARY UNIT: **Lats**
LIFE EXPECTANCY: **70.9**
LITERACY RATE: **100%**
DID YOU KNOW? **One of the three Baltic countries, Latvia is located in the far north of Europe.**

Lebanon

WHERE? **Middle East**
CAPITAL: **Beirut**
AREA: **4,015 sq mi (10,400 sq km)**
POPULATION ESTIMATE (2007): **3,921,278**
GOVERNMENT: **Republic**
LANGUAGES: **Arabic (official), French, English**
MONETARY UNIT: **Lebanese pound**
LIFE EXPECTANCY: **72.3**
LITERACY RATE: **87%**
DID YOU KNOW? **Lebanon is the only Middle Eastern country without a desert.**

Lesotho

WHERE? **Africa**
CAPITAL: **Maseru**
AREA: **11,720 sq mi (30,350 sq km)**
POPULATION ESTIMATE (2007): **2,012,649**
GOVERNMENT: **Monarchy**
LANGUAGES: **English and Sesotho (both official), Zulu, Xhosa**
MONETARY UNIT: **Loti**
LIFE EXPECTANCY: **36.8**
LITERACY RATE: **85%**
DID YOU KNOW? **This small African kingdom is surrounded on all sides by South Africa.**

Liberia

WHERE? **Africa**
CAPITAL: **Monrovia**
AREA: **43,000 sq mi (111,370 sq km)**
POPULATION ESTIMATE (2007): **3,193,942**
GOVERNMENT: **Republic**
LANGUAGES: **English (official), tribal dialects**
MONETARY UNIT: **Liberian dollar**
LIFE EXPECTANCY: **47.9**
LITERACY RATE: **58%**
DID YOU KNOW? **Liberia was founded by freed American slaves in 1847.**

Libya

WHERE? **Africa**
CAPITAL: **Tripoli**
AREA: **679,358 sq mi (1,759,540 sq km)**
POPULATION ESTIMATE (2007): **6,036,914**
GOVERNMENT: **Military dictatorship**
LANGUAGES: **Arabic, Italian, English**
MONETARY UNIT: **Libyan dinar**
LIFE EXPECTANCY: **76.3**
LITERACY RATE: **83%**
DID YOU KNOW? **The world's highest temperature ever recorded (136°F) was in Al Azizyah, Libya, in 1922.**

Liechtenstein

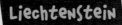

WHERE? **Europe**
CAPITAL: **Vaduz**
AREA: **62 sq mi (160 sq km)**
POPULATION ESTIMATE (2007): **34,247**
GOVERNMENT: **Constitutional monarchy**
LANGUAGES: **German (official), Alemannic dialect**
MONETARY UNIT: **Swiss franc**
LIFE EXPECTANCY: **79.4**
LITERACY RATE: **100%**
DID YOU KNOW? **This tiny kingdom has been neutral in all of Europe's wars since 1868.**

Countries of the World

For a look at the most populous cities in the world:
www.factmonster.com/populouscities

Lithuania

WHERE? **Europe**
CAPITAL: **Vilnius**
AREA: **25,174 sq mi (65,200 sq km)**
POPULATION ESTIMATE (2007): **3,575,439**
GOVERNMENT: **Parliamentary democracy**
LANGUAGES: **Lithuanian (official), Polish, Russian**
MONETARY UNIT: **Litas**
LIFE EXPECTANCY: **73.5**
LITERACY RATE: **100%**
DID YOU KNOW? **One of the three Baltic countries, Lithuania is located in northern Europe.**

Luxembourg

WHERE? **Europe**
CAPITAL: **Luxembourg**
AREA: **999 sq mi (2,586 sq km)**
POPULATION ESTIMATE (2007): **480,222**
GOVERNMENT: **Constitutional monarchy**
LANGUAGES: **Luxembourgian, French, German**
MONETARY UNIT: **Euro (formerly Luxembourg franc)**
LIFE EXPECTANCY: **78.6**
LITERACY RATE: **100%**
DID YOU KNOW? **This tiny kingdom is located in central Europe.**

Macedonia

WHERE? **Europe**
CAPITAL: **Skopje**
AREA: **9,781 sq mi (25,333 sq km)**
POPULATION ESTIMATE (2007): **2,055,915**
GOVERNMENT: **Emerging democracy**
LANGUAGES: **Macedonian, Albanian**
MONETARY UNIT: **Denar**
LIFE EXPECTANCY: **73.5**
LITERACY RATE: **Not available**
DID YOU KNOW? **Until Macedonia declared independence in 1991, it was part of Yugoslavia.**

Madagascar

WHERE? **Africa**
CAPITAL: **Antananarivo**
AREA: **226,660 sq mi (587,040 sq km)**
POPULATION ESTIMATE (2007): **19,448,815**
GOVERNMENT: **Republic**
LANGUAGES: **Malagasy and French (both official)**
MONETARY UNIT: **Malagasy franc**
LIFE EXPECTANCY: **56.5**
LITERACY RATE: **69%**
DID YOU KNOW? **Madagascar is the only home of ring-tailed lemurs and many other animal species.**

Malawi

WHERE? **Africa**
CAPITAL: **Lilongwe**
AREA: **45,745 sq mi (118,480 sq km)**
POPULATION ESTIMATE (2007): **13,603,181**
GOVERNMENT: **Multiparty democracy**
LANGUAGES: **English and Chichewa (both official)**
MONETARY UNIT: **Kwacha**
LIFE EXPECTANCY: **37.5**
LITERACY RATE: **63%**
DID YOU KNOW? **About 20% of Malawi is made up of a large lake named Nyasa.**

Malaysia

WHERE? **Asia**
CAPITAL: **Kuala Lumpur**
AREA: **127,316 sq mi (329,750 sq km)**
POPULATION ESTIMATE (2007): **24,821,286**
GOVERNMENT: **Constitutional monarchy**
LANGUAGES: **Malay (official), Chinese, Tamil, English**
MONETARY UNIT: **Ringgit**
LIFE EXPECTANCY: **72**
LITERACY RATE: **89%**
DID YOU KNOW? **Most of Malaysia is located in Southeast Asia; a smaller portion is located on the island of Borneo.**

Maldives

WHERE? Asia
CAPITAL: Male
AREA: 116 sq mi
(300 sq km)
POPULATION ESTIMATE (2007): 369,031
GOVERNMENT: Republic
LANGUAGES: Dhivehi (official), Arabic, Hindi, English
MONETARY UNIT: Maldivian rufiyaa
LIFE EXPECTANCY: 63.7
LITERACY RATE: 97%
DID YOU KNOW? Maldives, a group of low-lying islands, is threatened by rising sea levels associated with global warming.

Mali

WHERE? Africa
CAPITAL: Bamako
AREA: 478,764 sq mi
(1,240,000 sq km)
POPULATION ESTIMATE (2007): 11,995,402
GOVERNMENT: Republic
LANGUAGES: French (official), African languages
MONETARY UNIT: CFA franc
LIFE EXPECTANCY: 45.3
LITERACY RATE: 46%
DID YOU KNOW? The fabled, ancient city of Timbuktu is located in Mali.

Malta

WHERE? Europe
CAPITAL: Valletta
AREA: 122 sq mi
(316 sq km)
POPULATION ESTIMATE (2007): 401,880
GOVERNMENT: Republic
LANGUAGES: Maltese and English (both official)
MONETARY UNIT: Maltese lira
LIFE EXPECTANCY: 78.7
LITERACY RATE: 93%
DID YOU KNOW? The country is made up of five small islands in the Mediterranean.

Marshall Islands

WHERE? Pacific Islands
CAPITAL: Majuro
AREA: 70 sq mi
(181.3 sq km)
POPULATION ESTIMATE (2007): 61,782
GOVERNMENT: Constitutional government
LANGUAGES: Marshallese and English (both official)
MONETARY UNIT: U.S. dollar
LIFE EXPECTANCY: 69.7
LITERACY RATE: 94%
DID YOU KNOW? The Marshall Islands were once a dependency of the U.S.

Mauritania

WHERE? Africa
CAPITAL: Nouakchott
AREA: 397,953 sq mi
(1,030,700 sq km)
POPULATION ESTIMATE (2007): 3,270,065
GOVERNMENT: Republic
LANGUAGES: Arabic (official), French
MONETARY UNIT: Ouguiya
LIFE EXPECTANCY: 52.3
LITERACY RATE: 42%
DID YOU KNOW? This country's legal system is based on Islam.

Mauritius

WHERE? Africa
CAPITAL: Port Louis
AREA: 788 sq mi
(2,040 sq km)
POPULATION ESTIMATE (2007): 1,250,882
GOVERNMENT: Parliamentary democracy
LANGUAGES: English (official), French, Creole, Hindi, Urdu, Hakka, Bojpoori
MONETARY UNIT: Mauritian rupee
LIFE EXPECTANCY: 72.1
LITERACY RATE: 86%
DID YOU KNOW? Most of this island's population is of African or Indian descent.

Mexico

WHERE? **North America**
CAPITAL: **Mexico City**
AREA: **761,600 sq mi
(1,972,550 sq km)**
POPULATION ESTIMATE (2007): **108,700,891**
GOVERNMENT: **Republic**
LANGUAGES: **Spanish, Indian languages**
MONETARY UNIT: **Peso**
LIFE EXPECTANCY: **74.9**
LITERACY RATE: **92%**
DID YOU KNOW? **Most Mexicans are of mixed Native American and Spanish heritage.**

Micronesia

WHERE? **Pacific Islands**
CAPITAL: **Palikir**
AREA: **271 sq mi
(702 sq km)**
POPULATION ESTIMATE (2007): **107,862**
GOVERNMENT: **Constitutional government**
LANGUAGES: **English (official), native languages**
MONETARY UNIT: **U.S. dollar**
LIFE EXPECTANCY: **69.4**
LITERACY RATE: **89%**
DID YOU KNOW? **Four different island groups make up this country.**

Moldova

WHERE? **Europe**
CAPITAL: **Chisinau**
AREA: **13,067 sq mi
(33,843 sq km)**
POPULATION ESTIMATE (2007): **4,320,490**
GOVERNMENT: **Republic**
LANGUAGES: **Moldovan (official), Russian, Gagauz**
MONETARY UNIT: **Moldovan leu**
LIFE EXPECTANCY: **65**
LITERACY RATE: **99%**
DID YOU KNOW? **This Eastern European country was once a part of the Soviet Union.**

Monaco

WHERE? **Europe**
CAPITAL: **Monaco**
AREA: **0.75 sq mi
(1.95 sq km)**
POPULATION ESTIMATE (2007): **32,671**
GOVERNMENT: **Constitutional monarchy**
LANGUAGES: **French (official), English, Italian, Monégasque**
MONETARY UNIT: **French franc**
LIFE EXPECTANCY: **79.4**
LITERACY RATE: **99%**
DID YOU KNOW? **Bordering France, this tiny nation is famous for its casinos.**

Mongolia

WHERE? **Asia**
CAPITAL: **Ulaanbaatar**
AREA: **604,250 sq mi
(1,565,000 sq km)**
POPULATION ESTIMATE (2007): **2,874,127**
GOVERNMENT: **Parliamentary republic**
LANGUAGES: **Mongolian (official), Turkic, Russian, Chinese**
MONETARY UNIT: **Tugrik**
LIFE EXPECTANCY: **64.2**
LITERACY RATE: **99%**
DID YOU KNOW? **Mongolia is Asia's most sparsely populated country.**

Montenegro

WHERE? **Europe**
CAPITAL: **Podgorica**
AREA: **5,333 sq mi
(13,812 sq km)**
POPULATION ESTIMATE (2007): **684,736**
GOVERNMENT: **Republic**
LANGUAGES: **Serbian/Montenegrin, Ijekavian dialect (official)**
MONETARY UNIT: **Euro**
LIFE EXPECTANCY: **72.8**
LITERACY RATE: **94%**
DID YOU KNOW? **In 2006, Montenegrins voted in favor of independence from Serbia, and the country became the 192nd member of the United Nations.**

Morocco

WHERE? **Africa**

CAPITAL: **Rabat**

AREA: **172,413 sq mi (446,550 sq km)**

POPULATION ESTIMATE (2007): **33,757,175**

GOVERNMENT: **Constitutional monarchy**

LANGUAGES: **Arabic (official), French, Berber dialects, Spanish**

MONETARY UNIT: **Dirham**

LIFE EXPECTANCY: **70.3**

LITERACY RATE: **52%**

DID YOU KNOW? **The city of Fez contains the world's oldest university and mosque.**

Mozambique

WHERE? **Africa**

CAPITAL: **Maputo**

AREA: **309,494 sq mi (801,590 sq km)**

POPULATION ESTIMATE (2007): **20,905,585**

GOVERNMENT: **Republic**

LANGUAGES: **Portuguese (official), Bantu languages**

MONETARY UNIT: **Metical**

LIFE EXPECTANCY: **40.9**

LITERACY RATE: **48%**

DID YOU KNOW? **In 1992, Mozambique endured a devastating drought.**

Myanmar (Burma)

WHERE? **Asia**

CAPITAL: **Rangoon**

AREA: **261,969 sq mi (678,500 sq km)**

POPULATION ESTIMATE (2007): **47,373,9584**

GOVERNMENT: **Military regime**

LANGUAGES: **Burmese, minority languages**

MONETARY UNIT: **Kyat**

LIFE EXPECTANCY: **56**

LITERACY RATE: **83%**

DID YOU KNOW? **In 1989, the government changed the name of Burma to Myanmar.**

Namibia

WHERE? **Africa**

CAPITAL: **Windhoek**

AREA: **318,694 sq mi (825,418 sq km)**

POPULATION ESTIMATE (2007): **2,055,080**

GOVERNMENT: **Republic**

LANGUAGES: **Afrikaans, German, English (official), native languages**

MONETARY UNIT: **Namibian dollar**

LIFE EXPECTANCY: **44.8**

LITERACY RATE: **84%**

DID YOU KNOW? **Namibia achieved independence from South Africa in 1990.**

Nauru

WHERE? **Pacific Islands**

CAPITAL: **Yaren District (unofficial)**

AREA: **8.2 sq mi (21 sq km)**

POPULATION ESTIMATE (2007): **13,528**

GOVERNMENT: **Republic**

LANGUAGES: **Nauruan (official), English**

MONETARY UNIT: **Australian dollar**

LIFE EXPECTANCY: **62.3**

LITERACY RATE: **Not available**

DID YOU KNOW? **Nauru is the smallest island nation in the world.**

Nepal

WHERE? **Asia**

CAPITAL: **Kathmandu**

AREA: **54,363 sq mi (140,800 sq km)**

POPULATION ESTIMATE (2007): **28,901,790**

GOVERNMENT: **Constitutional monarchy**

LANGUAGES: **Nepali (official), Newari, Bhutia, Maithali**

MONETARY UNIT: **Nepalese rupee**

LIFE EXPECTANCY: **59.4**

LITERACY RATE: **45%**

DID YOU KNOW? **Mount Everest, on Nepal's border, is the world's highest mountain.**

The Netherlands

WHERE? **Europe**
CAPITAL: **Amsterdam**
AREA: **16,036 sq mi (41,532 sq km)**
POPULATION ESTIMATE (2007): **16,570,613**
GOVERNMENT: **Constitutional monarchy**
LANGUAGE: **Dutch**
MONETARY UNIT: **Euro (formerly guilder)**
LIFE EXPECTANCY: **78.7**
LITERACY RATE: **99%**
DID YOU KNOW? **About 40% of the Netherlands is land reclaimed from the sea.**

New Zealand

WHERE? **Pacific Islands**
CAPITAL: **Wellington**
AREA: **103,737 sq mi (268,680 sq km)**
POPULATION ESTIMATE (2007): **4,115,771**
GOVERNMENT: **Parliamentary democracy**
LANGUAGES: **English (official), Maori**
MONETARY UNIT: **New Zealand dollar**
LIFE EXPECTANCY: **78.5**
LITERACY RATE: **99%**
DID YOU KNOW? **The first people to inhabit New Zealand were the Maoris, who settled there about 1,200 years ago.**

Nicaragua

WHERE? **Central America**
CAPITAL: **Managua**
AREA: **49,998 sq mi (129,494 sq km)**
POPULATION ESTIMATE (2007): **5,675,356**
GOVERNMENT: **Republic**
LANGUAGE: **Spanish**
MONETARY UNIT: **Cordoba**
LIFE EXPECTANCY: **70**
LITERACY RATE: **68%**
DID YOU KNOW? **Nicaragua is the largest but most sparsely populated Central American country.**

Niger

WHERE? **Africa**
CAPITAL: **Niamey**
AREA: **489,189 sq mi (1,267,000 sq km)**
POPULATION ESTIMATE (2007): **12,894,865**
GOVERNMENT: **Republic**
LANGUAGES: **French (official), Hausa, Songhai, Arabic**
MONETARY UNIT: **CFA franc**
LIFE EXPECTANCY: **42.2**
LITERACY RATE: **18%**
DID YOU KNOW? **Most of Niger is located in the Sahara Desert.**

Nigeria

WHERE? **Africa**
CAPITAL: **Abuja**
AREA: **356,700 sq mi (923,770 sq km)**
POPULATION ESTIMATE (2007): **135,031,164**
GOVERNMENT: **Republic**
LANGUAGES: **English (official), Hausa, Yoruba, Ibo, more than 200 others**
MONETARY UNIT: **Naira**
LIFE EXPECTANCY: **46.5**
LITERACY RATE: **68%**
DID YOU KNOW? **Nigeria is Africa's most populous country.**

Norway

WHERE? **Europe**
CAPITAL: **Oslo**
AREA: **125,181 sq mi (324,220 sq km)**
POPULATION ESTIMATE (2007): **4,627,926**
GOVERNMENT: **Constitutional monarchy**
LANGUAGES: **Two official forms of Norwegian: Bokmål and Nynorsk**
MONETARY UNIT: **Krone**
LIFE EXPECTANCY: **79.2**
LITERACY RATE: **100%**
DID YOU KNOW? **Norway extends farther north than any other European country.**

Oman

WHERE? **Middle East**
CAPITAL: **Muscat**
AREA: **82,030 sq mi
(212,460 sq km)**
POPULATION ESTIMATE (2007): **3,204,897**
GOVERNMENT: **Monarchy**
LANGUAGES: **Arabic (official), English,
Indian languages**
MONETARY UNIT: **Omani rial**
LIFE EXPECTANCY: **72.8**
LITERACY RATE: **76%**
DID YOU KNOW? **Oman's major product is oil.**

Pakistan

WHERE? **Asia**
CAPITAL: **Islamabad**
AREA: **310,400 sq mi
(803,940 sq km)**
POPULATION ESTIMATE (2007): **3,204,897**
GOVERNMENT: **Republic**
LANGUAGES: **Punjabi, Sindhi, Siraiki,
Pashtu, Urdu (official), others**
MONETARY UNIT: **Pakistan rupee**
LIFE EXPECTANCY: **62.6**
LITERACY RATE: **46%**
DID YOU KNOW? **Pakistan means "pure
country."**

Palau

WHERE? **Pacific Islands**
CAPITAL: **Koror**
AREA: **177 sq mi
(458 sq km)**
POPULATION ESTIMATE (2007): **20,842**
GOVERNMENT: **Constitutional government**
LANGUAGES: **Palauan, English (official)**
MONETARY UNIT: **U.S. dollar**
LIFE EXPECTANCY: **69.8**
LITERACY RATE: **92%**
DID YOU KNOW? **Palau is made up of
200 islands.**

Panama

WHERE? **Central America**
CAPITAL: **Panama City**
AREA: **30,193 sq mi
(78,200 sq km)**
POPULATION ESTIMATE (2007): **3,242,173**
GOVERNMENT: **Constitutional democracy**
LANGUAGES: **Spanish (official), English**
MONETARY UNIT: **Balboa**
LIFE EXPECTANCY: **72.1**
LITERACY RATE: **93%**
DID YOU KNOW? **The Panama Canal links
the Atlantic and Pacific oceans and is
one of the world's most vital waterways.**

Papua New Guinea

WHERE? **Pacific Islands**
CAPITAL: **Port Moresby**
AREA: **178,703 sq mi
(462,840 sq km)**
POPULATION ESTIMATE (2007): **5,795,887**
GOVERNMENT: **Constitutional monarchy**
LANGUAGES: **English, Tok Pisin, Hiri Motu,
717 native languages**
MONETARY UNIT: **Kina**
LIFE EXPECTANCY: **64.6**
LITERACY RATE: **66%**
DID YOU KNOW? **More languages are
spoken in this country than in any other.**

Paraguay

WHERE? **South America**
CAPITAL: **Asunción**
AREA: **157,046 sq mi
(406,750 sq km)**
POPULATION ESTIMATE (2007): **6,667,147**
GOVERNMENT: **Republic**
LANGUAGES: **Spanish (official), Guaraní**
MONETARY UNIT: **Guaraní**
LIFE EXPECTANCY: **74.6**
LITERACY RATE: **94%**
DID YOU KNOW? **More than half of
Paraguay's workers are employed
in either agriculture or forestry.**

Peru

WHERE? South America
CAPITAL: Lima
AREA: 496,223 sq mi
(1,285,220 sq km)
POPULATION ESTIMATE (2007): 28,674,757
GOVERNMENT: Republic
LANGUAGES: Spanish and Quechua (both official), Aymara, other native languages
MONETARY UNIT: Nuevo sol
LIFE EXPECTANCY: 69.2
LITERACY RATE: 91%
DID YOU KNOW? Peru's Machu Picchu is an incredible ancient Incan fortress in the Andes mountains.

The Philippines

WHERE? Asia
CAPITAL: Manila
AREA: 115,830 sq mi
(300,000 sq km)
POPULATION ESTIMATE (2007): 91,077,287
GOVERNMENT: Republic
LANGUAGES: Filipino (based on Tagalog) and English (both official), regional languages
MONETARY UNIT: Peso
LIFE EXPECTANCY: 69.6
LITERACY RATE: 96%
DID YOU KNOW? The country is made up of more than 7,000 tropical islands.

Poland

WHERE? Europe
CAPITAL: Warsaw
AREA: 120,727 sq mi
(312,683 sq km)
POPULATION ESTIMATE (2007): 38,518,241
GOVERNMENT: Republic
LANGUAGE: Polish
MONETARY UNIT: Zloty
LIFE EXPECTANCY: 74.2
LITERACY RATE: 100%
DID YOU KNOW? The Polish name for the country is *Polska.*

Portugal

WHERE? Europe
CAPITAL: Lisbon
AREA: 35,672 sq mi
(92,391 sq km)
POPULATION ESTIMATE (2007): 10,642,836
GOVERNMENT: Parliamentary democracy
LANGUAGE: Portuguese
MONETARY UNIT: Euro (formerly escudo)
LIFE EXPECTANCY: 77.3
LITERACY RATE: 93%
DID YOU KNOW? Many of the world's famous explorers were Portuguese, including Magellan and Vasco da Gama.

Qatar

WHERE? Middle East
CAPITAL: Doha
AREA: 4,416 sq mi
(11,439 sq km)
POPULATION ESTIMATE (2007): 907,229
GOVERNMENT: Traditional monarchy
LANGUAGES: Arabic (official), English
MONETARY UNIT: Qatari riyal
LIFE EXPECTANCY: 73.4
LITERACY RATE: 83%
DID YOU KNOW? Qatar is home to Al Jazeera, a popular and controversial Arabic-language television network.

Romania

WHERE? Europe
CAPITAL: Bucharest
AREA: 91,700 sq mi
(237,500 sq km)
POPULATION ESTIMATE (2007): 22,276,056
GOVERNMENT: Republic
LANGUAGES: Romanian (official), Hungarian, German
MONETARY UNIT: Leu
LIFE EXPECTANCY: 71.1
LITERACY RATE: 98%
DID YOU KNOW? Romania was once a Roman province known as Dacia.

Russia

WHERE? **Europe and Asia**

CAPITAL: **Moscow**

AREA: **6,592,735 sq mi (17,075,200 sq km)**

POPULATION ESTIMATE (2007): **141,377,752**

GOVERNMENT: **Federation**

LANGUAGES: **Russian, others**

MONETARY UNIT: **Ruble**

LIFE EXPECTANCY: **66.8**

LITERACY RATE: **100%**

DID YOU KNOW? **Russia is the world's largest country.**

Rwanda

WHERE? **Africa**

CAPITAL: **Kigali**

AREA: **10,169 sq mi (26,338 sq km)**

POPULATION ESTIMATE (2007): **9,907,509**

GOVERNMENT: **Republic**

LANGUAGES: **Kinyarwanda, French, English (all official)**

MONETARY UNIT: **Rwandan franc**

LIFE EXPECTANCY: **46.6**

LITERACY RATE: **70%**

DID YOU KNOW? **Ethnic violence killed about 800,000 Rwandans in 1994.**

Saint Kitts and Nevis

WHERE? **North America**

CAPITAL: **Basseterre**

AREA: **101 sq mi (261 sq km)**

POPULATION ESTIMATE (2007): **39,349**

GOVERNMENT: **Constitutional monarchy**

LANGUAGE: **English**

MONETARY UNIT: **East Caribbean dollar**

LIFE EXPECTANCY: **71.9**

LITERACY RATE: **97%**

DID YOU KNOW? **Nevis is made up almost entirely of a single mountain, Nevis Peak.**

Saint Lucia

WHERE? **North America**

CAPITAL: **Castries**

AREA: **239 sq mi (620 sq km)**

POPULATION ESTIMATE (2007): **170,649**

GOVERNMENT: **Parliamentary democracy**

LANGUAGES: **English (official), French patois**

MONETARY UNIT: **East Caribbean dollar**

LIFE EXPECTANCY: **73.3**

LITERACY RATE: **67%**

DID YOU KNOW? **The major crop of this Caribbean island is bananas.**

Saint Vincent and the Grenadines

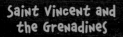

WHERE? **North America**

CAPITAL: **Kingstown**

AREA: **150 sq mi (389 sq km)**

POPULATION ESTIMATE (2007): **118,149**

GOVERNMENT: **Parliamentary democracy**

LANGUAGES: **English (official), French patois**

MONETARY UNIT: **East Caribbean dollar**

LIFE EXPECTANCY: **73.3**

LITERACY RATE: **96%**

DID YOU KNOW? **This country's highest point is the active volcano Soufrière.**

Samoa

WHERE? **Pacific Islands**

CAPITAL: **Apia**

AREA: **1,104 sq mi (2,860 sq km)**

POPULATION ESTIMATE (2007): **176,615**

GOVERNMENT: **Constitutional monarchy**

LANGUAGES: **Samoan, English**

MONETARY UNIT: **Tala**

LIFE EXPECTANCY: **70.4**

LITERACY RATE: **100%**

DID YOU KNOW? **Samoa, now independent, was once ruled by Germany and New Zealand.**

 For a list of kingdoms and monarchs of the world:
www.factmonster.com/monarchs

Countries of the World

San Marino

WHERE? **Europe**
CAPITAL: **San Marino**
AREA: **24 sq mi (61 sq km)**
POPULATION ESTIMATE (2007): **29,615**
GOVERNMENT: **Republic**
LANGUAGE: **Italian**
MONETARY UNIT: **Italian lira**
LIFE EXPECTANCY: **81.5**
LITERACY RATE: **96%**

DID YOU KNOW? **San Marino, founded around 350 A.D., is the world's oldest republic.**

São Tomé and Príncipe

WHERE? **Africa**
CAPITAL: **São Tomé**
AREA: **386 sq mi (1,001 sq km)**
POPULATION ESTIMATE (2007): **199,579**
GOVERNMENT: **Republic**
LANGUAGE: **Portuguese**
MONETARY UNIT: **Dobra**
LIFE EXPECTANCY: **66.6**
LITERACY RATE: **79%**

DID YOU KNOW? **The recent discovery of oil may bring wealth to this poor nation.**

Saudi Arabia

WHERE? **Middle East**
CAPITAL: **Riyadh**
AREA: **756,981 sq mi (1,960,582 sq km)**
POPULATION ESTIMATE (2007): **27,601,038**
GOVERNMENT: **Monarchy**
LANGUAGE: **Arabic**
MONETARY UNIT: **Riyal**
LIFE EXPECTANCY: **75.2**
LITERACY RATE: **79%**

DID YOU KNOW? **This country contains two of Islam's holiest cities, Mecca and Medina.**

Senegal

WHERE? **Africa**
CAPITAL: **Dakar**
AREA: **75,749 sq mi (196,190 sq km)**
POPULATION ESTIMATE (2007): **12,521,851**
GOVERNMENT: **Republic**
LANGUAGES: **French (official), Wolof, Serer, other dialects**
MONETARY UNIT: **CFA franc**
LIFE EXPECTANCY: **56.6**
LITERACY RATE: **40%**

DID YOU KNOW? **Senegal's capital, Dakar, is the westernmost point of Africa.**

Serbia

WHERE? **Europe**
CAPITAL: **Belgrade**
AREA: **34,116 sq mi (88,361 sq km)**
POPULATION ESTIMATE (2007): **9,465,529**
GOVERNMENT: **Republic**
LANGUAGES: **Serbian, Albanian**
MONETARY UNIT: **Yugoslav new dinar**
LIFE EXPECTANCY: **74.4**
LITERACY RATE: **93%**

DID YOU KNOW? **In 2003, Yugoslavia changed its name to Serbia and Montenegro. The two republics divided into separate countries in 2006.**

Seychelles

WHERE? **Africa**
CAPITAL: **Victoria**
AREA: **176 sq mi (455 sq km)**
POPULATION ESTIMATE (2007): **81,895**
GOVERNMENT: **Republic**
LANGUAGES: **English and French (both official), Seselwa**
MONETARY UNIT: **Seychelles rupee**
LIFE EXPECTANCY: **71.5**
LITERACY RATE: **58%**

DID YOU KNOW? **This island nation is located in the Indian Ocean.**

Sierra Leone

WHERE? **Africa**

CAPITAL: **Freetown**

AREA: **27,699 sq mi (71,740 sq km)**

POPULATION ESTIMATE (2007): **6,144,562**

GOVERNMENT: **Constitutional democracy**

LANGUAGES: **English (official), Mende, Temne, Krio**

MONETARY UNIT: **Leone**

LIFE EXPECTANCY: **42.7**

LITERACY RATE: **31%**

DID YOU KNOW? **This nation is one of the poorest countries in the world.**

Singapore

WHERE? **Asia**

CAPITAL: **Singapore**

AREA: **267 sq mi (692.7 sq km)**

POPULATION ESTIMATE (2007): **4,553,009**

GOVERNMENT: **Parliamentary republic**

LANGUAGES: **Malay, Chinese (Mandarin), Tamil, English (all official)**

MONETARY UNIT: **Singapore dollar**

LIFE EXPECTANCY: **81.5**

LITERACY RATE: **93%**

DID YOU KNOW? **Singapore is the second most densely populated country in the world.**

Slovakia

WHERE? **Europe**

CAPITAL: **Bratislava**

AREA: **18,859 sq mi (48,845 sq km)**

POPULATION ESTIMATE (2007): **5,447,502**

GOVERNMENT: **Parliamentary democracy**

LANGUAGES: **Slovak (official), Hungarian**

MONETARY UNIT: **Koruna**

LIFE EXPECTANCY: **74.2**

LITERACY RATE: **99%**

DID YOU KNOW? **Until 1993, the country was part of Czechoslovakia, which no longer exists.**

Slovenia

WHERE? **Europe**

CAPITAL: **Ljubljana**

AREA: **7,820 sq mi (20,253 sq km)**

POPULATION ESTIMATE (2007): **2,009,245**

GOVERNMENT: **Parliamentary republic**

LANGUAGES: **Slovenian, Serbo-Croatian**

MONETARY UNIT: **Euro**

LIFE EXPECTANCY: **75.9**

LITERACY RATE: **100%**

DID YOU KNOW? **Slovenia was part of Yugoslavia until declaring independence in 1991.**

Solomon Islands

WHERE? **Pacific Islands**

CAPITAL: **Honiara**

AREA: **10,985 sq mi (28,450 sq km)**

POPULATION ESTIMATE (2007): **566,842**

GOVERNMENT: **Parliamentary democracy**

LANGUAGES: **English, Solomon pidgin, more than 60 Melanesian languages**

MONETARY UNIT: **Solomon Islands dollar**

LIFE EXPECTANCY: **72.4**

LITERACY RATE: **Not available**

DID YOU KNOW? **Experts think people have lived here since about 2000 B.C.**

Somalia

WHERE? **Africa**

CAPITAL: **Mogadishu**

AREA: **246,199 sq mi (637,657 sq km)**

POPULATION ESTIMATE (2007): **9,118,773**

GOVERNMENT: **Transitional government**

LANGUAGES: **Somali (official), Arabic, English, Italian**

MONETARY UNIT: **Somali shilling**

LIFE EXPECTANCY: **47.7**

LITERACY RATE: **38%**

DID YOU KNOW? **Between January 1991 and August 2000, Somalia had no working government.**

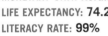

South Africa

WHERE? **Africa**
CAPITAL: **Pretoria (administrative), Cape Town (legislative)**
AREA: **471,008 sq mi (1,219,912 sq km)**
POPULATION ESTIMATE (2007): **43,997,828**
GOVERNMENT: **Republic**
LANGUAGES: **11 official languages: Afrikaans, English, Ndebele, Pedi, Sotho, Swazi, Tsonga, Tswana, Venda, Xhosa, Zulu**
MONETARY UNIT: **Rand**
LIFE EXPECTANCY: **44.1**
LITERACY RATE: **86%**

DID YOU KNOW? **South Africa is the world's largest producer of gold.**

Spain

WHERE? **Europe**
CAPITAL: **Madrid**
AREA: **194,896 sq mi (504,782 sq km)**
POPULATION ESTIMATE (2007): **40,448,191**
GOVERNMENT: **Parliamentary monarchy**
LANGUAGES: **Castilian Spanish (official), Catalan, Galician, Basque**
MONETARY UNIT: **Euro (formerly peseta)**
LIFE EXPECTANCY: **79.4**
LITERACY RATE: **98%**

DID YOU KNOW? **Spain is the closest European country to Africa.**

Sri Lanka

WHERE? **Asia**
CAPITAL: **Colombo**
AREA: **25,332 sq mi (65,610 sq km)**
POPULATION ESTIMATE (2007): **20,926,315**
GOVERNMENT: **Republic**
LANGUAGES: **Sinhala (official), Tamil, English**
MONETARY UNIT: **Sri Lankan rupee**
LIFE EXPECTANCY: **72.9**
LITERACY RATE: **92%**

DID YOU KNOW? **Sri Lanka was once called Serendip, and then Ceylon.**

Sudan

WHERE? **Africa**
CAPITAL: **Khartoum**
AREA: **967,493 sq mi (2,505,810 sq km)**
POPULATION ESTIMATE (2007): **42,292,929**
GOVERNMENT: **Authoritarian regime**
LANGUAGES: **Arabic (official), English, tribal dialects**
MONETARY UNIT: **Sudanese dinar**
LIFE EXPECTANCY: **58.1**
LITERACY RATE: **61%**

DID YOU KNOW? **Civil War has plagued Sudan for decades. Recently, as many as 300,000 people have been killed by Arab militias in the Darfur region.**

Suriname

WHERE? **South America**
CAPITAL: **Paramaribo**
AREA: **63,039 sq mi (163,270 sq km)**
POPULATION ESTIMATE (2007): **470,784**
GOVERNMENT: **Constitutional democracy**
LANGUAGES: **Dutch (official), Surinamese, English**
MONETARY UNIT: **Suriname guilder**
LIFE EXPECTANCY: **69.1**
LITERACY RATE: **93%**

DID YOU KNOW? **Suriname is named after its earliest inhabitants, the Surinen Indians.**

Swaziland

WHERE? **Africa**
CAPITAL: **Mbabane**
AREA: **6,704 sq mi (17,360 sq km)**
POPULATION ESTIMATE (2007): **1,133,066**
GOVERNMENT: **Monarchy**
LANGUAGES: **Swazi (official), English**
MONETARY UNIT: **Lilangeni**
LIFE EXPECTANCY: **37.5**
LITERACY RATE: **82%**

DID YOU KNOW? **The nation's King Mswati III is the world's last absolute monarch.**

Sweden

WHERE? Europe
CAPITAL: Stockholm
AREA: 173,731 sq mi
(449,964 sq km)
POPULATION ESTIMATE (2007): 9,031,088
GOVERNMENT: Constitutional monarchy
LANGUAGE: Swedish
MONETARY UNIT: Krona
LIFE EXPECTANCY: 80.3
LITERACY RATE: 99%
DID YOU KNOW? The Nobel Prizes (except the Peace Prize) are awarded each year in Sweden.

Switzerland

WHERE? Europe
CAPITAL: Bern
AREA: 15,942 sq mi
(41,290 sq km)
POPULATION ESTIMATE (2007): 7,554,661
GOVERNMENT: Federal republic
LANGUAGES: German, French, Italian (all official), Romansch
MONETARY UNIT: Swiss franc
LIFE EXPECTANCY: 80.3
LITERACY RATE: 99%
DID YOU KNOW? The Red Cross emblem was created by reversing the colors of Switzerland's flag.

Syria

WHERE? Middle East
CAPITAL: Damascus
AREA: 71,498 sq mi
(185,180 sq km)
POPULATION ESTIMATE (2007): 19,314,747
GOVERNMENT: Republic
LANGUAGES: Arabic (official), French, English
MONETARY UNIT: Syrian pound
LIFE EXPECTANCY: 69.7
LITERACY RATE: 77%
DID YOU KNOW? Damascus is considered the oldest capital city in the world.

Taiwan

WHERE? Asia
CAPITAL: Taipei
AREA: 13,892 sq mi
(35,980 sq km)
POPULATION ESTIMATE (2007): 23,174,294
GOVERNMENT: Multiparty democracy
LANGUAGE: Chinese (Mandarin)
MONETARY UNIT: New Taiwan dollar
LIFE EXPECTANCY: 77.1
LITERACY RATE: 86%
DID YOU KNOW? The nation was once called Formosa. The name, meaning "the beautiful," was given by Portuguese explorers.

Tajikistan

WHERE? Asia
CAPITAL: Dushanbe
AREA: 55,251 sq mi
(143,100 sq km)
POPULATION ESTIMATE (2007): 7,076,598
GOVERNMENT: Republic
LANGUAGE: Tajik
MONETARY UNIT: Somoni
LIFE EXPECTANCY: 64.5
LITERACY RATE: 99%
DID YOU KNOW? Once part of the Soviet Union, its name means "land of the Tajiks."

Tanzania

WHERE? Africa
CAPITAL: Dar es Salaam
AREA: 364,898 sq mi
(945,087 sq km)
POPULATION ESTIMATE (2007): 38,139,640
GOVERNMENT: Republic
LANGUAGES: Swahili and English (both official), local languages
MONETARY UNIT: Tanzanian shilling
LIFE EXPECTANCY: 44.9
LITERACY RATE: 78%
DID YOU KNOW? Tanzania's Mount Kilimanjaro is the highest mountain in Africa.

Countries of the World

Thailand

WHERE? **Asia**
CAPITAL: **Bangkok**
AREA: **198,455 sq mi
(514,000 sq km)**
POPULATION ESTIMATE (2007): **65,068,149**
GOVERNMENT: **Constitutional monarchy**
LANGUAGES: **Thai (Siamese), Chinese,
English**
MONETARY UNIT: **Baht**
LIFE EXPECTANCY: **71.4**
LITERACY RATE: **96%**
DID YOU KNOW? **Thailand was once known
as Siam.**

Togo

WHERE? **Africa**
CAPITAL: **Lomé**
AREA: **21,925 sq mi
(56,790 sq km)**
POPULATION ESTIMATE (2007): **5,701,579**
GOVERNMENT: **Republic**
LANGUAGES: **French (official), Éwé, Mina,
Kabyé, Cotocoli**
MONETARY UNIT: **CFA franc**
LIFE EXPECTANCY: **53**
LITERACY RATE: **61%**
DID YOU KNOW? **The Danes, Germans,
British and French once ruled Togo.**

Tonga

WHERE? **Pacific
Islands**
CAPITAL: **Nuku'alofa**
AREA: **290 sq mi
(748 sq km)**
POPULATION ESTIMATE (2007): **116,921**
GOVERNMENT: **Constitutional monarchy**
LANGUAGES: **Tongan, English**
MONETARY UNIT: **Pa'anga**
LIFE EXPECTANCY: **69.2**
LITERACY RATE: **99%**
DID YOU KNOW? **Polynesians have lived
on Tonga for at least 3,000 years.**

Trinidad and Tobago

WHERE? **North America**
CAPITAL: **Port-of-Spain**
AREA: **1,980 sq mi
(5,130 sq km)**
POPULATION ESTIMATE (2007): **1,056,608**
GOVERNMENT: **Parliamentary democracy**
LANGUAGES: **English (official), Hindi,
French, Spanish**
MONETARY UNIT: **Trinidad and Tobago
dollar**
LIFE EXPECTANCY: **69.3**
LITERACY RATE: **99%**
DID YOU KNOW? **Columbus explored
Trinidad in 1498.**

Tunisia

WHERE? **Africa**
CAPITAL: **Tunis**
AREA: **63,170 sq mi
(163,610 sq km)**
POPULATION ESTIMATE (2007): **71,158,647**
GOVERNMENT: **Republic**
LANGUAGES: **Arabic (official), French**
MONETARY UNIT: **Tunisian dinar**
LIFE EXPECTANCY: **74.7**
LITERACY RATE: **74%**
DID YOU KNOW? **Bordering the
Mediterranean, Tunisia stretches south
into the Sahara.**

Turkey

WHERE? **Europe
and Asia**
CAPITAL: **Ankara**
AREA: **301,388 sq mi (780,580 sq km)**
POPULATION ESTIMATE (2007): **71,158,647**
GOVERNMENT: **Parliamentary democracy**
LANGUAGE: **Turkish**
MONETARY UNIT: **Turkish lira**
LIFE EXPECTANCY: **72.1**
LITERACY RATE: **87%**
DID YOU KNOW? **Turkey was once the
home of the Byzantine and the
Ottoman empires.**

Turkmenistan

WHERE? **Asia**
CAPITAL: **Ashgabat**
AREA: **188,455 sq mi**
(488,100 sq km)
POPULATION ESTIMATE (2007): **5,136,262**
GOVERNMENT: **Republic**
LANGUAGES: **Turkmen, Russian, Uzbek**
MONETARY UNIT: **Manat**
LIFE EXPECTANCY: **61.3**
LITERACY RATE: **98%**
DID YOU KNOW? **About nine-tenths of the country is desert, mainly the Kara-Kum.**

Tuvalu

WHERE? **Pacific Islands**
CAPITAL: **Funafuti**
AREA: **10 sq mi**
(26 sq km)
POPULATION ESTIMATE (2007): **11,992**
GOVERNMENT: **Constitutional monarchy**
LANGUAGES: **Tuvaluan, English**
MONETARY UNIT: **Tuvaluan dollar**
LIFE EXPECTANCY: **67.7**
LITERACY RATE: **Not available**
DID YOU KNOW? **Tuvalu was formerly named the Ellice Islands.**

Uganda

WHERE? **Africa**
CAPITAL: **Kampala**
AREA: **91,135 sq mi**
(236,040 sq km)
POPULATION ESTIMATE (2007): **30,262,610**
GOVERNMENT: **Republic**
LANGUAGES: **English (official), Swahili, Luganda, Ateso, Luo**
MONETARY UNIT: **Ugandan shilling**
LIFE EXPECTANCY: **50.4**
LITERACY RATE: **70%**
DID YOU KNOW? **Uganda's brutal former dictator, Idi Amin, ruled the country from 1971 to 1978. He died in 2003.**

Ukraine

WHERE? **Europe**
CAPITAL: **Kyiv (Kiev)**
AREA: **233,089 sq mi**
(603,700 sq km)
POPULATION ESTIMATE (2007): **46,299,862**
GOVERNMENT: **Republic**
LANGUAGE: **Ukrainian**
MONETARY UNIT: **Hryvnia**
LIFE EXPECTANCY: **66.7**
LITERACY RATE: **100%**
DID YOU KNOW? **In 1986, a reactor blew at Chernobyl, causing the worst nuclear power accident in history.**

United Arab Emirates

WHERE? **Middle East**
CAPITAL: **Abu Dhabi**
AREA: **32,000 sq mi**
(82,880 sq km)
POPULATION ESTIMATE (2007): **2,642,566**
GOVERNMENT: **Federation**
LANGUAGES: **Arabic (official), English**
MONETARY UNIT: **U.A.E. dirham**
LIFE EXPECTANCY: **75**
LITERACY RATE: **78%**
DID YOU KNOW? **This country is made up of seven Gulf states.**

United Kingdom

WHERE? **Europe**
CAPITAL: **London**
AREA: **94,525 sq mi**
(244,820 sq km)
POPULATION ESTIMATE (2007): **60,776,238**
GOVERNMENT: **Constitutional monarchy**
LANGUAGES: **English, Welsh, Scots Gaelic**
MONETARY UNIT: **British pound**
LIFE EXPECTANCY: **78.3**
LITERACY RATE: **99%**
DID YOU KNOW? **The United Kingdom is made up of England, Wales, Scotland and Northern Ireland.**

United States

WHERE? **North America**
CAPITAL: **Washington, D.C.**
AREA: **3,717,792 sq mi
(9,629,091 sq km)**
POPULATION ESTIMATE (2007): **301,139,947**
GOVERNMENT: **Republic**
LANGUAGES: **English, Spanish (spoken
by a sizable minority)**
MONETARY UNIT: **U.S. dollar**
LIFE EXPECTANCY: **77.4**
LITERACY RATE: **97%**
DID YOU KNOW? **The U.S. is the world's
third largest country, and the world's third
most populous country.**

Uruguay

WHERE? **South America**
CAPITAL: **Montevideo**
AREA: **68,040 sq mi
(176,220 sq km)**
POPULATION ESTIMATE (2007): **3,447,496**
GOVERNMENT: **Republic**
LANGUAGE: **Spanish**
MONETARY UNIT: **Peso**
LIFE EXPECTANCY: **75.9**
LITERACY RATE: **98%**
DID YOU KNOW? **Uruguay hosted the first
World Cup soccer tournament in 1930.**

Uzbekistan

WHERE? **Asia**
CAPITAL: **Tashkent**
AREA: **172,741 sq mi
(447,400 sq km)**
POPULATION ESTIMATE (2007): **27,780,059**
GOVERNMENT: **Republic**
LANGUAGES: **Uzbek, Russian, Tajik**
MONETARY UNIT: **Uzbekistani som**
LIFE EXPECTANCY: **64.1**
LITERACY RATE: **99%**
DID YOU KNOW? **In 2001, Uzbekistan gave
the U.S. a base to fight the Taliban and
al-Qaeda in Afghanistan.**

Vanuatu

WHERE? **Pacific Islands**
CAPITAL: **Port Vila**
AREA: **5,700 sq mi
(14,760 sq km)**
POPULATION ESTIMATE (2007): **211,971**
GOVERNMENT: **Republic**
LANGUAGES: **English and French (both
official), Bislama**
MONETARY UNIT: **Vatu**
LIFE EXPECTANCY: **62.1**
LITERACY RATE: **53%**
DID YOU KNOW? **Vanuatu is an
archipelago of 83 islands.**

Vatican City (Holy See)

WHERE? **Europe**
CAPITAL: **None**
AREA: **0.17 sq mi
(0.44 sq km)**
POPULATION ESTIMATE (2007): **890**
GOVERNMENT: **Ecclesiastical**
LANGUAGES: **Latin, Italian**
MONETARY UNIT: **Italian lira**
LIFE EXPECTANCY: **77.5**
LITERACY RATE: **100%**
DID YOU KNOW? **This nation is the world's
smallest country.**

Venezuela

WHERE? **South America**
CAPITAL: **Caracas**
AREA: **352,143 sq mi
(912,050 sq km)**
POPULATION ESTIMATE (2007): **26,084,662**
GOVERNMENT: **Republic**
LANGUAGES: **Spanish (official), native
languages**
MONETARY UNIT: **Bolivar**
LIFE EXPECTANCY: **74.1**
LITERACY RATE: **93%**
DID YOU KNOW? **Venezuela's Angel Falls
is the world's highest waterfall.**

For country profiles, go to:
www.factmonster.com/countries

Vietnam

WHERE? Asia
CAPITAL: Hanoi
AREA: 127,243 sq mi
(329,560 sq km)
POPULATION ESTIMATE (2007): 85,262,356
GOVERNMENT: Communist state
LANGUAGES: Vietnamese (official), French, English, Khmer, Chinese
MONETARY UNIT: Dong
LIFE EXPECTANCY: 70.4
LITERACY RATE: 94%
DID YOU KNOW? The country was divided into North and South Vietnam in 1954 and reunified in 1976.

Yemen

WHERE? Middle East
CAPITAL: Sanaa
AREA: 203,850 sq mi
(527,970 sq km)
POPULATION ESTIMATE (2007): 22,211,743
GOVERNMENT: Republic
LANGUAGE: Arabic
MONETARY UNIT: Rial
LIFE EXPECTANCY: 61.4
LITERACY RATE: 50%
DID YOU KNOW? In 1990, North and South Yemen joined to form the Republic of Yemen.

Zambia

WHERE? Africa
CAPITAL: Lusaka
AREA: 290,584 sq mi
(752,610 sq km)
POPULATION ESTIMATE (2007): 11,477,447
GOVERNMENT: Republic
LANGUAGES: English (official), local dialects
MONETARY UNIT: Kwacha
LIFE EXPECTANCY: 39.4
LITERACY RATE: 81%
DID YOU KNOW? Zambia changed its name from Northern Rhodesia after it gained independence in 1964.

Zimbabwe

WHERE? Africa
CAPITAL: Harare
AREA: 150,803 sq mi
(390,580 sq km)
POPULATION ESTIMATE (2007): 12,311,143
GOVERNMENT: Parliamentary democracy
LANGUAGES: English (official), Ndebele, Shona
MONETARY UNIT: Zimbabwean dollar
LIFE EXPECTANCY: 37.8
LITERACY RATE: 91%
DID YOU KNOW? This country has the world's lowest life expectancy.

Most Livable and Least Livable Countries

The United Nations' Human Development Index ranks nations according to their citizens' quality of life. The rankings are based on life expectancy, education and income.

MOST LIVABLE
1. Norway
2. Iceland
3. Australia
4. Ireland
5. Sweden
6. Canada
7. Japan
8. United States
9. Switzerland
10. Netherlands

Norway

Source: Human Development Report, 2006, United Nations

LEAST LIVABLE
1. Niger
2. Sierra Leone
3. Mali
4. Burkina Faso
5. Guinea-Bissau
6. Central African Republic
7. Chad
8. Ethiopia
9. Burundi
10. Mozambique

Niger

Countries of the World

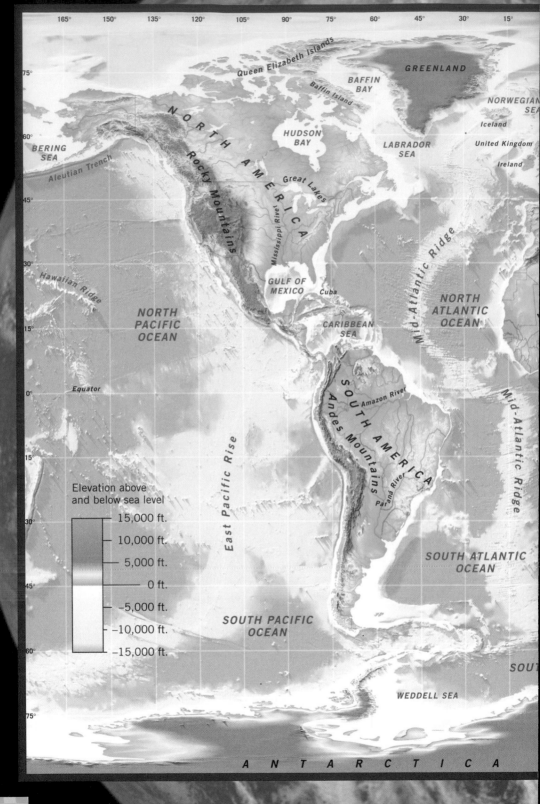

Elevation above
and below sea level

- 15,000 ft.
- 10,000 ft.
- 5,000 ft.
- 0 ft.
- −5,000 ft.
- −10,000 ft.
- −15,000 ft.

165° 150° 135° 120° 105° 90° 75° 60° 45° 30° 15°

75°
60°
45°
30°
15°
0°
15°
30°
45°
60°
75°

Queen Elizabeth Islands

GREENLAND

BAFFIN BAY

Baffin Island

NORWEGIAN SEA

Iceland

HUDSON BAY

LABRADOR SEA

United Kingdom

Ireland

BERING SEA

Aleutian Trench

NORTH AMERICA

Rocky Mountains

Great Lakes

Mississippi River

GULF OF MEXICO

Cuba

CARIBBEAN SEA

Mid-Atlantic Ridge

NORTH ATLANTIC OCEAN

NORTH PACIFIC OCEAN

Hawaiian Ridge

Equator

East Pacific Rise

SOUTH AMERICA

Andes Mountains

Amazon River

Paraná River

Mid-Atlantic Ridge

SOUTH ATLANTIC OCEAN

SOUTH PACIFIC OCEAN

SOUT

WEDDELL SEA

ANTARCTICA

ARCTIC OCEAN

15° 30° 45° 60° 75° 90° 105° 120° 135° 150° 165°

75°

60°

EUROPE

Baltic Sea

North Sea

Alps

Mediterranean Sea

Black Sea

Sahara

Nile River

Red Sea

AFRICA

Congo River

Kalahari Desert

Madagascar

Central Indian Ridge

INDIAN OCEAN

Southwest Indian Ridge

N OCEAN

Ural Mts.

Caspian Sea

Aral Sea

Euphrates R.

Persian Gulf

Indus River

Himalayas

Ganges R.

ARABIAN SEA

S i b e r i a

A S I A

Lena River

Mt. Everest
World's highest point
29,035 ft.

Gobi

Huang River

Chang River

Mekong R.

BAY OF BENGAL

Ninety East Ridge

Sumatra

Java Trench

Java

Borneo

South China Sea

Sea of Okhotsk

Kuril-Kamchatka Trench

Honshu

Japan Trench

NORTH PACIFIC OCEAN

Challenger Deep
World's greatest ocean depth
-36,198 ft.

Equator

New Guinea

Great Barrier Reef

AUSTRALIA

North Island

South Island

Maps always show a
distorted view of the
Earth because they
are not curved in
three dimensions.

45°

30°

15°

0°

15°

30°

45°

60°

75°

THE WORLD

ATLANTIC OCEAN

BLACK SEA

MEDITERRANEAN SEA

RED SEA

MOLDOVA
ROMANIA
BULGARIA
MACEDONIA
YUGOSLAVIA
ALBANIA
GREECE
Crete
HUNGARY
BOSNIA AND HERZEGOVINA
CROATIA
SLOVENIA
AUSTRIA
SWITZERLAND
ITALY
Sicily
MALTA
Corsica
Sardinia
Majorca
FRANCE
SPAIN
PORTUGAL

GEORGIA
ARMENIA
AZERBAIJAN
TURKEY
CYPRUS
LEBANON
ISRAEL
SYRIA
JORDAN
IRAQ
IRAN
KUWAIT
BAHRAIN
QATAR
SAUDI ARABIA
YEMEN

SOMALIA
Mogadishu

ERITREA
Asmara
DJIBOUTI
Djibouti
Addis Ababa
Harer
Gore
ETHIOPIA
KENYA
UGANDA

Port Sudan
Khartoum
Nile R.
SUDAN
Juba

EGYPT
Cairo
Suez
Alexandria
Luxor
Aswan
Al Jawf

S   A   H   A   R   A

LIBYA
Tripoli
Banghazi
Qafsah
TUNISIA
Tunis
Constantine
Algiers
Oran

ALGERIA

MOROCCO
Tangier
Rabat
Fès
Casablanca
Erfoud
Marrakech
Canary Is.
Madeira Islands
Laayoune (El Aaiún)
WESTERN SAHARA
Nouakchott

MAURITANIA

MALI
Timbuktu
Bamako
Gaoua
Niger R.

NIGER
Agadez
Niamey
Zinder

CHAD
N'Djamena

CENTRAL AFRICAN REPUBLIC
Bangui
Congo R.

CAMEROON
Yaoundé
Douala
Benue R.
Malabo
EQUATORIAL GUINEA

NIGERIA
Kano
Abuja
Ibadan
Lagos
Niger R.

BENIN
Porto-Novo
TOGO
GHANA
Accra
Kumasi
BURKINA FASO
Ouagadougou
CÔTE D'IVOIRE
Yamoussoukro
Abidjan
LIBERIA
Monrovia
SIERRA LEONE
Freetown
GUINEA
Conakry
GUINEA-BISSAU
Bissau
THE GAMBIA
Banjul
SENEGAL
Dakar

AFRICA

INDIAN OCEAN

Antananarivo

MADAGASCAR

Mombasa
Dar es Salaam
Nairobi

Moroni
COMOROS

Zanzibar

TANZANIA

Kigoma

Lake Nyasa

Cidade de Nacala

MALAWI
Lilongwe

Blantyre

Lake Victoria

RWANDA
Kigali
Bukavu
BURUNDI
Bujumbura

Lake Tanganyika

Beira

MOZAMBIQUE

Maputo

Harare

ZIMBABWE

SWAZILAND
Mbabane

Durban

Pretoria

Johannesburg

LESOTHO
Maseru

Lubumbashi

DEMOCRATIC REPUBLIC OF THE CONGO

Kananga

Kinshasa

Brazzaville

Pointe-Noire

Kitwe

Lusaka

ZAMBIA

BOTSWANA

Gaborone

Port Elizabeth

SOUTH AFRICA

ANGOLA

NAMIBIA

Windhoek

Cape Town

Luanda

Namibe

Lubango

Walvis Bay

Malabo
(EQUATORIAL GUINEA)

ATLANTIC OCEAN

Mozambique Channel

0 mi.   500 mi.   1,000 mi.

0 km   500 km   1,000 km

NORWAY
SWEDEN
UNITED KINGDOM
DENMARK
FINLAND
NETHERLANDS
BELGIUM
GERMANY
RUSSIA
ESTONIA
FRANCE LUXEMBOURG
POLAND
LATVIA
LITHUANIA
SWITZERLAND
CZECH REPUBLIC
BELARUS
RUSSIA
Khanty-Mansiysk
AUSTRIA SLOVAKIA
UKRAINE
Yakaterinburg
SLOVENIA CROATIA
HUNGARY
Chelyabinsk
ITALY
ROMANIA
MOLDOVA
Magnitogorsk
Omsk
Tom Kem
BOSNIA AND HERZEGOVINA
SERBIA
Novosibirsk
MONTENEGRO
BULGARIA
ALBANIA
Imeni Gastello
Astana
MACEDONIA
Black Sea
KAZAKHSTAN
Qaraghandy (Karaganda)
GREECE
Istanbul
Ankara
GEORGIA
Caspian Sea
Tyuratam
Mediterranean Sea
Izmir
T'bilisi
Aral Sea
TURKEY
ARMENIA
Yerevan
Baku
Nukus
UZBEKISTAN
Bishkek
Almaty
Adana
Tabriz
AZERBAIJAN
Tashkent
KYRGYZSTAN
CYPRUS
Nicosia
Aleppo
TURKMENISTAN
Samarkand
Fergana
LEBANON
Beirut
Mosul
ISRAEL
SYRIA
Irbil
Tehran
Ashgabat
Dushanbe
TAJIKISTAN
LIBYA
Tel Aviv
Damascus
Kirkuk
Mashhad
Jerusalem
Amman
Baghdad
Kermanshah
Herat
Kabul
Claimed by India
JORDAN
IRAQ
Esfahan
Islamabad
Tabuk
Srinagar
EGYPT
Al Basrah
IRAN
AFGHANISTAN
Kuwait
Shiraz
Kerman
Quetta
Faisalabad
KUWAIT
Persian Gulf
Multan
Red Sea
Manama
BAHRAIN
PAKISTAN
Jiddah
Riyadh
Doha
Abu Dhabi
Delhi
NEPAL
Mecca
QATAR
Kanpur
Kathma
AFRICA
SAUDI ARABIA
Muscat
Karachi
Abha
Karachi
INDIA
SUDAN
OMAN
Arabian Sea
Nagpur
Sanaa
Mumbai (Bombay)
Pune
ERITREA
Taizz
YEMEN
Al Makalla
Hyderabad
DJIBOUTI
Aden
UNITED ARAB EMIRATES
ETHIOPIA
Bay of Benga
0 mi.   500 mi.   1,000 mi.
Bangalore
Chennai (Madras)
Cochin
Madurai
0 km   500 km   1,000 km
Jaffna
UGANDA
KENYA
SOMALIA
INDIAN OCEAN
Colombo
SRI LANK

ARCTIC OCEAN

Bering
Sea

Cherskiy

Tiksi

Verkhoyansk

oril'sk

RUSSIA

Magadan

Kamchatka
Peninsula

Yakutsk

Petropavlovsk-
Kamchatskiy

S I B E R I A

Sea of
Okhotsk

Krasnoyarsk

okuznetsk

Irkutsk

Khabarovsk

Sakhalin

Harbin

Sapporo

Ulaanbaatar

Changchun

Vladivostok

MONGOLIA

Gobi

Shenyang

qi

Jinxi

N. KOREA

JAPAN

Hohhot

Beijing

Pyongyang

Tokyo

Tianjin

Seoul

Nagoya

Taiyuan

Jinan

S. KOREA

Taegu
Pusan

Kyoto
Kobe Osaka

PACIFIC
OCEAN

Lanzhou

Qingdao

Fukuoka

Hiroshima

Xi'an

Nagasaki

CHINA

Hefei

Shanghai

hasa

Wuhan

Chengdu

Chongqing

Naha

imphu

BHUTAN

Fuzhou

Taipei

Xiamen

BANGLADESH

Dhaka

Liuzhou

TAIWAN

Mandalay

Nanning

Guangzhou

Kao-hsiung

tta Chittagong

Macao

MYANMAR
(BURMA)

Hanoi

Hong Kong

LAOS

Luzon

Chiang Mai

Vientiane

Baguio

Quezon City

Rangoon

THAILAND

Da Nang

Manila

Bangkok

VIETNAM

PHILIPPINES

CAMBODIA

Cebu

Phnom
Penh

Ho Chi Minh City

Davao

Phuket

Songkhla

Borneo

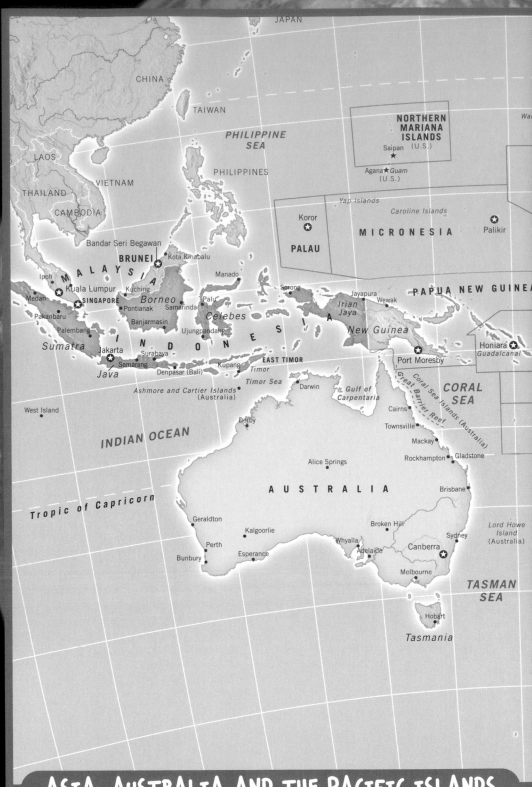

JAPAN

CHINA

TAIWAN

LAOS

VIETNAM

THAILAND

CAMBODIA

PHILIPPINE
SEA

PHILIPPINES

NORTHERN
MARIANA
ISLANDS
(U.S.)

Saipan ★

Agana ★ Guam
(U.S.)

Wak

Bandar Seri Begawan

BRUNEI

MALAYSIA

Ipoh

Medan

Kuala Lumpur

SINGAPORE

Pakanbaru

Palembang

Sumatra

Jakarta

Surabaya

Semarang

Java

Kota Kinabalu

Kuching

Pontianak

Borneo

Samarinda

Banjarmasin

Manado

Palu

Celebes

Ujungpandang

I N D O N E S I A

Denpasar (Bali)

Kupang

Sorong

Yap Islands

Koror

PALAU

MICRONESIA

Caroline Islands

Palikir

PAPUA NEW GUINEA

Jayapura

Wewak

Irian
Jaya

New Guinea

Port Moresby

Honiara

Guadalcanal

EAST TIMOR

Timor

Timor Sea

Ashmore and Cartier Islands
(Australia)

Darwin

Gulf of
Carpentaria

Coral Sea Islands (Australia)

Great Barrier Reef

CORAL
SEA

West Island

INDIAN OCEAN

Derby

Cairns

Townsville

Mackay

Alice Springs

Rockhampton

Gladstone

Brisbane

AUSTRALIA

Tropic of Capricorn

Geraldton

Kalgoorlie

Broken Hill

Whyalla

Lord Howe
Island
(Australia)

Sydney

Perth

Esperance

Adelaide

Canberra

Bunbury

Melbourne

TASMAN
SEA

Hobart

Tasmania

ASIA, AUSTRALIA AND THE PACIFIC ISLANDS

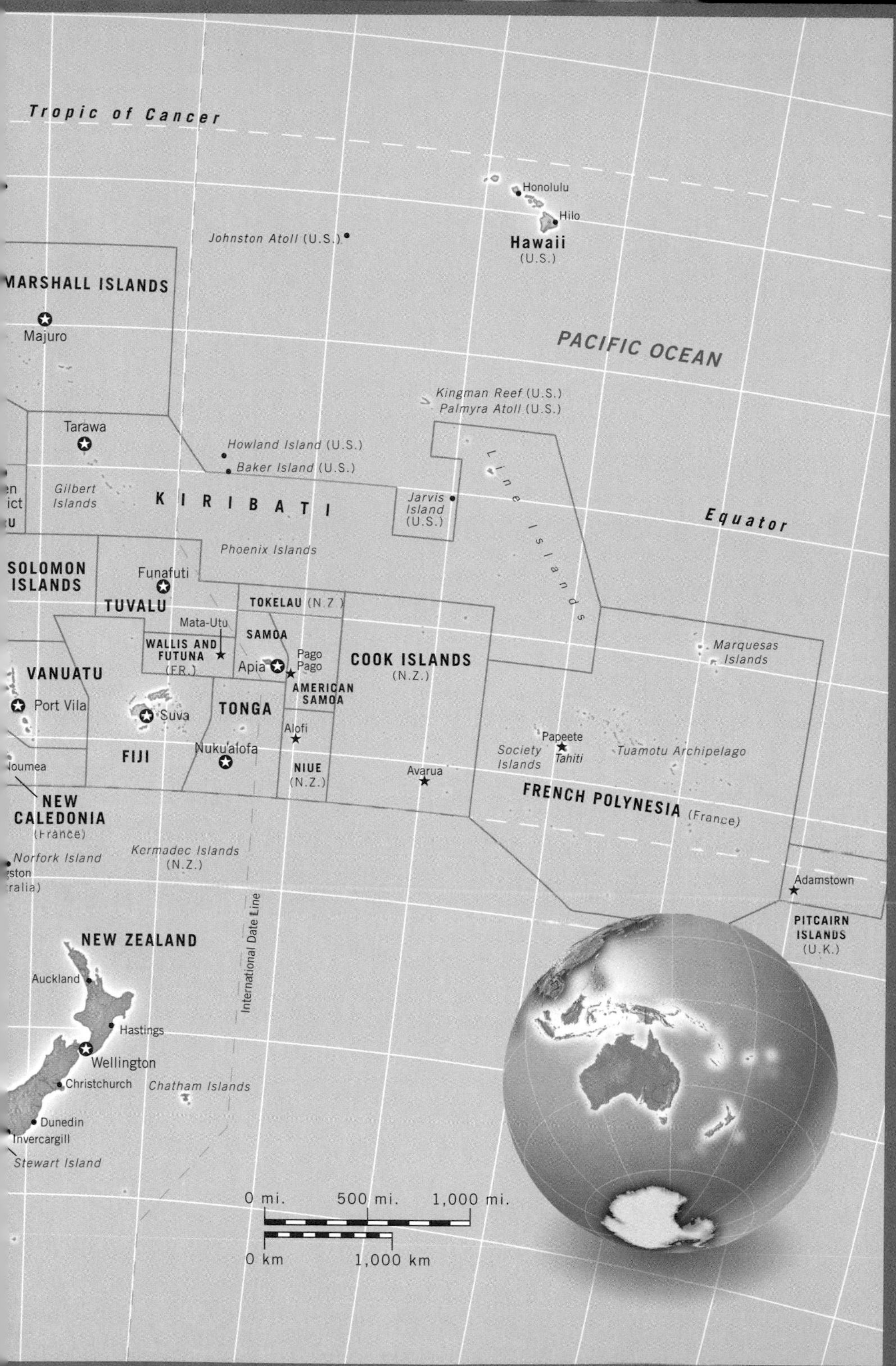

Tropic of Cancer

MARSHALL ISLANDS
● Majuro

Johnston Atoll (U.S.) ●

Honolulu ●
● Hilo
HAWAII
(U.S.)

PACIFIC OCEAN

Tarawa
●

Gilbert
Islands

KIRIBATI

Kingman Reef (U.S.)
Palmyra Atoll (U.S.)

Line Islands

Equator

SOLOMON
ISLANDS

Howland Island (U.S.) ●
● Baker Island (U.S.)

Jarvis
Island
(U.S.) ●

TUVALU

Funafuti
●

Phoenix Islands

TOKELAU (N.Z.)

Mata-Utu

WALLIS AND
FUTUNA
(FR.)

SAMOA

Apia ●

Pago
Pago ★

AMERICAN
SAMOA

COOK ISLANDS
(N.Z.)

Marquesas
Islands

VANUATU
● Port Vila

Suva
●

TONGA

Alofi
★

Society
Islands

Papeete
● Tahiti

Tuamotu Archipelago

FIJI

Nuku'alofa
●

NIUE
(N.Z.)

Avarua
★

FRENCH POLYNESIA (France)

Noumea

NEW
CALEDONIA
(France)

Norfolk Island
(Australia)

Kermadec Islands
(N.Z.)

Adamstown
★

PITCAIRN
ISLANDS
(U.K.)

NEW ZEALAND

Auckland ●

International Date Line

Hastings
●

Wellington
●

● Christchurch

Chatham Islands

● Dunedin
Invercargill ●

Stewart Island

0 mi.   500 mi.   1,000 mi.

0 km   1,000 km

EUROPE

Murmansk

Pechora

Oulu

ASIA

Arkhangel'sk

INLAND

R   U   S   S   I   A

Izhevsk

sinki

St. Petersburg

Tallinn

Kazan

STONIA

Nizhniy Novgorod

LATVIA

Moscow

Samara

IA

Smolensk

ilnius

Lipetsk

Saratov

Minsk

Voronezh

KAZAKHSTAN

BELARUS

Homyel'

st

Kiev

Kharkiv

Volgograd

Derazhnya

Voroshilovgrad

UKRAINE

Gorlovka

Makeyevka

Chisinau

Zhdanov

Rostov

Iasi

Odessa

Mykolavia

MOLDOVA

Kerch

Groznyy

MANIA

Simferopol

Bucharest

Sevastopol

a

Constanta

BLACK SEA

Varna

BULGARIA

Istanbul

T   U   R   K   E   Y

Izmir

hens

SYRIA

IRAN

Crete

CYPRUS

IRAQ

LEBANON

ICELAND

Greenland Sea

Tasiilaq
(Ammassalik)

Narsarsuaq

*Labrador
Sea*

*Island of
Newfoundland*

St. John's

Saint-Pierre

GREENLAND
(Denmark)

Nuuk (Godthåb)

Happy Valley
Goose Bay

Baffin Bay

Davis Strait

Qaanaaq (Thule)

CANADA

Iqaluit

Alert

Chisasibi
(Fort George)

Baffin Island

Queen Elizabeth Islands

HUDSON
BAY

Moosonee

Kangiqtugaapik (Resolute)

Churchill

Winnipeg

*ARCTIC
OCEAN*

Arctic Circle

Victoria Island

Banks Island

*Beaufort
Sea*

Echo Bay

Yellowknife

Saskatoon

Regina

Bismarck

Inuvik

Edmonton

Barrow

Prudhoe Bay

Calgary

Helena

RUSSIA

Alaska (U.S.)

Whitehorse

Fairbanks

Juneau

Boise

Nome

Anchorage

Valdez

Vancouver

Seattle

Victoria

Bethel

Olympia

Portland

Kodiak

Salem

*Bering
Sea*

Aleutian Islands

80

NORTH AMERICA AND CENTRAL AMERICA

ATLANTIC OCEAN

Halifax

Augusta
Concord
Montpelier
Ottawa
Montreal
Albany
Toronto
Buffalo
Hartford
Rochester
Boston
Providence
New York
Philadelphia
Dover
Harrisburg
Cleveland
Pittsburgh
Baltimore
Washington, DC
Detroit
Toledo
Columbus
Cincinnati
Richmond
Norfolk
Milwaukee
Indianapolis
Frankfort
Charleston
Raleigh
Madison
Chicago
Louisville
Nashville
Columbia
Springfield
Saint Louis
Atlanta
Des Moines
Memphis
Birmingham
Montgomery
Savannah
Omaha
Kansas City
Jefferson City
Jackson
Tallahassee
Lincoln
Topeka
Little Rock
Baton Rouge
Jacksonville
Cheyenne
Oklahoma City
Dallas
New Orleans
Miami
Denver
Santa Fe
Austin
Houston
Freeport
Nassau
Phoenix
El Paso
San Antonio
Ciudad Juárez
Hermosillo
Monterrey
Tampico
Veracruz
León
Guadalajara
Mexico City
Puebla
Oaxaca
Mazatlán
Puerto Vallarta
Acapulco
La Paz

UNITED STATES

MEXICO

GULF OF MEXICO

Gulf of California

Tropic of Cancer

PACIFIC OCEAN

BERMUDA (U.K.)
Hamilton

1,000 mi.
500 mi.
0 mi.
0 km
500 km
1,000 km

TURKS AND CAICOS ISLANDS (U.K.)
Grand Turk

BAHAMAS

VIRGIN ISLANDS (U.S., U.K.)
SAINT MAARTEN/ SAINT MARTIN (Neth. Antilles)/(Guad.)
SAINT BARTHELEMY (Guad.)
ANGUILLA (U.K.)
ANTIGUA AND BARBUDA
SAINT KITTS AND NEVIS
MONTSERRAT (U.K.)
GUADELOUPE (Fr.)
DOMINICA
MARTINIQUE (Fr.)
SAINT LUCIA
SAINT VINCENT AND THE GRENADINES
GRENADA
BARBADOS

San Juan
PUERTO RICO (U.S.)
DOMINICAN REPUBLIC
Santiago
Santo Domingo
Port-au-Prince
HAITI

CUBA
Havana
Camagüey
Guantánamo
Montego Bay
Kingston
JAMAICA

CAYMAN ISLANDS (U.K.)
George Town

Cancún
Mérida

BELIZE
Belize City
Belmopan
GUATEMALA
Guatemala City
HONDURAS
Tegucigalpa
San Salvador
EL SALVADOR
NICARAGUA
Managua
COSTA RICA
San José
PANAMA
Panama City

CARIBBEAN SEA

NETHERLANDS ANTILLES (Neth.)
ARUBA (Neth.)

TRINIDAD AND TOBAGO
GUYANA
VENEZUELA
COLOMBIA

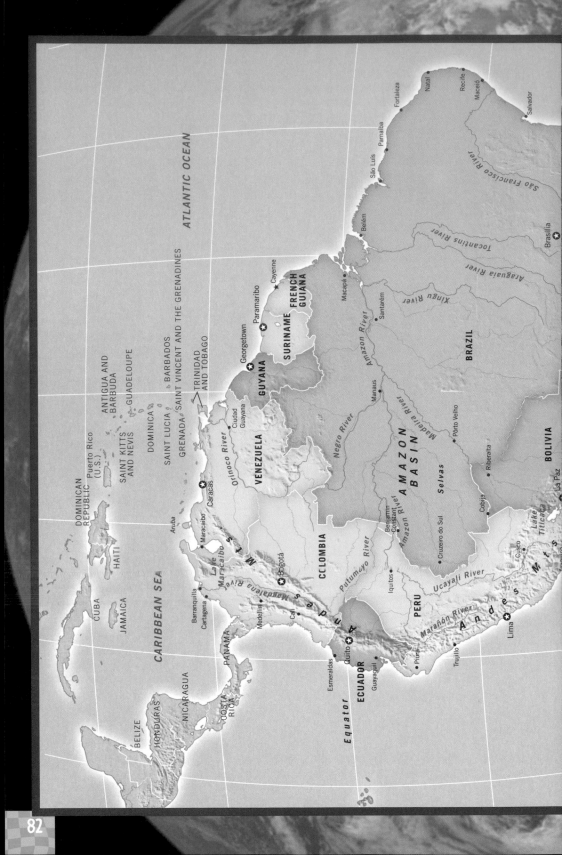

ATLANTIC OCEAN

Natal
Recife
Maceió
Fortaleza
Salvador

São Luís
Parnaíba

São Francisco River

Belém
Brasília

Tocantins River

Araguaia River

Cayenne
Macapá

FRENCH GUIANA

SURINAME
Santarém

Paramaribo
Xingu River

Georgetown
Amazon River

GUYANA
BRAZIL

Manaus

Ciudad
Guayana
Negro River

AMAZON
BASIN

VENEZUELA
Madeira River
Pôrto Velho

Caracas
Selvas
Riberalta

Orinoco River
Cobija

Aruba
Maracaibo
Lake
Maracaibo
Benjamin
Constant
Amazon River
Cruzeiro do Sul
BOLIVIA
La Paz

DOMINICAN
REPUBLIC
Puerto Rico
(U.S.)

ANTIGUA AND
BARBUDA
GUADELOUPE

SAINT KITTS
AND NEVIS
DOMINICA

SAINT LUCIA
BARBADOS

GRENADA SAINT VINCENT AND THE GRENADINES
TRINIDAD
AND TOBAGO

COLOMBIA

Bogotá
Putumayo River
Iquitos

Magdalena River
Ucayali River

CARIBBEAN SEA
Barranquilla
Cartagena
Medellín
Cali

CUBA
Piura
Cusco
Lake
Titicaca

JAMAICA
PERU
Marañón River
Trujillo

HAITI
Lima

A n d e s   M t s

BELIZE
PANAMA
NICARAGUA
COSTA
RICA
HONDURAS

Esmeraldas
Quito
Guayaquil

ECUADOR

Equator

SOUTH AMERICA

PACIFIC OCEAN

ATLANTIC OCEAN

Highlands

Belo Horizonte
Rio de Janeiro
São Paulo
Curitiba
Pôrto Alegre

Paraná River

Paraguay R.

PARAGUAY
Asunción
Formosa
Ciudad del Este
Encarnación
Resistencia
Salto

URUGUAY
Montevideo
Río de la Plata
Mar del Plata

Sucre

San Miguel de Tucumán
Córdoba
Rosario
Buenos Aires
Paraná River

ARGENTINA
Bahía Blanca

Iquique
Antofagasta

A n d e s   M t s .

CHILE
Valparaíso
Santiago
Concepción
Puerto Montt

Comodoro Rivadavia

Río Gallegos
Punta Arenas
Ushuaia
Cape Horn

Strait of Magellan

Stanley
Falkland Is.
(Islas Malvinas)
(Administered by U.K.;
claimed by Argentina)

0 mi.   500 mi.   1,000 mi.

0 km   500 km   1,000 km

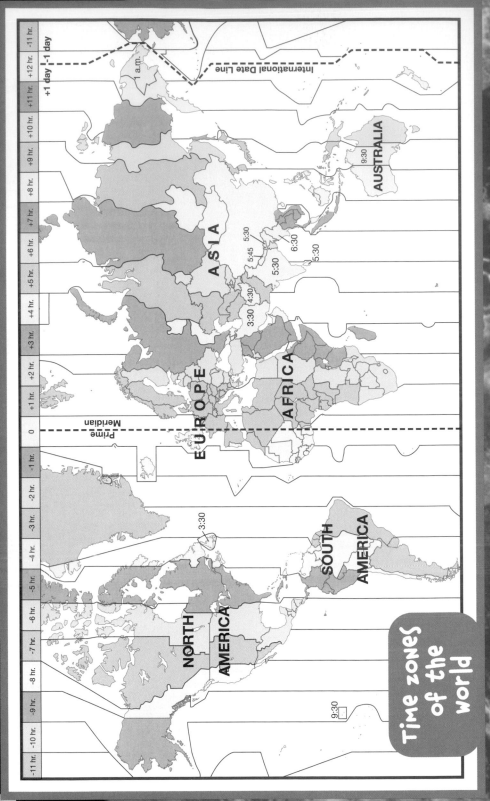

United Nations

The United Nations (U.N.) was created after World War II to provide a meeting place to help develop good relations between countries, promote peace and security around the world and encourage international cooperation in solving problems.

The major organizations of the U.N. are the Secretariat, the Security Council and the General Assembly.

The **Secretariat** is the management center of U.N. operations and is headed by the Secretary-General, who is the director of the U.N.

The **Security Council** is responsible for making and keeping international peace. Its main purpose is to prevent war by settling disputes between nations. The Security Council has 15 members. There are five permanent members: the U.S., the Russian Federation, Britain, France and China. There are also ten temporary members that serve two-year terms.

The **General Assembly** is the world's forum for discussing matters that affect world peace and security and for making recommendations concerning both. The U.N. has no power of its own to enforce decisions. Including the 51 original member nations, it is made up of a total of 192 countries.

The U.N. Headquarters in New York City

World Population Milestones

1 BILLION in 1804

2 BILLION in 1927   123 years later

3 BILLION in 1960   33 years later

4 BILLION in 1974   14 years later

5 BILLION in 1987   13 years later

6 BILLION in 1999   12 years later

Source: United Nations Population Division

Countries by Size

Biggest

COUNTRY	SQUARE MILES
1. Russia	6,592,735
2. Canada	3,855,081
3. United States	3,718,691
4. China	3,705,386
5. Brazil	3,286,470

Smallest

COUNTRY	SQUARE MILES
1. Vatican City	0.17
2. Monaco	0.75
3. Nauru	8.11
4. Tuvalu	10.0
5. San Marino	23.6

FROM TFK MAGAZINE

GLOBAL WARMING WARNING

Scientists say the effects of global warming are causing species to disappear quicker than originally thought

Warmer temperatures threaten polar bears.

Global warming is causing hundreds of species to die off or change more quickly than scientists predicted, a new study shows. "I feel as though we are staring crisis in the face," said Douglas Futuyma, a professor at the State University of New York in Stony Brook. "It's not just down the road somewhere. It is just hurtling toward us."

Extinction Evidence

At least 70 species of frogs have become extinct because of climate change, according to a study in the scientific journal *Annual Review of Ecology, Evolution and Systematics*. The study also reports that between 100 and 200 cold-dependent animal species, such as penguins and polar bears, are in serious danger.

"We are finally seeing species going extinct," said University of Texas biologist Camille Parmesan, author of the study. "Now we've got the evidence."

Parmesan looked at 866 studies and saw trends of animal populations moving north to cooler climates. She also saw adaptations such as plants blooming earlier than usual and an increase in pests and parasites.

Parmesan said she worries most about cold-weather species. Emperor penguins have dropped from 300 breeding pairs to just nine in the western Antarctic Peninsula. Polar bears are dropping in numbers and weight in the Arctic.

Animals that adapt better to warmth or can move and live farther north are managing better than other populations in the same species, she said.

Conference on Climate

Leaders from more than 180 nations met in Nairobi, Kenya, in 2006 to discuss global warming at a United Nations climate conference. The leaders agreed on the next steps to cut global-warming gases.

Leaders agreed to take a new look at the Kyoto Protocol, an energy agreement, by 2008. The goal will be to set new rules on the release of carbon dioxide and other gases after Kyoto expires in 2012.

Germany's Environment Minister Sigmar Gabriel said the timeline set at the meeting is too long. "Urgent action is necessary," he said.

—BY JILL EGAN

U.S. Power

Here's a breakdown of the sources of energy in the United States.
Source: *The New York Times*

Source	Percentage
OIL	39%
NATURAL GAS	24%
COAL	23%
NUCLEAR	8%
HYDROPOWER	3%
OTHER	3%

■ nonrenewable sources
■ renewable sources
■ other

ENERGY AND THE EARTH

Energy is the power we use for transportation, to heat and light our homes and to manufacture all kinds of products. Energy sources come in two types: **nonrenewable** and **renewable**.

NONRENEWABLE SOURCES OF ENERGY

Most of the energy we use comes from fossil fuels such as coal, natural gas and petroleum. Once these natural resources are used up, they are gone forever. Uranium, a metallic chemical element, is another nonrenewable source, but it is not a fossil fuel. Uranium is converted to a fuel and used in nuclear power plants.

The process of gathering these fuels can be harmful to the environment. In addition, to produce energy, fossil fuels are put through a process called combustion. Combustion releases pollution, such as carbon monoxide and sulfur dioxide, and probably contributes to acid rain and global warming.

RENEWABLE SOURCES OF ENERGY

Renewable sources of energy can be used over and over again. Renewable resources include solar energy, wind turbines, geothermal energy, biomass and hydropower. They generate much less pollution—in both their gathering and in production—than do nonrenewable sources.

→ **Solar energy** comes from the Sun. Some people use solar panels on their homes to convert sunlight into electricity.

→ **Wind turbines,** which look like giant windmills, generate electricity.

→ **Geothermal energy** comes from the Earth's core. Engineers extract steam or very hot water from the Earth's crust and use the steam to produce electricity.

→ **Biomass** includes natural products such as wood, manure and corn. These materials are burned and used for heat.

→ Dams and rivers generate **hydropower.** When water flows through a dam, it activates a turbine, which runs an electric generator.

Top Energy Producers and Consumers

The United States produces the most energy in the world, and it also uses the most— almost double the amount used by China, the world's second largest energy consumer.

PRODUCERS

COUNTRY	% OF TOTAL WORLD ENERGY PRODUCED
1. United States	16%
2. Russia	13%
3. China	12%
4. Saudi Arabia	5%
5. Canada	4%

Source: U.S. Department of Energy

CONSUMERS

COUNTRY	% OF TOTAL WORLD ENERGY CONSUMED
1. United States	25%
2. China	13%
3. Russia	7%
4. Japan	5%
5. India	3%

Source: U.S. Department of Energy

TOP 5 TFK Oil Reliance

Each day, the United States uses about 21 million barrels of oil—more than any other country in the world. We import just over half of it. Here's where we got the oil in 2006.

SOURCE OF OIL	NUMBER OF BARRELS THE U.S. IMPORTS A DAY
1. Canada	1,616,000
2. Mexico	1,598,000
3. Saudi Arabia	1,495,000
4. Venezuela	1,297,000
5. Nigeria	1,078,000

Source: U.S. Department of Energy

Environment & Energy

PERILS OF POLLUTION

→ Many scientists think human-caused pollution has contributed to global warming, which is a rise in the Earth's surface temperature. A world that continues to warm up could mean big trouble. Hotter temperatures are causing some ice at the North and South Poles to melt and the oceans to rise. The warmer climate is changing our weather patterns and could result in dangerous tornadoes and droughts.

Glaciers are melting.

→ The Earth stays warm the same way a greenhouse does. Gases in the atmosphere, such as carbon dioxide, methane and nitrogen, act like the glass of a greenhouse: they let in the Sun's light and warmth, but they keep the Earth's heat from escaping. This is known as the greenhouse effect. Scientists think that if too many of these greenhouse gases are released into the atmosphere, from pollution, for example, the gases can trap too much heat, causing temperatures to rise.

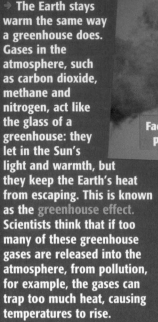

Factory emissions pollute the air.

Dumping garbage is harmful to plants and wildlife.

Top Carbon Dioxide Emitters

Carbon dioxide is a heat-trapping gas that contributes to the greenhouse effect. These are the countries that emit the most carbon dioxide.

1. United States
2. China
3. Russia
4. India
5. Japan
6. Germany
7. Canada
8. United Kingdom
9. South Korea
10. Italy

Source: U.S. Department of Energy

→ Acid rain occurs when rainwater is contaminated with pollutants like nitrogen oxide and sulfur dioxide. These gases come from fuels being burned at high temperatures, as in car exhausts. When acid rain falls, it can damage wildlife and erode buildings.

→ Pollution is the contamination of air or water by harmful substances. One source of pollution is hazardous waste—anything thrown away that could be dangerous to the environment, such as paint and pesticides. These materials can seep into water supplies and contaminate them.

→ The ozone layer, a thin sheet of an invisible gas called ozone, surrounds Earth about 15 miles above its surface. Ozone protects us from the Sun's harmful rays. In recent years, the amount of ozone in the atmosphere has decreased, probably due to human-made gases called chlorofluorocarbons (CFCs). As the ozone level decreases, the Sun's rays become more dangerous to humans.

Smog hangs over Los Angeles.

Did You Know?

About 97% of all water on Earth is saltwater, which humans can't use in the home or for drinking. Nearly 2% of the world's freshwater is frozen in the ice caps of Antarctica and Greenland, and still more is deep in the ground. Only about one-third of 1% of all water on Earth is available for human use.

The Most Polluted Places in the World

The Blacksmith Institute, an environmental organization based in New York City, put together this list. It is based on the size of the affected population, the toxins involved and the health problems associated with the pollution.

1. CHERNOBYL, UKRAINE
The world's worst nuclear disaster took place on April 26, 1986, when a reactor blew at the nuclear power plant in Chernobyl. The explosion ripped open the core, blew the roof off the building, started more than 30 fires and allowed radioactive material to leak into the air. About 30 people were killed and nearly 300 people were treated for radiation poisoning.

The Chernobyl disaster

2. DZERZHINSK, RUSSIA
This major Russian chemical manufacturing center produced sarin and other deadly poisons during the cold war. Between 1930 and 1998, nearly 300,000 tons of chemical waste were improperly disposed of.

3. HAINA, DOMINICAN REPUBLIC
This urban area was severely contaminated with lead from an automobile battery recycling plant, which is now closed.

4. KABWE, ZAMBIA
Zambia's second largest city is heavily contaminated with lead from the mining industry.

5. LA OROYA, PERU
Lead, copper, zinc and sulfur dioxide from mining have contaminated the town.

Dirty Cities

Are you breathing dirty air? Below are lists of the dirtiest cities in the United States and the world.

UNITED STATES

RANK	METROPOLITAN AREA
1.	Bakersfield, California
2.	Los Angeles–Long Beach–Riverside, California
3.	Visalia-Porterville, California
4.	Fresno-Madera, California
5.	Merced, California

Source: American Lung Association

WORLD

RANK	METROPOLITAN AREA
1.	Mexico City, Mexico
2.	São Paulo, Brazil
3.	Cairo, Egypt
4.	New Delhi, India
5.	Shanghai, China

Source: World Health Organization

WHAT AMERICANS THROW AWAY

	% OF ALL TRASH
Paper products and cardboard	36%
Yard waste	20%
Food waste	9%
Metals	9%
Glass	8%
Plastics	7%
Rubber and leather goods	3%
Other	8%

Did You Know?

Pollution caused nearly 20,000 beach closings in 2004, the highest number in 15 years.

... AND WHERE TRASH GOES

About 55% of our trash ends up in **landfills,** better known as dumps. Landfills are shallow holes that are often lined with plastic to prevent toxic substances from seeping into the soil or water supply. The country's landfills are quickly filling up, and cities and towns are faced with a big problem since most people oppose plans to open landfills in their neighborhoods.

Some garbage—about 14% of it—is burned in **incinerators,** or large furnaces. The good thing about incinerators is that the trash is gone once it's burned. The downside is that the ash and smoke released in the burning process sometimes contain harmful chemicals. The other 31% of the trash we produce is recycled.

Environment & Energy

The Three Rs

Recycling is a great way to conserve resources and help the environment. Remember the three Rs:

1. REDUCE
Reducing waste is the best way to help the environment. Buy large containers of food whenever possible. For example, buy one 32-ounce container of yogurt rather than four 8-ounce cups.

2. REUSE
Rather than throw things away, find ways to use them again.
→ Use food containers for paint cups or for storing toys or art supplies.
→ Cut old clothes into pieces and use them as rags.

3. RECYCLE
Recycled items are new products made out of the materials from old ones. Recycle all of your used paper and your aluminum, plastic and glass containers.

A LOOK AT THE RECYCLING PROCESS

Did you ever wonder what happens to the objects that you toss into recycling bins? Here's a look at how glass, plastic, aluminum and paper are recycled.

GLASS

As long as 3,000 years ago, Egyptians used glass to make jewelry, cups and other items. Glass is made of sand, soda ash and limestone and is one of the easiest materials to recycle.

→ At recycling centers, glass is sorted by color.
→ The glass is transported to a processing facility where it is cleaned and crushed into what is called cullet.
→ The cullet is brought to a manufacturing plant and mixed with more sand, soda ash and limestone.
→ The mixture is heated in a furnace and turned into a thick liquid.
→ The liquid flows out of the furnace and into an automatic feeder, where it is cut into bottle-size portions.
→ These portions flow down a chute into molds, where they are shaped and cooled.
→ A machine makes a small hole in the center, and air is blown into the bottle to hollow it out. A neck is shaped for a cap or lid.
→ An annealing oven, or leer, slowly heats, then cools, the glassware, making it strong.

PLASTIC

Unlike glass, which is made entirely of natural substances, plastic is composed of man-made and raw materials, including petroleum and crude oil.

→ Plastic collected at recycling centers is brought to a recycling plant where it is washed and inspected.

A plastic recycling plant

→ The recyclable plastic is washed and chopped into tiny flakes.
→ The flakes are separated in a flotation tank.
→ The flakes are dried and then melted into a liquid.
→ The liquid is fed through a screen for even more cleaning. It comes out in long strands.
→ The strands are cooled and cut into pellets.
→ The pellets then make their way to manufacturers who use them to make new products.

ALUMINUM

Making an aluminum can from recycled aluminum uses 96% less energy than it does to produce one for the first time.

→ Recycled cans are moved from a recycling center to a recycling plant where they are shredded into dime-size pieces.

　→ The pieces are placed in a furnace and melted into a liquid metal.

　→ The liquid flows into molds that form ingots, or bars of metal.

→ Rollers squeeze the ingots into sheets.

→ Sheets are rolled into coils and sent to a plant, where they are shaped into cans again.

A paper recycling plant

PAPER

Paper is made of tiny fibers. Because these fibers eventually become weak, paper cannot be recycled forever. Most types of paper can be recycled. Some types— those with a glossy or waxy coating—are sometimes too expensive to recycle. When you recycle paper, you should try to separate newsprint, white paper and cardboard.

→ The paper you bring to a recycling center is sorted and sent to a paper mill.

→ The paper is soaked and heated in a huge vat, called a hydrapulper.

→ Detergents and chemicals remove inks. The paper is now pulp, which looks like cottage cheese.

→ The pulp is screened and cleaned to remove glue, other debris and any remaining ink.

→ The pulp is bleached with chlorine or other chemicals to make it white. It is washed again.

→ The pulp is fed into a machine that spits out the pulp onto a flat moving screen where it forms sheets.

→ The sheets are rolled and dried.

→ Paper is cut to size, wrapped and shipped.

Recycle These Facts!

A ton of paper made from recycled paper saves:
• 7,000 gallons of water.
• Between 17 and 31 trees.
• 60 pounds of air pollutants.

Recycling a pound of steel saves enough energy to light a 60-watt light bulb for 26 hours.

Americans recycle only 5% of all the plastics produced in this country.

Americans use 100 million steel cans and 200 million aluminum beverage cans every day.

More than 30 million trees are cut down to produce a year's supply of newspapers.

One drip per second from a faucet wastes 540 gallons of water a year.

It takes between 400 and 500 years for a Styrofoam cup to decompose. It takes an orange peel six months to decompose.

Using recycled glass uses 40% less energy than making products from all new materials.

Today, almost 22% of the glass produced in the United States is recycled.

TFK MYSTERY PERSON

CLUE 1: I was born in Springdale, Pennsylvania, in 1907.

CLUE 2: I worked as an aquatic biologist at the Fish and Wildlife Service for 16 years.

CLUE 3: I wrote seven books about life under the sea. My best-selling book, *Silent Spring*, exposed the dangers of pesticides to the environment.

WHO AM I? (See Answer Key on page 242.)

Environment & Energy

91

CLOTHES ENCOUNTERS

FASHION THROUGH THE DECADES

1900s
- corsets for tiny waists
- tight collars
- lots of lace
- long lightweight "duster" coats
- upswept hair
- narrow shoes for both men and women
  - straw "boater" hats for men
  - feathered hats for women

1900s

1910s
- bathing costumes
- lace-up boots
- decorated stockings
- narrow "hobble" skirts
- trenchcoats
- beaded handbags
- Middle Eastern patterns
- V-neck sweaters

1920s
- drop-waist flapper dresses
- cloches (close-fitting hats) for women
- baggy flannel trousers for men
- long, wide coats
- costume jewelry
- T-strap shoes
- sheer stockings
- bobbed hair

1930s
- hats worn at an angle
- patterned sweaters
- one-piece wool bathing suits
- long, flowing gowns
- sandals
- fox-fur collars
- wide overcoats for men
- rectangular wristwatches

1940s

1940s

- matching skirts and sweaters
- fur muffs
- rolled-up blue jeans
- narrow "drainpipe" trousers
- the "pompadour" hairstyle
- sleek evening dresses
- cork-soled "wedge" shoes
- baggy pull-over sweaters
- Hawaiian shirts for men

1950s
- white T-shirts
- motorcycle jackets
- pedal pushers (Capri pants)
- Bermuda shorts
- poodle skirts
- saddle shoes
- full skirts with petticoats
- strapless evening gowns
- jeans

1960s

1960s

- bell-bottoms
- miniskirts
- T-shirts with messages
- pale lipstick and dark eyeliner
- long hair for men and women
- white vinyl "go-go" boots
- peace signs
- paisley and Indian prints

1970s
- Western boots
- lots of lip gloss and blush
- T-shirts with logos
- denim, denim, denim
- leg warmers
- pantsuits
- earth tones
- leotards with wraparound skirts

1980s

1980s

- big hair and lots of hairspray
- fingerless lace gloves
- frills on collars and hems
- bright vests and shirts for men
- "power suits" with big shoulder pads for women
- long fake-pearl necklaces
- tunics over leggings

1990s

- baggy pants
- designer athletic shoes
- puffy jackets
- chain wallets
- lots of flannel
- small eyeglasses
- hooded sweatshirts
- henna tattoos

2000s

- low-rise pants
- blazers
- graphic T-shirts
- hooded tops
- bare midriffs

2000s

Centuries of Jeans

Jeans have a long history, unlike most fashion fads, which tend to be fleeting. Denim and jean fabrics originated in Europe in the late 16th century.

19th century

18TH CENTURY
American mills begin producing their own jean. Laborers wear the durable clothing.

19TH CENTURY
San Francisco dry goods merchant Levi Strauss produces "waist overalls"–the early name for jeans. They become a hit with gold miners eager to strike it rich in California.

In 1886, Strauss adds a brown leather patch to the back of his waist overalls. The label is still sewn on Levi's jeans today.

20TH CENTURY
John Wayne and Gary Cooper play rugged, waist overalls-wearing cowboys in 1930s Hollywood Westerns. Eager to imitate these movie stars, American men don the pants, too.

1940s
American troops pack their waist overalls when they travel overseas to fight in World War II. The trend catches on in Europe. Lee and Wrangler make their own jeans to compete with Levi's.

1950s

1950s
No longer called waist overalls, jeans become a symbol of the teenage rebel, particularly after James Dean wears them in the 1955 film *Rebel Without a Cause*. Some schools ban jeans.

1960s
Jeans dominate college campuses. Students begin to personalize their jeans with paint, embroidery and patches.

1980s

1980s
Designer jeans, such as Sassoon, Jordache and Calvin Klein, emerge. Straight-leg, tight-fitting styles give jeans a new look.

1990s
Jeans are everywhere–on babies, parents, teachers and executives–and in a wide variety of styles, from boot-cut to bell bottoms, from dark-rinse to stonewashed.

2000s
The decade begins with low-rise, boot-cut or bell-bottom jeans. By 2006, skinny jeans are all the rage.

2006

Fashion

The Seven Continents

CONTINENT	APPROXIMATE AREA	HIGHEST POINT	LOWEST POINT
1. AFRICA	11,608,000 square miles (30,065,000 sq km)	Mount Kilimanjaro, Tanzania: 19,340 feet (5,895 m)	Lake Assal, Djibouti: 512 feet (156 m) below sea level
2. ANTARCTICA	5,100,000 square miles (13,209,000 sq km)	Vinson Massif: 16,066 feet (4,897 m)	Ice covering: 8,327 feet (2,538 m) below sea level
3. ASIA (includes the Middle East)	17,212,000 square miles (44,579,000 sq km)	Mount Everest, bordering China and Nepal: 29,035 feet (8,850 m)	Dead Sea, bordering Israel and Jordan: 1,349 feet (411 m) below sea level
4. AUSTRALIA (includes Oceania)	3,132,000 square miles (8,112,000 sq km)	Mount Kosciusko, Australia: 7,316 feet (2,228 m)	Lake Eyre, Australia: 52 feet (16 m) below sea level
5. EUROPE (Ural Mountains divide Europe from Asia)	3,837,000 square miles (9,938,000 sq km)	Mount Elbrus, bordering Russia and Georgia: 18,510 feet (5,642 m)	Caspian Sea, bordering Russia and Kazakhstan: 92 feet (28 m) below sea level
6. NORTH AMERICA (includes Central America and the Caribbean)	9,449,000 square miles (24,474,000 sq km)	Mount McKinley, Alaska, U.S.: 20,320 feet (6,194 m)	Death Valley, California, U.S.: 282 feet (86 m) below sea level
7. SOUTH AMERICA	6,879,000 square miles (17,819,000 sq km)	Mount Aconcagua, Argentina: 22,834 feet (6,960 m)	Valdes Peninsula, Argentina: 131 feet (40 m) below sea level

Source: WorldAtlas.com

Mount Aconcagua

In 2000, the International Hydrographic Organization delimited (marked the boundaries of) a fifth ocean. The new ocean, called the Southern Ocean, surrounds Antarctica and extends north to 60 degrees south latitude. It is the fourth largest ocean, bigger only than the Arctic Ocean.

The Five Oceans

OCEAN	AREA	AVERAGE DEPTH
1. PACIFIC OCEAN	60,060,700 square miles (155,557,000 sq km)	13,215 feet (4,028 m)
2. ATLANTIC OCEAN	29,637,900 square miles (76,762,000 sq km)	12,880 feet (3,926 m)
3. INDIAN OCEAN	26,469,500 square miles (68,556,000 sq km)	13,002 feet (3,963 m)
4. SOUTHERN OCEAN	7,848,300 square miles (20,327,000 sq km)	13,100–16,400 feet* (4,000–5,000 m)
5. ARCTIC OCEAN	5,427,000 square miles (14,056,000 sq km)	3,953 feet (1,205 m)

*Official depths of the Southern Ocean are in dispute.

Record Breakers

→ **LARGEST LAKE: CASPIAN SEA**
Between Russia and Japan,
152,239 square miles (394,299 sq km)

→ **LONGEST RIVER: THE NILE**
Africa, 4,180 miles
(6,690 km)

→ **SHORTEST RIVER:**
THE ROE Montana, U.S.,
201 feet (61 m)

→ **LARGEST ISLAND: GREENLAND**
839,999 square miles (2,175,600 sq km)

→ **LONGEST MOUNTAIN RANGE: THE ANDES**
South America, more than 5,000 miles
(8,000 km)

→ **HIGHEST WATERFALL: ANGEL FALLS**
(SALTO ANGEL)
Venezuela, 3,212 feet (979 m) high

→ **BIGGEST DESERT: SAHARA**
Africa, 3.5 million square miles
(9.1 million sq km)

→ **HIGHEST MOUNTAIN: MOUNT EVEREST,**
HIMALAYAN MOUNTAINS
Bordering Nepal and China, 29,035 feet
(8,850 m) above sea level

→ **LOWEST POINT ON LAND: THE DEAD SEA**
Bordering Israel and Jordan, water
surface 1,349 feet (411 meters) below
sea level

→ **LARGEST SEA: THE MEDITERRANEAN SEA**
1,144,800 square miles (2,966,000 sq km)

→ **LARGEST ARCHIPELAGO: INDONESIA**
3,500-mile (5,632-km) stretch of 13,000
islands

→ **DEEPEST LAKE: LAKE BAIKAL**
Russia, 5,315 feet
(1,620 m) deep

→ **LARGEST GULF:**
GULF OF MEXICO
615,000 square miles
(1,502,200 sq km)

→ **LARGEST PENINSULA:**
ARABIA Southwest Asia,
1,250,000 square miles (3,237,500 sq km)

IMPORTANT EXPLORERS

1000 Leif Eriksson (Viking) explored
Labrador and Newfoundland in Canada.

1271 Marco Polo (Italian) explored
China.

1325–1349 Ibn Batuta (Arab)
explored Africa, the Middle East,
Europe and parts of Asia.

1488 Bartholomeu Dias (Portuguese)
rounded South Africa's Cape of Good Hope.

1492 Christopher Columbus (Italian) arrived in
the West Indies.

1498 Vasco da Gama (Portuguese) explored the
coast of India.

1513 Ponce de León (Spanish) reached Florida.

1519–1521 Hernando Cortés (Spanish)
conquered Mexico.

1519–1522 The expedition led by Ferdinand
Magellan (Portuguese) circled the globe.

1532–1533 Francisco Pizarro (Spanish)
conquered Peru.

1535–1536 Jacques Cartier (French)
sailed up Canada's St. Lawrence River.

1539–1542 Hernando de Soto (Spanish)
explored the southeastern United States

1607 John Smith (British) settled Jamestown,
Virginia.

1609–1610 Henry Hudson (British) explored the
river, strait and bay that bear his name.

1769 James Cook (British) explored New
Zealand.

1804–1806 Meriwether Lewis and
William Clark (American) explored the
northwest U.S.

1909 Robert
E. Peary
(American)
reached the
North Pole.

1911 Roald
Amundsen
(Norwegian)
reached the South Pole.

Aceh, Indonesia

Kapaau, Hawaii

Earthquakes

There are millions of earthquakes each year, ranging on average from 18 major quakes annually to more than two million minor ones that are barely felt. We can usually expect one exceptionally large earthquake per year.

An earthquake is a trembling movement of Earth's rocky outer layer, called the crust. The crust is divided into several plates that are slowly and continuously shifting. Most earthquakes occur along a fault—a crack in the crust between two plates—when two plates crash together or move in opposite directions. A quake begins at a point called the focus.

A **tsunami** is a series of giant sea waves that follows an earthquake or a volcanic eruption. The waves can be up to 50 feet tall and move at about 600 miles per hour. The waves can cause massive destruction when they break on land.

Earth on the Move

If you look at a map of the world, you'll see that the continents look as if they are pieces of a big puzzle. For example, if you pushed South America and Africa into each other, they would fit together as one land mass.

Many scientists believe that until about 200 million years ago, the world was made up of a single supercontinent called Pangaea. It eventually separated and drifted apart into the seven continents we have today. This movement is called continental drift.

According to the theory of plate tectonics, the Earth's lithosphere—the crust and the outer part of the mantle—is not one giant piece of rock. Instead, it's broken into several moving slabs, or plates. These plates slide above a hot layer of the mantle. The plates move as much as a few inches every year. The oceans and the continents sit on top of the plates and move with them.

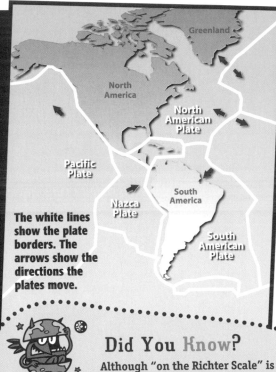

The white lines show the plate borders. The arrows show the directions the plates move.

Did You Know?

Although "on the Richter Scale" is still a common expression, the scale developed by Charles Richter in 1935 is no longer the most widely used magnitude measurement. It was found to be imprecise in measuring the biggest earthquakes.

Volcanoes

Mauna Loa

A volcano is a cone-shaped hill or mountain with a vent (opening) at the top called a crater. The crater connects with magma, or molten rock, dozens of miles below the surface of Earth.

Magma mixes with gases, crystals and chunks of rock and other debris and is forced upward through weaknesses and cracks in Earth's crust. As magma rises, it creates more pressure and upward movement, pushing rocks aside and building toward eruption. When enough pressure accumulates, an eruption occurs and the molten rock either pours from the crater as lava flows, or it shoots violently into the air in chunks of lava.

Lava is red-hot when it pours or blasts from the top of a volcano but soon changes to dark red, gray, black or some other color as it cools and turns into a solid. Very hot, gas-rich lava is fluid and flows like hot tar. Cooler, gas-poor lava flows slowly, like thick honey.

Mauna Loa in Hawaii is the world's largest volcano. It measures about 6 miles tall from the sea floor to the top, which is about 2.5 miles above sea level.

Did You Know?

Many of the world's volcanoes are lined up along the "ring of fire," a belt that encircles the Pacific Ocean. This region experiences frequent earthquakes and volcanic activity. About 75% of the world's volcanoes are located here.

Krakatau

Deadliest Volcanoes

VOLCANO, LOCATION	YEAR	NUMBER OF DEATHS
Tambora, Indonesia	1815	92,000
Krakatau, Indonesia	1883	36,400
Mount Pelee, Martinique	1902	29,000
Ruiz, Colombia	1985	25,000
Unzen, Japan	1792	14,300

Geography

The Roof of the World

Mount Everest

In 1852, scientists declared Mount Everest the highest mountain in the world. This announcement captured the international imagination, and soon the idea of reaching the summit of the "roof of the world" was viewed as the ultimate geographic feat.

It wasn't until 101 years later that someone achieved that lofty goal. On May 29, 1953, **Edmund Hillary,** a beekeeper from New Zealand, and **Tenzing Norgay,** an acclaimed Sherpa climber, became the first to reach the roof of the world.

Hillary and Tenzing

Sherpas are a people of Tibetan ancestry who migrated to Nepal about 600 years ago. They are known for their ability to tolerate high altitudes, their mountaineering skills and their extraordinary bravery.

The dangers of climbing Everest, which measures 29,035 feet, include avalanches, crevasses, ferocious winds up to 125 miles per hour, sudden storms and temperatures of -40°F. In addition, climbers face oxygen deprivation. They spend months getting used to the climate. Most climbers attempt Everest only in May and October, to avoid the winter snows and the summer monsoons.

EVEREST TRIVIA

→ More than 2,000 people have reached the summit of Everest; almost 200 have died on the mountain.

→ The sons of Hillary and Tenzing also reached the summit of Everest.

→ According to *National Geographic*, Everest grows about 4 millimeters a year.

→ In 1963, James Whittaker became the first American to summit Everest.

→ In 1975, Junko Tabei of Japan became the first woman to reach the summit of Everest.

Time Zones

Before railways were established in the 1800s, all time was local. Noon was simply when the Sun was directly overhead in what is called solar time.

ENGINEERING TIME All that changed when railroads began to move people across great distances quickly. In 1878, Sir Sandford Fleming, a Canadian railway engineer, developed the system of worldwide time zones that we still use today. He proposed that the world be divided into 24 time zones, each spaced 15 degrees of longitude apart. He came to this idea because Earth completes a rotation every 24 hours and there are 360 degrees of longitude, so each hour Earth rotates 1/24th of a circle or 15 degrees. Railroad companies in the United States began using Sir Fleming's standard time zones in 1883. A conference was held in Washington, D.C., in 1884, to standardize time around the world and select the prime meridian, which runs through Greenwich, England. The prime meridian is 0 degrees longitude, and all other lines of longitude are measured by their distance from the prime meridian.

SETTING THE STANDARD In the U.S., most states began using the Eastern, Central, Mountain and Pacific time zones by 1895, but the use of time zones did not become mandatory until Congress passed the Standard Time Act of 1918. Today the U.S. and its territories cover nine time zones.

Types of Maps

There are several types of maps. Each one serves a different purpose. Most maps include a compass rose, which indicates which way is north, south, east and west. They also include a scale so you can estimate distances. Here's a look at some different types of maps.

POLITICAL MAPS

do not show physical features. Instead, they indicate state and national boundaries and capital and major cities. A capital city is usually marked with a star within a circle.

CLIMATE MAPS

give general information about climate and precipitation (rain and snow) of a region. Cartographers, or mapmakers, use colors to show different climate or precipitation zones.

ROAD MAPS show major—and some minor—highways and roads, airports, railroad tracks, cities and other points of interest in an area. People use road maps to plan trips and for driving directions.

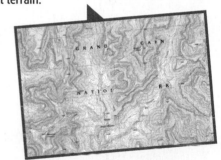

ECONOMIC OR RESOURCE MAPS feature

the types of natural resources or economic activity that dominate an area. Cartographers use symbols to show the locations of natural resources or economic activities.

PHYSICAL MAPS illustrate

the physical features of an area, such as mountains, rivers and lakes. The water is usually shown in blue. Colors are used to show relief—differences in land elevations. Green is typically used at lower elevations, and orange or brown indicates higher elevations.

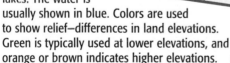

TOPOGRAPHIC MAPS include

contour lines to show the shape and elevation of an area. Lines that are close together indicate steep terrain, and lines that are far apart denote flat terrain.

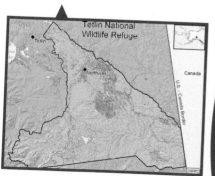

TFK MYSTERY PERSON

CLUE 1: I was born in 1454 in Florence, Italy. I was an explorer, a merchant and a mapmaker.

CLUE 2: I went on several early voyages to the New World. At the time, many people thought that it was part of Asia. I was one of the first explorers to declare that it was a new continent.

CLUE 3: In 1507, a German mapmaker named the New World America in my honor.

WHO AM I? (See Answer Key on page 242.)

THE CONSTITUTION

In 1787 leaders of the states gathered to write the Constitution—a set of principles that described how the new nation would be governed. The Constitution went into effect in 1789. The Constitution begins with a famous section called the preamble. The preamble says that the U.S. government was created by the people and for the benefit of the people:

> We the people of the United States, in order to form a more perfect Union, establish justice, insure domestic tranquility, provide for the common defense, promote the general welfare and secure the blessings of liberty to ourselves and our posterity, do ordain and establish this Constitution for the United States of America.

The leaders of the states wanted a strong and fair national government. But they also wanted to protect individual freedoms and prevent the government from abusing its power. They believed they could do this by having three separate branches of government: the Executive, the Legislative and the Judicial. This separation is described in the first three articles, or sections, of the Constitution.

 THE CONSTITUTION WAS ORIGINALLY MADE UP OF SEVEN ARTICLES.

ARTICLE I creates the Legislative Branch—the House of Representatives and the Senate—and describes its powers and responsibilities.

ARTICLE II creates the Executive Branch, which is led by the President, and describes its powers and responsibilities.

ARTICLE III creates the Judicial Branch, which is led by the Supreme Court, and describes its powers and responsibilities.

ARTICLE IV describes the rights and powers of the states.

ARTICLE V explains how amendments (changes or additions) can be made to the Constitution.

ARTICLE VI says the Constitution is "the supreme law of the land."

ARTICLE VII tells how the Constitution would be ratified (approved and made official) by the states.

 For the complete Constitution, including all the amendments:
www.factmonster.com/constitution

As Article V shows, the authors of the Constitution expected from the beginning that amendments would be made to the document. There are now 27 Amendments.

The first 10 Amendments are known as the Bill of Rights. They list individual freedoms promised by the new government. The Bill of Rights was approved in 1791.

Other Notable Amendments

AMENDMENT XIII (approved 1865) declares slavery illegal.

AMENDMENT I guarantees freedom of religion, speech and the press.

AMENDMENT II guarantees the right of the people to have firearms.

AMENDMENT III says that soldiers may not stay in a house without the owner's permission.

AMENDMENT IV says that the government cannot search people and their homes without a strong reason.

AMENDMENT V says that every person has the right to a trial and to protection of his or her rights while waiting for a trial. Also, private property cannot be taken without payment.

AMENDMENT VI says that every person shall have the right to "a speedy and public trial."

AMENDMENT VII guarantees the right to a trial in various types of legal cases.

AMENDMENT VIII outlaws all "cruel and unusual punishment."

AMENDMENT IX says that people have rights in addition to those listed in the Constitution.

AMENDMENT X says that the powers the Constitution does not give to the national government belong to the states and to the people.

AMENDMENT XIX (approved 1920) grants women the right to vote.

AMENDMENT XXII (approved 1951) says that a President may serve no more than two four-year terms.

AMENDMENT XXVI (approved 1971) sets the voting age to 18.

Unusual Amendments

Since 1789, members of Congress have proposed about 10,000 amendments to the Constitution. These are just a few that Congress did not approve.

→ 1893: to rename the U.S. the "United States of the Earth"

→ 1914: to make divorce illegal

→ 1916: to put all acts of war to a national vote. Those who vote "yes" must register for military service.

→ 1933: to limit personal wealth to $1 million

→ 1971: to give Americans the right to a pollution-free environment

An amendment to ban the burning of the U.S. flag has been proposed several times.

THE LEGISLATIVE BRANCH

CONGRESS

SENATE

100 MEMBERS
6-YEAR TERMS

HOUSE OF REPRESENTATIVES

435 MEMBERS
2-YEAR TERMS

President Pro Tempore	Senate Majority Leader	Senate Minority Leader	Speaker of the House	House Majority Leader	House Minority Leader

Robert Byrd (D)	Harry Reid (D)	Trent Lott (R)	Nancy Pelosi (D)	Steny Hoyer (D)	John Boehner (R)

The Legislative Branch is made up of the two houses of Congress—the **Senate** and the **House of Representatives.** The most important duty of the Legislative Branch is to make laws. Laws are written, discussed and voted on in Congress.

There are **100 Senators** in the Senate, two from each state. Senators are elected by their states and serve six-year terms. The Vice President of the U.S. is considered the head of the Senate but does not vote in the Senate unless there is a tie. The President Pro Tempore of the Senate presides over the chamber in the absence of the Vice President. The Senator in the majority party who has served the longest is usually elected to the position.

The Senate approves nominations made by the President to the Cabinet, the Supreme Court, federal courts and other posts. The Senate must ratify all treaties by a two-thirds vote.

The House of Representatives has **435 Representatives.** The number of Representatives each state gets is based on its population. For example, California has many more Representatives than Montana has. When Census figures determine that the population of a state has changed significantly, the number of Representatives in that state may shift proportionally.

Representatives are elected by their states and serve two-year terms. The Speaker of the House, elected by the Representatives, is considered the head of the House.

Both parties in the Senate and the House of Representatives elect leaders. The leader of the party that controls the House is called the Majority Leader. The other party leader is called the Minority Leader.

Both houses of Congress elect Whips. The Whips keep track of votes on bills, try to persuade party members to vote along the party line and make sure lawmakers show up for votes.

"Whip" comes from the British term for the person who whips dogs to keep them running with the pack during a fox hunt.

go Go to Congress Connection and find out who represents you at timeforkids.com/congress

Did You Know?

Alaska, Delaware, North Dakota, South Dakota, Montana, Vermont and Wyoming each only have one Representative in the House. California has 53.

THE EXECUTIVE BRANCH

The President is the head of the Executive Branch, which makes laws official. The President is elected by the electoral college (see pages 106-107)and serves a four-year term. The President cannot serve more than two four-year terms. He or she approves and carries out laws passed by the Legislative Branch, appoints or removes Cabinet members and officials, negotiates treaties and acts as head of state and Commander-in-Chief of the armed forces.

THE PRESIDENT

George W. Bush

THE VICE PRESIDENT

Richard Cheney

The Executive Branch also includes the **Vice President** and other officials, such as members of the **Cabinet.** The Cabinet is made up of the heads of the 15 major departments of the government.

The Cabinet gives advice to the President about important matters.

THE CABINET

Department of Agriculture	Department of Commerce	Department of Defense	Department of Education	Department of Energy
			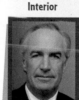	
Secretary Mike Johanns	Secretary Carlos Gutierrez	Secretary Robert Gates	Secretary Margaret Spellings	Secretary Samuel W. Bodman
Department of Health and Human Services	Department of Homeland Security	Department of Housing and Urban Development	Department of the Interior	Department of Justice
Secretary Michael O. Leavitt	Secretary Michael Chertoff	Secretary Alphonso Jackson	Secretary Dirk Kempthorne	Attorney General Alberto Gonzales
Department of Labor	Department of State	Department of Transportation	Department of the Treasury	Department of Veterans Affairs
Secretary Elaine Chao	Secretary Condoleezza Rice	Secretary Mary E. Peters	Secretary Henry M. Paulson Jr.	Secretary Jim Nicholson

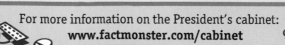
For more information on the President's cabinet:
www.factmonster.com/cabinet

Government

103

THE JUDICIAL BRANCH

Supreme Court Justices (from left to right, front row then back row): Anthony M. Kennedy, John Paul Stevens, Chief Justice John Roberts, Antonin Scalia, David Souter; Stephen G. Breyer, Clarence Thomas, Ruth Bader Ginsburg, Samuel A. Alito Jr.

Supreme Court Building

The Judicial Branch oversees the court system of the United States. Through court cases, the Judicial Branch explains the meaning of the Constitution and laws passed by Congress. **The Supreme Court** is the head of the Judicial Branch. Unlike a criminal court, the Supreme Court rules whether something is constitutional or unconstitutional—that is, whether or not it is permitted under the Constitution.

On the Supreme Court there are **nine Justices,** or judges: eight associate Justices and one Chief Justice. The judges are nominated by the President and approved by the Senate. They have no term limits.

The Supreme Court is the highest court in the land. Its decisions are final, and no other court can overrule those decisions. Decisions of the Supreme Court set precedents—new ways of interpreting the law.

Students demonstrate while the Justices consider the role of race in college admissions.

Significant Supreme Court Decisions

1803 *Marbury v. Madison*
The first time a law passed by Congress was declared unconstitutional

1857 *Dred Scott v. Sandford*
Declared that a slave was not a citizen and that Congress could not outlaw slavery in U.S. territories

1896 *Plessy v. Ferguson*
Said that racial segregation was legal

1954 *Brown v. Board of Education*
Made racial segregation in schools illegal

1966 *Miranda v. Arizona*
Stated that criminal suspects must be informed of their rights before being questioned by police

2003 *Grutter v. Bollinger* and *Gratz v. Bollinger*
Ruled that colleges can, under certain conditions, consider race and ethnicity in admissions

For other Supreme Court cases:
www.factmonster.com/courtdecisions

HOW A BiLL BECOMES A LAW

1. A MEMBER OF CONGRESS INTRODUCES THE BiLL.

When a Senator or Representative introduces a bill, it is sent to the clerk of the Senate or House, who gives it a number and title. Next, the bill goes to the appropriate committee.

2. COMMITTEES REVIEW AND VOTE ON THE BiLL.

Committees specialize in different areas, such as foreign relations or agriculture, and are made up of small groups of Senators or Representatives.

The committee may reject the bill and "table" it, meaning it is never discussed again. Or the committee may hold hearings to listen to facts and opinions, make changes in the bill and cast votes. If most committee members vote in favor of the bill, it is sent back to the Senate and the House for debate.

3. THE SENATE AND THE HOUSE DEBATE AND VOTE ON THE BiLL.

Separately, the Senate and the House debate the bill, offer amendments and cast votes. If the bill is defeated in either the Senate or the House, the bill dies.

Sometimes, the House and the Senate pass the same bill but with different amendments. In these cases, the bill goes to a conference committee made up of members of both houses of Congress. The conference committee works out differences between the two versions of the bill.

Then the bill goes before all of Congress for a vote. If a majority of both the Senate and the House votes for the bill, it goes to the President for approval.

4. THE PRESIDENT SIGNS THE BiLL— OR NOT.

If the President approves the bill and signs it, the bill becomes a law. However, if the President disapproves, he or she can veto the bill by refusing to sign it.

Congress can try to overrule a veto. If both the Senate and the House pass the bill by a two-thirds majority, the President's veto is overruled and the bill becomes a law.

Presidential Succession

Who would take over if the President died, resigned or was removed from office? The list of who is next in line is known as presidential succession.

- → Vice President
- → Speaker of the House
- → President Pro Tempore of the Senate
- → Secretary of State
- → Secretary of the Treasury
- → Secretary of Defense
- → Attorney General
- → Secretary of the Interior
- → Secretary of Agriculture
- → Secretary of Commerce
- → Secretary of Labor
- → Secretary of Health and Human Services
- → Secretary of Housing and Urban Development
- → Secretary of Transportation
- → Secretary of Energy
- → Secretary of Education
- → Secretary of Veterans Affairs
- → Secretary of Homeland Security

Who on the current Cabinet was not born in the U.S. and therefore cannot become President?

(See Answer Key on page 242.)

President Truman signing a bill

President Clinton approving NAFTA

HOW THE PRESIDENT GETS ELECTED

McKinley campaign poster

→ → → → → 1. ← ← ← ← ←

CANDIDATE ANNOUNCES PLAN TO RUN FOR OFFICE.

This announcement launches the candidate's official campaign. Speeches, debates and baby kissing begin.

→ → → → → 2. ← ← ← ← ←

CANDIDATE CAMPAIGNS TO WIN DELEGATE SUPPORT.

The first stage of a presidential campaign is the nomination campaign. At this time the candidate is competing with other candidates in the same party, hoping to get the party's nomination. The candidate works to win delegates—representatives who pledge to support the candidate's nomination at the national party convention—and to persuade potential voters in general.

1952 Republican National Convention

→ → → → → 3. ← ← ← ← ←

CAUCUSES AND PRIMARY ELECTIONS TAKE PLACE IN THE STATES.

Caucuses and primaries are ways for the general public to take part in nominating presidential candidates.

At a caucus, local party members gather to nominate a candidate. A caucus is a lively event at which party leaders and activists debate issues and consider candidates. The rules governing caucus procedures vary by party and by state.

A primary is more like a general election. Voters go to the polls to cast their votes for a presidential candidate (or delegates who will represent that candidate at the party convention).

A primary election is the main way voters choose a nominee.

Jimmy Carter on his campaign plane

→ → → → → 4. ← ← ← ← ←

NOMINEE FOR PRESIDENT IS ANNOUNCED AT NATIONAL PARTY CONVENTION.

There are two primary political parties in the United States—the Democratic Party and the Republican Party. The main goal of a national party convention is to unify party members. Thousands of delegates gather to rally support for the party's ideas and to formally nominate party candidates for President and Vice President.

After the convention, the second stage of the presidential campaign begins: the election campaign. In this stage, candidates from different parties compete against each other as they try to get elected President.

→ → → → → 5. ← ← ← ← ←

CITIZENS CAST THEIR VOTES.

Presidential elections are held every four years on the Tuesday after the first Monday of November.

Many Americans think that when they cast their ballot, they are voting for their chosen candidate. Actually, they are selecting groups of electors in the Electoral College.

THE ELECTORAL COLLEGE CASTS ITS VOTES.

Some Founding Fathers wanted Congress to elect the President. Others wanted the President to be elected by popular vote. The Electoral College represents a compromise between these ideas.

Every state has a number of electors equal to its number of Senators and Representatives. In addition, there are three electors for the District of Columbia. Laws vary by state, but electors are usually chosen by popular vote. An elector may not be a Senator, Representative or other person holding a national office.

In most cases, the electoral votes from a particular state go to the candidate who leads the popular vote in that state. (Only Maine and Nebraska divide electoral votes among candidates.)

This "winner takes all" system can produce surprising results; in the elections of 1824, 1876, 1888 and 2000, the candidate who had the greatest popular vote did not win the greatest Electoral College vote and so lost the presidency.

On the first Monday after the second Wednesday in December, the electors cast their ballots. At least 270 electoral votes are required to elect a President. If this majority is not reached, the House of Representatives chooses the President.

THE PRESIDENT IS INAUGURATED.

On January 20, the President enters office in a ceremony that is known as the Inauguration and takes the presidential oath: "I do solemnly swear (or affirm) that I will faithfully execute the office of President of the United States, and will to the best of my ability, preserve, protect and defend the Constitution of the United States."

George H. W. Bush's Inauguration

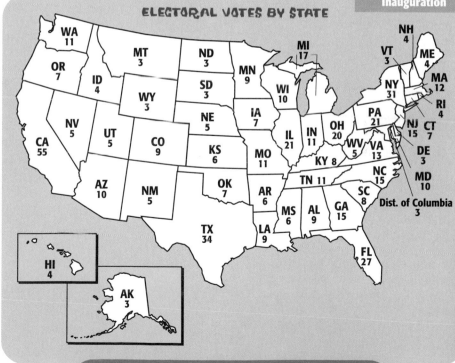

ELECTORAL VOTES BY STATE

For the results of past presidential elections:
www.factmonster.com/elections

Government

107

Pay Day

Senator John Warner

Considering that many business leaders make millions each year, the salaries of government officials seem quite low in comparison.

POSITION	2006 SALARY
President	$400,000
Vice President	$202,900
Senator	$158,100
U.S. Representative	$158,100
Majority and Minority Leaders	$175,600
Speaker of the House	$202,900
Chief Justice, U.S. Supreme Court	$202,900
Associate Justice, U.S. Supreme Court	$194,200

Source: U.S. Office of Personnel Management

You're Out

President Clinton

The President, the Vice President and other U.S. officials can be impeached—that is, formally charged with "high crimes and misdemeanors," which include bribery, perjury, treason and abuse of power.

Under the Constitution, only the House of Representatives has the power to impeach a federal official. If a majority of the House votes for impeachment, then the Senate holds a trial and votes on whether to convict the official. If two-thirds of the Senate votes for conviction, the official will be removed from office.

Only two Presidents have been impeached: Andrew Johnson and Bill Clinton. However, neither was convicted by the Senate.

Hiram Revels

Jeannette Rankin

FAMOUS FIRSTS

African American member of the U.S. Senate: Hiram Revels, 1870, Mississippi

African American member of the U.S. House of Representatives: Jefferson Long, Georgia, 1870

African American Associate Justice of the U.S. Supreme Court: Thurgood Marshall, 1967

African American Cabinet member: Robert C. Weaver, Secretary of Housing and Urban Development, 1966

Hispanic member of the U.S. House of Representatives: Romualdo Pacheco, California, was elected in 1876 by a one-vote margin.

Hispanic member of the U.S. Senate: Octaviano Larrazolo, New Mexico, 1928

Hispanic Cabinet member: Lauro F. Cavazos, 1988, Secretary of Education

Woman member of the U.S. House of Representatives: Jeannette Rankin, Montana, 1916

Woman member of the U.S. Senate: Rebecca Latimer Felton, Georgia, appointed 1922

Woman Associate Justice of the U.S. Supreme Court: Sandra Day O'Connor, 1981

Woman Cabinet member: Frances Perkins, Secretary of Labor, 1933

Woman Speaker of the House of Representatives: Nancy Pelosi, California, 2007

Muslim member of Congress: Rep. Keith Ellison, Minnesota, 2007

Buddhist members of Congress: Rep. Mazie Hirono, Hawaii, and Rep. Hank Johnson, Georgia, both 2007

Speaker Nancy Pelosi (left) and Rep. Keith Ellison reenact Ellison's swearing-in ceremoney using Thomas Jefferson's Koran.

Sandra Day O'Connor

Riding into History

In 1955, laws in some states forced blacks and whites to sit separately in restaurants, on buses and in other public places. Rosa Parks helped change those laws. Read the timeline to learn more about Parks and how her action affected history. Then answer the questions.

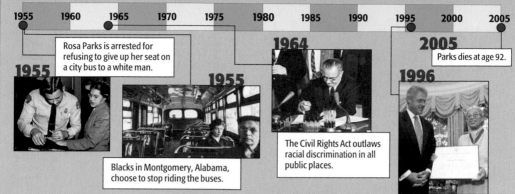

1955 — 1960 — 1965 — 1970 — 1975 — 1980 — 1985 — 1990 — 1995 — 2000 — 2005

1955
Rosa Parks is arrested for refusing to give up her seat on a city bus to a white man.

1955
Blacks in Montgomery, Alabama, choose to stop riding the buses.

1964
The Civil Rights Act outlaws racial discrimination in all public places.

2005
Parks dies at age 92.

1996
Parks is awarded the Presidential Medal of Freedom.

1. Blacks and whites could sit together in all public places starting in which year? _____

2. True or false: Parks received the Presidential Medal of Freedom in 1955. _____

3. How many years ago did Parks challenge the seating laws on buses? _____

(See Answer Key on page 242.)

Who Can Vote and Be Elected

WHO CAN VOTE?
ANYONE WHO IS
→ 18 years of age
→ a citizen of the U.S. and meets the residency requirements of his or her state

WHO CAN BE PRESIDENT?
SOMEONE WHO IS
→ a natural-born citizen of the U.S.
→ at least 35 years of age
→ a resident of the U.S. for at least 14 years

WHO CAN BE SENATOR?
SOMEONE WHO IS
→ at least 30 years old
→ a citizen of the U.S. for at least nine years
→ a resident of the state where he or she is elected

In 1818, 28-year-old John Henry Eaton was appointed to the Senate—in violation of the constitution.

WHO CAN BE A U.S. REPRESENTATIVE?
SOMEONE WHO IS
→ at least 25 years old
→ a citizen of the U.S. for at least seven years
→ a resident of the state where he or she is elected

TFK MYSTERY PERSON

CLUE 1: I was born on October 11, 1884, in New York City.

CLUE 2: In 1905, I married a man who became the 32nd President of the United States.

CLUE 3: I was a socially active First Lady. I championed the rights of women, minorities and the poor.

WHO AM I? (See Answer Key on page 242.)

FACT MONSTER™

FACT MONSTER ASKED PEDIATRICIAN
BRIAN ORR TO ANSWER SOME
QUESTIONS KIDS OFTEN ASK.

why do men go bald?

Men can lose their hair at any time in their lives, not only when they grow old. Bald men have an inherited trait that makes them lose their hair in a special pattern. That pattern is called male pattern baldness. When a young man starts to lose his hair, his body is following the instructions of his genetic code—just like when your body makes blonde or black hair, blue or brown eyes. If you're a lucky male, you might someday get a perfect bald head like mine!

what is athlete's foot?

Athlete's foot is a disease of the feet caused by a fungus (yuck!) called *tinea pedis*. This fungus takes advantage of the warm, moist soles of your feet. It invades the skin layers and makes your skin crack and peel. Just because your feet peel doesn't mean you have athlete's foot, however. It is the cracking of the skin that is painful and the main symptom of the illness. To get athlete's foot you do not need to be an athlete, but you do have to have moist feet. To avoid it, just air out your sneakers and feet every day.

why does my nose run?

The nose serves as one of the body's first barriers against infection. Your nose makes more mucus when a foreign substance, such as a virus, enters the body. That mucus, combined with an increased flow of blood to the nose caused by the infection, makes your nose "run" with excess liquid. And it keeps tissue companies in business.

Is a healthy person's temperature always 98.6°F?

Healthy or sick, our temperatures change in a rhythm throughout the day. When we are healthy, our average temperature is 98.6°F, but even when we are healthy our temperature could go up to 99°F or down to 97°F. When we are sick, our temperatures rise to higher points. Someone has a fever when their body temperature is over 100.5°F, so a temperature of 99°F is not a reason to stay home from school!

why do we blink?

Blinking protects our eyes from foreign objects, sweeps up dirt that gets in our eyes and lubricates our eyes by spreading tears across their surface. Isn't that a lot to accomplish in the "blink of an eye?"

why does a bruise turn colors?

A bruise is actually a pocket of blood under the skin caused by a broken blood vessel. It changes color and fades as the body reabsorbs the blood from the bruise.

Did You Know?

Every person has five sense organs that take in information from the environment and send it to the brain. The five senses are: sight (eyes), hearing (ears), smell (nose), taste (tongue) and touch (skin).

Body Count

Robert Ladlow, who was born in 1918, was the tallest person on record. He grew to be 8 feet 11 inches, and he weighed 439 pounds.

Kids have 20 first teeth. Adults have 32 teeth.

About 400 gallons of blood flow through your kidneys in one day.

You blink your eyes about 20,000 times a day.

Your heart beats about 100,000 times a day.

The four taste zones on your tongue are bitter (back), sour (back sides), salty (front sides) and sweet (front).

Your body contains eight pints of blood.

The strongest muscle in the body is the masseter muscle, which is located in the jaw.

Muscles normally account for 40% of one's body weight.

There are 230 joints in the body.

Most people shed 40 pounds of skin in a lifetime.

Your body is 70% water

The small intestines are about 25 feet long.

The large intestines are five feet long and three times wider than the small intestines.

Jeanne Louise Calment lived longer than any other human in history! She died in August 1997 at an astounding 122 years and 164 days.

Your brain sends messages to other parts of your body at the rate of 240 m.p.h.

Humans breathe 20 times per minute, more than 10 million times per year and about 700 million times in a lifetime.

There are ten million nerve cells in your brain.

You have about 100,000 hairs on your head.

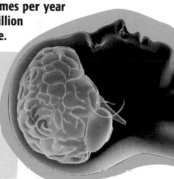

Leading Causes of Death

in the U.S.

CAUSE OF DEATH	PERCENT OF TOTAL DEATHS
1. Heart disease	28%
2. Cancer	23%
3. Stroke	6%
4. Chronic lower respiratory disease	5%
5. Accidents	4%

Source: U.S. National Center for Health Statistics

in the World

CAUSE OF DEATH	PERCENT OF TOTAL DEATHS
1. Heart disease	13%
2. Stroke	10%
3. Lower respiratory infections	7%
4. HIV/AIDS	5%
5. Chronic obstructive pulmonary disease	5%

Source: World Health Organization

Your Body

If you could peek inside your own body, what would you see? Hundreds of bones, miles of blood vessels and trillions of cells, all of which are constantly working together.

Skin

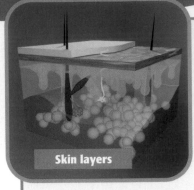

Skin layers

MAIN JOB: To protect your internal organs from drying up and to prevent harmful bacteria from getting inside your body

HOW MUCH: The average person has about six pounds of skin.

MAIN LAYERS:
- Epidermis: Outer two layers of skin, cells, hair and nails
- Dermis: Inner layer of living tissue, containing nerves, sweat glands and blood vessels

Joints

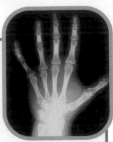

MAIN JOB: To allow bones to move in different directions

DID YOU KNOW? Bones don't bend. Joints allow two bones next to each other to move.

Ligaments

MAIN JOB: To hold joints together. These bands of tough tissue are strong and flexible.

Cells

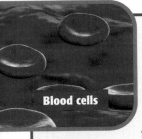

Blood cells

MAIN JOB: To perform the many jobs necessary to stay alive, such as moving oxygen around your body, taking care of your energy supply and waste removal

DID YOU KNOW? There are 26 billion cells in a newborn baby and 50 trillion cells in an adult.

SOME DIFFERENT CELLS:
- Bone cells produce the fibers and minerals from which bone is made.
- Fat cells contain fat, which is burned to create energy.
- Muscle cells are organized into muscles, which move body parts.
- Nerve cells pass nerve messages around your body.
- Red blood cells carry oxygen around your body.

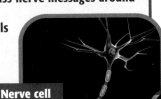

Nerve cell

Muscles

MAIN JOB: To make body movement possible

HOW MANY: Your body has more than 650 muscles.

KINDS OF MUSCLES:
- Skeletal muscles help the body move. You have about 400 skeletal muscles.
- Smooth muscles are located inside organs, like the stomach.
- The cardiac muscle is found only in the heart.

Tendons

MAIN JOB: To hold your muscles to your bones

DID YOU KNOW? Tendons look like rubber bands.

 go Show what you know about staying healthy at timeforkids.com/triviafever

Viscera

This term refers to the organs that fill your body's chest and abdominal cavity.

MAIN JOB: To provide your body with food and oxygen and to remove waste

PARTS: The viscera include the trachea (windpipe), lungs, liver, kidneys, gallbladder, spleen, stomach, large intestine, small intestine and bladder.

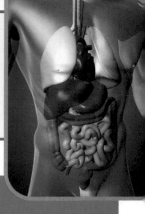

Bones

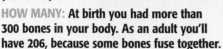

MAIN JOB: To give shape and support to your body

HOW MANY: At birth you had more than 300 bones in your body. As an adult you'll have 206, because some bones fuse together.

DID YOU KNOW? The largest bone in the body is the femur, or thighbone. In a 6-foot-tall person, it is 20 inches long. The smallest bone is the stirrup bone in the ear. It is one-tenth of an inch long.

KINDS OF BONES:

- Long bones are thin; they are found in your legs, arms and fingers.
- Short bones are wide and chunky; they are found in your feet and wrists.
- Flat bones are flat and smooth, like your shoulder blades.
- Irregular bones, like the bones in your inner ear and the vertebrae in your spine, come in many different shapes.

Dr. What?

→ An **anesthesiologist** specializes in the use of anesthetic drugs and techniques, which prevent people from feeling pain. Before an operation, people are usually given anesthesia.

→ A **cardiologist** specializes in the treatment of heart disease.

→ A **dermatologist** specializes in all aspects of skin care and problems of the skin and hair.

→ A **gastroenterologist** treats problems of the stomach, intestines and related organs.

→ An **internist** specializes in the diagnosis, prevention and treatment of all forms of adult disease.

→ A **neurologist** specializes in disorders affecting the nervous system.

→ An **obstetrician** specializes in obstetrics, the branch of medicine that deals with human birth.

→ An **ophthalmologist** diagnoses and treats eye problems.

→ An **orthopedist** is trained to treat the entire skeletal system.

→ An **otologist** specializes in the treatment of the ear.

→ A **podiatrist** specializes in the treatment of foot problems.

→ A **psychiatrist** treats people with emotional problems.

→ A **radiologist** specializes in making and explaining x-rays and other pictures that show areas inside the body.

Glands

MAIN JOB: To manufacture substances that help your body to function

KINDS OF GLANDS:

- Endocrine glands make hormones, which tell the different parts of your body when to work.
- Oil glands keep your skin from drying out.
- Salivary glands make saliva, which helps you to digest and swallow food.
- Sweat glands make perspiration, which regulates your body temperature.

Health

113

The Food Pyramid

In 2005, the Department of Agriculture introduced a new food pyramid—pyramids, to be precise. Instead of a one-size-fits-all pyramid, there are now 12 different versions. Each one is slightly different, depending on a person's age, gender and level of physical activity. The pyramids are designed to help people with different lifestyles and nutritional needs live healthier lives. The new nutritional guideline system is called MyPyramid.

For an 11-year-old girl who exercises for 30 to 60 minutes each day, the pyramid recommends that she eat daily:

→ about six ounces of grains, including three ounces of whole grains rather than products made out of white flour

→ three servings (one cup equals one serving) of fruit and five servings of vegetables

→ three cups of milk

→ five ounces of lean meat or beans

→ a small amount of fats and oils and added sugars

Check out www.mypyramid.gov to see what it recommends for you.

| GRAINS | VEGETABLES | FRUITS | MILK | MEAT & BEANS |

OIL   Oils are not a food group, but you need some for good health. Get your oils from fish, nuts and liquid oils such as corn oil, soybean oil and canola oil.

Counting Calories

A calorie is a type of measurement that indicates how much energy we get from food. Nutrition labels tell you how many calories a food contains. In general, kids age 7 to 12 should take in about 2,200 calories each day. Teenage girls need about 2,200 calories, while teenage boys require about 2,800.

Did You Know?

In 2006, Coca-Cola, PepsiCo and Cadbury Schweppes all said they would remove sweetened sodas and other drinks from schools by 2009.

Protein, Carbohydrates, Fat

→ **PROTEIN** helps the body grow, builds muscle and gives us energy. Protein-rich foods include meats, eggs, nuts and beans.

→ **CARBOHYDRATES** are sugars that the body uses for energy. Simple carbohydrates, also called simple sugars, provide the body with quick energy. They are found in fruit, milk and white sugar. Complex carbohydrates, known as fiber and starch, break down slower than simple carbohydrates. They are found in vegetables, bread, rice, oatmeal, whole grains and peas.

→ Your body needs **FAT** for energy, to grow and to process vitamins. There are many different kinds of fats. Polyunsaturated and monounsaturated fats are good for your body. These fats are found in nuts and fish, as well as in olive, peanut, safflower and canola oil. Saturated fats are mostly found in food from animals, such as meat and butter. Saturated fats can increase the risk of certain diseases. You should try to stay away from hydrogenated oils and trans fats, which are found in fast foods, baked goods and chips. They also can increase the risk of health problems.

Super-Sized Americans

Many Americans eat too much and don't exercise enough. If you have a hard time believing that, take a look around. About 15% of kids age 6 to 19 are obese and 20% are overweight. As for adults, 64% are either obese or overweight.

Obesity can lead to serious health problems, such as heart disease, stroke, diabetes and high blood pressure. Type 2 diabetes, once considered an adult disease, increasingly affects kids.

Health professionals put much of the blame for the super-sizing of America on junk food, enormous portion sizes and not enough exercise. The U.S. Department of Heath and Human Services reports that about half of all American kids aren't active enough.

The next time you're hungry for a snack, consider these facts:

A 2-ounce bag of chips has about 310 calories and about 21 grams of fat.

A medium-size apple has about 70 calories and less than 1 gram of fat.

A WHATCHAMACALLIT candy bar has 237 calories and about 11 grams of fat.

20 baby carrots have about 70 calories and no fat.

A 12-ounce can of cola has 132 calories and 33 grams of sugar.

Water has NO calories or sugar.

Health

115

Eating fast food once in a while won't hurt you, but too much of it can cause serious problems. Most fast food contains too many calories and too much salt and artery-clogging cholesterol to eat every day—or even once a week. Here's a look at how many calories and grams of fat are packed into fast food. Keep in mind that kids age 7 to 12 should eat about 2,200 calories a day.

FOOD	CALORIES	FAT
McDonald's Big Mac	540	29
Medium-size McDonald's French fries	380	21
Medium-size McDonald's vanilla shake	740	18
TOTAL FOR ONE MEAL	1,660 CALORIES	68 GRAMS
Burger King Whopper with cheese	760	47
Medium-size Burger King French fries	360	20
Medium-size Burger King vanilla shake	560	21
TOTAL FOR ONE MEAL	1,680 CALORIES	88 GRAMS
COMPARE THAT TO A MEAL PREPARED AT HOME:		
1/2 of a roasted chicken breast	142	3
Medium-size baked white potato with 1 teaspoon butter	175	3
1/2 cup of green peas	67	0
8-ounce glass of 1% milk	102	2
1 cup of unsweetened applesauce	105	0
TOTAL FOR ONE MEAL	591 CALORIES	8 GRAMS

Exercise: It's Fun and Good for You!

Not only is exercise fun, but it also helps your mind, body and overall well-being. Kids who exercise regularly often do better in school, sleep better, are less likely to be overweight or obese and are stronger than less-active kids. Exercise can also relieve stress and improve your mood.

Federal health officials recently reported that most kids spend a shocking four hours each day watching TV, using a computer or playing video games! They recommend that kids exercise for at least 30 minutes almost every day. So get up and get moving!

There are two types of exercise: aerobic and anaerobic. When you do aerobic exercises, such as running, swimming, biking and playing soccer, you increase your heart rate and the flow of oxygen-rich blood to your muscles. Aerobic exercise also builds endurance and burns fat and calories. Anaerobic exercise, such as weight-lifting, involves short bursts of effort. It helps to build strength and muscle mass.

Playing on a team is a great way to exercise and meet new friends, but it's not for everyone. If you prefer to work out alone, try dancing, jumping rope, jogging, yoga, swimming or inline skating.

Other Ways to Move

Let's face it, not everyone likes to exercise. If you're one of those people, there are many ways to get your heart pumping that don't require heading to a gym or putting on sweats. Give one of these a try:

• dancing
• gardening
• inline skating
• kayaking
• kickboxing
• martial arts
• raking leaves (you can also earn money doing this)
• walking your dog

Ouch!

Millions of kids are rushed to emergency rooms every year when they get hurt playing a sport. Here are the sports that send the most kids to the hospital.

1. Basketball
2. Cycling
3. Football
4. Baseball or softball
5. Ice skating, inline skating or skateboarding

Source: National Center for Health Statistics

Move and Burn

Here's a look at how many calories you can burn per hour when doing certain activities.

ACTIVITY	CALORIES BURNED
Sleeping	90
Swimming (25 yards per minute)	180
Dancing	210
Walking (4 m.p.h.)	240
Downhill skiing	288
Hiking	288
Inline skating (9 m.p.h.)	336
Playing soccer	360
Playing basketball	380
Jumping rope	400
Jogging (6 m.p.h.)	790

Kids on the Move

Here's a look at how often kids age 10 to 17 exercise. The information is based on activities that caused sweating and hard breathing for at least 20 minutes.

Percent of kids who participate in a physical activity three or more days a week

Boys	76.8%
Girls	65.6%
Kids	
age 10-11	78.2%
12-14	74.2%
15-17	63.3%

Percent of kids who participate in a team sport or sport lesson

Age		
	10-11	61.5%
	12-14	61.6%
	15-17	53.4%

Source: U.S. Department of Health and Human Services

TFK MYSTERY PERSON

CLUE 1: I am a doctor. I was born in Harrow, England, in 1929.

CLUE 2: I am the first person to run a mile in less than 4 minutes. On May 6, 1954, I set a world record of 3 minutes and 59.4 seconds.

CLUE 3: I retired from racing in December 1954 to practice medicine. I was knighted in 1975.

WHO AM I? (See Answer Key on page 242.)

For tips on staying healthy:
www.factmonster.com/healthtips

Health

A model of the memorial

FROM **TFK** MAGAZINE

A KING-SIZED MEMORIAL

Work begins in the nation's capital to create a monument honoring civil rights leader, the Reverend Martin Luther King Jr.

More than 40 years after Reverend Martin Luther King Jr. gave his famous "I Have a Dream" speech at the National Mall in Washington, D.C., a monument is being built there in his honor.

King with Malcolm X

Members of the King family, Presidents, civil rights leaders, celebrities and ordinary citizens gathered at a groundbreaking ceremony. King's children, Bernice Albertine King, Yolanda Denise King and Martin Luther King III, were joined by President George W. Bush, former President Bill Clinton, Oprah Winfrey, Condoleezza Rice and others. King's wife, Coretta Scott King, died in January 2006.

"Honoring Dr. King's legacy requires more than building a monument," President Bush said at the ceremony. "It requires the ongoing commitment of every American. So we will continue to work for the day when the dignity and humanity of every person is respected and the American promise is denied to no one."

Honoring King's Message

The memorial will be built on a four-acre site near the Lincoln Memorial.

The entrance to the memorial will include a sculpture of massive split stones called *The Mountain of Despair.* The sculpture will represent the separated America that inspired King to help all people overcome racial and social barriers.

After passing the split stones, visitors will reach a third stone of hope. "With this faith, we will be able to hew out of the mountain of despair a stone of hope" will be carved into one side. Carved into the other side will be the words, "Let justice roll down like waters and righteousness like a mighty stream."

Construction of the $100 million monument is scheduled to be complete in 2008 but more money is needed for the project. Organizers have already raised more than $64 million. The money has come from businesses such as Tommy Hilfiger and General Motors.

The King monument is the first to honor an African American civilian on the National Mall.

–BY JILL EGAN

King with President Johnson

Milestones from
150, 100 and 50 Years Ago

1858

LINCOLN AND DOUGLAS SQUARE OFF IN A SERIES OF DEBATES

One hundred and fifty years ago, Abraham Lincoln and Senator Stephen Douglas competed for one of Illinois's seats in the U.S. Senate. They faced each other in a series of seven debates. Lincoln, a Republican, argued against the expansion of slavery and supported the Union cause. Douglas, a Democrat, believed in popular sovereignty, a doctrine that said settlers should decide if their territory should be free or slave. Douglas won the election by a small margin. Lincoln, however, was elected President in 1860. Both men spoke eloquently, and a style of debate was named in honor of the Lincoln-Douglas debates.

Douglas

Lincoln

1908

HENRY FORD REVOLUTIONIZES THE AUTO INDUSTRY

From an early age, Henry Ford loved experimenting with machines. While working as a machinist and an engineer for the Edison Illuminating Company, Ford tinkered in his spare time with his ideas for a car. In 1896, he introduced the Quadricycle, a four-wheeled cart powered by a gas engine. In 1903, he started the Ford Motor Company. One hundred years ago, in 1908, Ford introduced the Model T. The car, which sold for $850, was the first one mass-produced on an assembly line. Between 1908 and 1928, Ford Motor Company produced about 20 million Model T cars.

Henry Ford

Model T

TFK MYSTERY PERSON

CLUE 1: I was born on January 12, 1737, in Massachusetts.

CLUE 2: I was the first person to sign the Declaration of Independence, in 1776. I signed the historic document in bold, clear strokes. My name is used as a slang term for "signature."

CLUE 3: I served as the governor of my home state twice, for a total of 11 years.

WHO AM I? (See Answer Key on page 242.)

1958

BILLBOARD DEBUTS THE HOT 100 CHART

On August 4, 1958, *Billboard*, the music industry's leading magazine, introduced the Hot 100 chart. The chart, still published each week, lists the most popular songs based on airplay and sales. The first No. 1 hit was Ricky Nelson's "Poor Little Fool." Musicians are often judged by the number of No. 1 hits they have recorded.

Ricky Nelson

History

119

ANCIENT HISTORY

10,000–4000 B.C. ➜	In Mesopotamia, settlements develop into cities.
ca* 3800–3600 B.C. ➜	People learn to use the wheel.
4500–4000 B.C. ➜	Earliest known civilization arises in Sumer.
3000–2000 B.C. ➜	The rule of the pharaohs begins in Egypt. King Khufu completes construction of the Great Pyramid at Giza (ca. 2680 B.C.), and King Khafre builds the **Great Sphinx of Giza** (ca. 2540 B.C.).
3000–1500 B.C. ➜	The Indus Valley civilization flourishes in what is today Pakistan. In Britain, **Stonehenge** is erected.
1500–1000 B.C. ➜	Moses leads the Israelites out of Egypt and delivers the Ten Commandments. Chinese civilization develops under the Shang Dynasty.
1000–900 B.C. ➜	Hebrew elders begin to write the books of the Hebrew Bible.
900–800 B.C. ➜	Phoenicians establish Carthage (ca. 810 B.C.). The *Iliad* and the *Odyssey* are composed, probably by the Greek poet Homer.
800–700 B.C. ➜	The first recorded Olympic games (776 B.C.) take place.
700–600 B.C. ➜	Lao-tse, Chinese philosopher and founder of Taoism, is born (604 B.C.).
600–500 B.C. ➜	**Confucius** (551–479 B.C.) develops his philosophy in China. Buddha (ca. 563–483 B.C.) founds Buddhism in India.
500–400 B.C. ➜	Greek culture flourishes during the age of Pericles (450–400 B.C.). The Parthenon is built in Athens as a temple of the goddess Athena (447–432 B.C.).
400–300 B.C. ➜	Alexander the Great (356–323 B.C.) destroys Thebes (335 B.C.), conquers Tyre and Jerusalem (332 B.C.), occupies Babylon (330 B.C.) and invades India.
300–250 B.C. ➜	The Temple of the Sun is built at Teotihuacán, Mexico (ca. 300 B.C.).
250–200 B.C. ➜	The Great Wall of China is built (ca. 215 B.C.).
100–31 B.C. ➜	Julius Caesar (100–44 B.C.) invades Britain (55 B.C.) and conquers Gaul (France) (ca. 50 B.C.). Cleopatra rules Egypt from 51–31 B.C.
44 B.C. ➜	Julius Caesar is murdered.

3000–2000 B.C.

3000–1500 B.C.

600–500 B.C.

*ca. stands for circa, which means approximately.

WORLD HISTORY A.D. 1–999

50–99

500–549

600–649

ca. A.D. 1–30 ➜	Life of Jesus Christ. Emperor Kuang Wu Ti founds the Han dynasty in China. Buddhism is introduced to China.
50–99 ➜	Jews revolt against the Romans; **Jerusalem is destroyed** (A.D. 70).
100–149 ➜	The great Emperor Hadrian rules Rome (A.D. 117–138).
150–199 ➜	The earliest Mayan temples are built in Central America.
200–249 ➜	Goths invade Asia Minor (ca. A.D. 220).
250–299 ➜	Mayan civilization (A.D. 250–900) has advances in art, architecture and science.
300–349 ➜	Constantine the Great (rules A.D. 312–337) unites eastern and western Roman empires, with a new capital at Constantinople (A.D. 330).
350–399 ➜	Huns (Mongols) invade Europe (ca. A.D. 360).
400–449 ➜	St. Patrick returns to Ireland (A.D. 432) and brings Christianity to the island.
450–499 ➜	Vandals destroy Rome (A.D. 455).
500–549 ➜	**Arthur,** king of the Britons, is killed (ca. A.D. 537).
550–599 ➜	After killing about half the European population, the plague subsides (A.D. 594).
600–649 ➜	**Muhammad,** founder of Islam, flees from Mecca to Medina (the Hegira, A.D. 622). Arabs conquer Jerusalem (A.D. 637) and destroy the Alexandrian library (A.D. 641).
650–699 ➜	Arabs attack North Africa (A.D. 670) and destroy Carthage (A.D. 697).
700–749 ➜	Arab empire extends from Lisbon to China (by A.D. 716).
750–799 ➜	The city of Machu Picchu flourishes in Peru.
800–849 ➜	Charlemagne is crowned the first Holy Roman Emperor in Rome (A.D. 800).
850–899 ➜	The Russian nation is founded by Vikings under Prince Rurik (A.D. 855–879).
900–949 ➜	Vikings discover Greenland (ca. A.D. 900). Arab Spain under Abd al-Rahman III becomes a center of learning (A.D. 912–961).
950–999 ➜	Erik the Red establishes the first Viking colony in Greenland (A.D. 982).

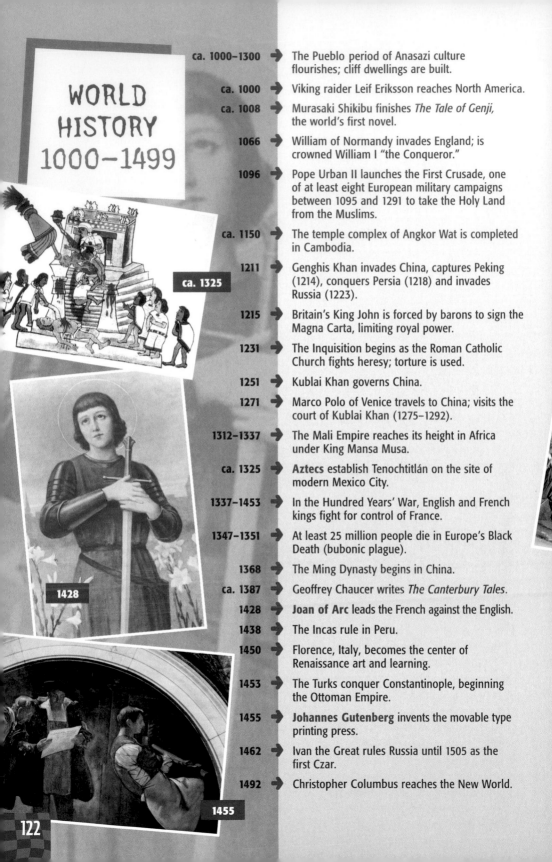

ca. 1000–1300	➡	The Pueblo period of Anasazi culture flourishes; cliff dwellings are built.
ca. 1000	➡	Viking raider Leif Eriksson reaches North America.
ca. 1008	➡	Murasaki Shikibu finishes *The Tale of Genji*, the world's first novel.
1066	➡	William of Normandy invades England; is crowned William I "the Conqueror."
1096	➡	Pope Urban II launches the First Crusade, one of at least eight European military campaigns between 1095 and 1291 to take the Holy Land from the Muslims.
ca. 1150	➡	The temple complex of Angkor Wat is completed in Cambodia.
1211	➡	Genghis Khan invades China, captures Peking (1214), conquers Persia (1218) and invades Russia (1223).
1215	➡	Britain's King John is forced by barons to sign the Magna Carta, limiting royal power.
1231	➡	The Inquisition begins as the Roman Catholic Church fights heresy; torture is used.
1251	➡	Kublai Khan governs China.
1271	➡	Marco Polo of Venice travels to China; visits the court of Kublai Khan (1275–1292).
1312–1337	➡	The Mali Empire reaches its height in Africa under King Mansa Musa.
ca. 1325	➡	**Aztecs** establish Tenochtitlán on the site of modern Mexico City.
1337–1453	➡	In the Hundred Years' War, English and French kings fight for control of France.
1347–1351	➡	At least 25 million people die in Europe's Black Death (bubonic plague).
1368	➡	The Ming Dynasty begins in China.
ca. 1387	➡	Geoffrey Chaucer writes *The Canterbury Tales*.
1428	➡	**Joan of Arc** leads the French against the English.
1438	➡	The Incas rule in Peru.
1450	➡	Florence, Italy, becomes the center of Renaissance art and learning.
1453	➡	The Turks conquer Constantinople, beginning the Ottoman Empire.
1455	➡	**Johannes Gutenberg** invents the movable type printing press.
1462	➡	Ivan the Great rules Russia until 1505 as the first Czar.
1492	➡	Christopher Columbus reaches the New World.

ca. 1325

1428

1455

WORLD HISTORY 1500–1899

1620

1789

1861

1501 ➔	The first African slaves are brought to America, to the Spanish colony of Santo Domingo.
ca. 1503 ➔	Leonardo Da Vinci paints the *Mona Lisa*.
1509 ➔	Henry VIII takes the English throne. Michelangelo begins painting the ceiling of the Sistine Chapel.
1517 ➔	Martin Luther objects to wrongdoing in the Catholic Church; start of Protestantism.
1519 ➔	Hernando Cortés conquers Mexico for Spain.
1520 ➔	Suleiman I "the Magnificent" becomes Sultan of Turkey.
1522 ➔	Portuguese explorer Ferdinand Magellan's expedition circumnavigates the globe.
1543 ➔	Copernicus publishes his theory that Earth revolves around the Sun.
1547 ➔	Ivan IV "the Terrible" is crowned Czar of Russia.
1588 ➔	The Spanish Armada is defeated by the English.
1609 ➔	Galileo makes the first astronomical observations using a telescope.
1618 ➔	The Thirty Years' War begins. European Protestants revolt against Catholic oppression.
1620 ➔	After a three-month voyage aboard the Mayflower, **pilgrims land** at Plymouth Rock.
1775 ➔	The American Revolution begins with the Battle of Lexington and Concord.
1776 ➔	The U.S. Declaration of Independence is signed.
1783 ➔	The American Revolution is brought to an end with the Treaty of Paris.
1789 ➔	The **French Revolution** begins with the storming of the Bastille.
1819 ➔	Simón Bolívar leads wars for independence throughout South America.
1824 ➔	Mexico becomes a republic, three years after declaring independence from Spain.
1846 ➔	A potato crop failure causes famine in Ireland.
1861 ➔	The **U.S. Civil War** begins as attempts to reach a compromise on slavery fail.
1865 ➔	The U.S. Civil War ends.
1884 ➔	The Berlin West Africa Conference is held; Europe colonizes the African continent.
1893 ➔	New Zealand becomes the first country in the world to give women the right to vote.
1898 ➔	The Spanish-American War begins.

WORLD HISTORY 1900–1959

1909

1912

1949

1903 ➡ The Wright brothers fly the first powered airplane at Kitty Hawk, North Carolina.

1904 ➡ The Russo-Japanese War begins, as competition for Korea and Manchuria heats up.

1909 ➡ U.S. explorers Robert E. Peary and **Matthew Henson** reach the North Pole. The National Association for the Advancement of Colored People (NAACP) is founded in New York City.

1912 ➡ The *Titanic* sinks on its maiden voyage; more than 1,500 drown.

1914 ➡ World War I begins.

1917 ➡ U.S. enters World War I. The Russian Revolution begins.

1918 ➡ World War I fighting ends. A worldwide flu epidemic strikes; by 1920, about 20 million are dead.

1919 ➡ Mahatma Gandhi begins his nonviolent resistance against British rule in India.

1924 ➡ Joseph Stalin begins his rule as Soviet dictator, which lasts until his death in 1953.

1929 ➡ In the U.S., stock market prices collapse and the Depression begins.

1933 ➡ Adolf Hitler is appointed German Chancellor; Nazi oppression begins. Franklin D. Roosevelt is sworn in as U.S. President; he launches the New Deal.

1937 ➡ The Nazis open their first concentration camp (Buchenwald); by 1945, the Nazis murder some 6 million Jews in what is now called the Holocaust.

1939 ➡ World War II begins.

1941 ➡ A Japanese attack on the U.S. fleet at Pearl Harbor in Hawaii (December 7) brings the U.S. into World War II. The Manhattan Project (atom bomb research) begins.

1945 ➡ War ends in Europe on V-E Day (May 8). The U.S. drops the atom bomb on Hiroshima, Japan (August 6), and Nagasaki, Japan (August 9). The war ends in the Pacific on V-J day (September 2).

1947 ➡ The U.S. Marshall Plan is proposed to help Europe recover from the war. India and Pakistan gain independence from Britain.

1948 ➡ The existence of the nation of Israel is proclaimed.

1949 ➡ The North Atlantic Treaty Organization (NATO) is founded. Communist People's Republic of China is proclaimed by Chairman Mao Zedong. **South Africa sets up apartheid** (a policy of discrimination against nonwhites).

1950 ➡ Korean War begins when North Korean Communist forces invade South Korea. It lasts three years.

1957 ➡ The Russians launch *Sputnik I*, the first Earth-orbiting satellite; the space race begins.

WORLD HISTORY 1960– Present

1989

1989

2003

1963 ➡ Martin Luther King Jr. delivers his "I Have a Dream" speech in Washington, D.C. President John F. Kennedy is killed by a sniper in Dallas.

1965 ➡ U.S. planes begin combat missions in the Vietnam War.

1967 ➡ Israeli and Arab forces battle; Six-Day War ends with Israel occupying the Sinai Peninsula, Golan Heights, Gaza Strip and part of the Suez Canal.

1969 ➡ *Apollo 11* astronauts take man's first walk on the Moon.

1973 ➡ Vietnam War ends with the signing of peace pacts. The Yom Kippur War begins as Egyptian and Syrian forces attack Israel.

1979 ➡ Muslim leader Ayatollah Khomeini takes over Iran, where U.S. citizens are seized and held hostage.

1981 ➡ Scientists identify the AIDS virus.

1989 ➡ Thousands rallying for democracy are killed in **Tiananmen Square,** China. After 28 years, the **Berlin Wall** that divided Germany is torn down.

1990 ➡ South Africa frees Nelson Mandela, who was imprisoned for 27 years. Iraqi troops invade Kuwait, setting off the nine-month Persian Gulf War.

1991 ➡ The Soviet Union breaks up after President Mikhail Gorbachev resigns. In Yugoslavia, Slovenia and Croatia secede; a four-year war with Serbia begins.

1994 ➡ South Africa holds its first interracial national election; Nelson Mandela is elected President.

2000 ➡ Elections in Yugoslavia formally end the brutal rule of Slobodan Milosevic.

2001 ➡ On September 11, hijackers crash two jetliners into New York City's World Trade Center, another into the Pentagon and a fourth in rural Pennsylvania. In response, U.S. and British forces attack the Taliban government and bomb al-Qaeda terrorist camps in Afghanistan.

2003 ➡ The U.S. and Britain lead an **invasion of Iraq.** Their forces topple Saddam Hussein's government within weeks. U.S. troops capture the former dictator.

2004 ➡ The U.S. transfers power of Iraq to an interim Iraqi government. Hamid Karzai is elected President of Afghanistan. An underwater earthquake in the Indian Ocean causes a raging tsunami that devastates several Asian countries and parts of East Africa; more than 225,000 people die in the disaster.

2005 ➡ Iraqi voters elect a 275-seat National Assembly, approve a constitution and elect a Parliament.

2006 ➡ Montenegrins vote for independence from Serbia, and Montenegro becomes the world's newest country. Saddam Hussein is found guilty of crimes against humanity and is later executed.

U.S HISTORY

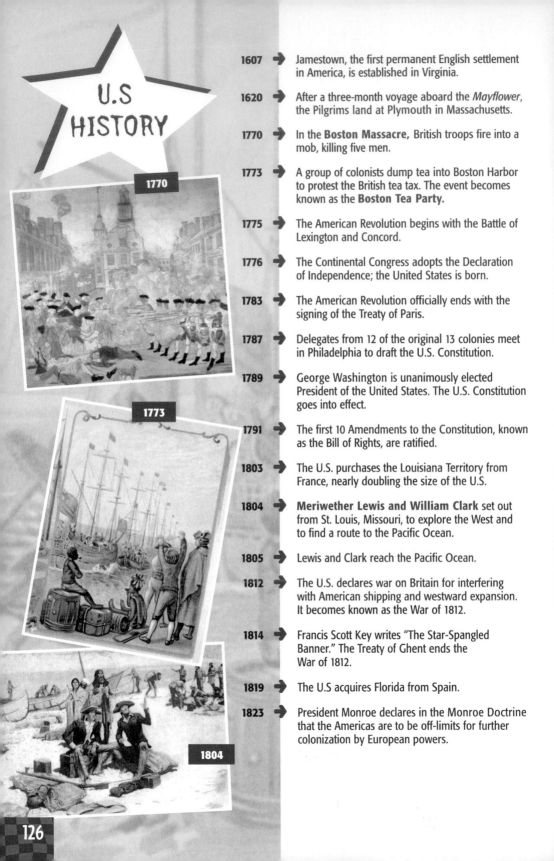

1607 → Jamestown, the first permanent English settlement in America, is established in Virginia.

1620 → After a three-month voyage aboard the *Mayflower*, the Pilgrims land at Plymouth in Massachusetts.

1770 → In the **Boston Massacre,** British troops fire into a mob, killing five men.

1773 → A group of colonists dump tea into Boston Harbor to protest the British tea tax. The event becomes known as the **Boston Tea Party.**

1775 → The American Revolution begins with the Battle of Lexington and Concord.

1776 → The Continental Congress adopts the Declaration of Independence; the United States is born.

1783 → The American Revolution officially ends with the signing of the Treaty of Paris.

1787 → Delegates from 12 of the original 13 colonies meet in Philadelphia to draft the U.S. Constitution.

1789 → George Washington is unanimously elected President of the United States. The U.S. Constitution goes into effect.

1791 → The first 10 Amendments to the Constitution, known as the Bill of Rights, are ratified.

1803 → The U.S. purchases the Louisiana Territory from France, nearly doubling the size of the U.S.

1804 → **Meriwether Lewis and William Clark** set out from St. Louis, Missouri, to explore the West and to find a route to the Pacific Ocean.

1805 → Lewis and Clark reach the Pacific Ocean.

1812 → The U.S. declares war on Britain for interfering with American shipping and westward expansion. It becomes known as the War of 1812.

1814 → Francis Scott Key writes "The Star-Spangled Banner." The Treaty of Ghent ends the War of 1812.

1819 → The U.S acquires Florida from Spain.

1823 → President Monroe declares in the Monroe Doctrine that the Americas are to be off-limits for further colonization by European powers.

1770

1773

1804

U.S HISTORY

1836 → Texas declares its independence from Mexico. All the Texan defenders of the Alamo are killed in a siege by the Mexican Army.

1838 → More than 15,000 Cherokee Indians are forced to march from Georgia to Indian Territory in present-day Oklahoma. About 4,000 die from starvation and disease along the "Trail of Tears."

1845 → Texas becomes a state.

1846 → The U.S. declares war on Mexico to gain territory in the Southwest.

1848 → The Mexican War ends; the U.S. gains territory comprising present-day California, Nevada, Utah, most of New Mexico and Arizona and parts of Colorado and Wyoming.

1849 → Gold is discovered at Sutter's Mill in California.

1854 → Congress establishes the territories of Kansas and Nebraska. Tensions rise between those who want them to be free states and those who want them to be slave states.

1857 → Abolitionist John Brown and 21 followers try to spark a slave revolt by capturing a government arms depot in Harpers Ferry, West Virginia.

1860 → Following the election of Abraham Lincoln as President, South Carolina secedes from the U.S.

1861 → More Southern states secede from the U.S. and form the Confederate States of America, with Jefferson Davis as President. The Civil War, a conflict between the North (the Union) and the South (the Confederacy) over the expansion of slavery and the imposition of high tariffs on imported goods, begins when the **Confederates attack Fort Sumter** in Charleston, South Carolina.

1863 → Lincoln issues the Emancipation Proclamation, freeing slaves in the Confederate states.

1865 → **The Civil War ends** with the surrender of Confederate general Robert E. Lee to Union general Ulysses S. Grant. **Lincoln is assassinated** by John Wilkes Booth. The 13th Amendment to the Constitution is ratified, prohibiting slavery.

1867 → The U.S. purchases Alaska from Russia.

1869 → The Central Pacific and Union Pacific railroads are joined at Promontory, Utah, creating the first transcontinental (cross-country) railroad.

U.S HISTORY

1920

1955

1969

1890 →	The last major battle of the Indian Wars occurs at Wounded Knee in South Dakota.
1898 →	The U.S.S. *Maine* is blown up in Havana harbor, which leads the U.S. to declare war on Spain. As a result of winning the Spanish-American War, the U.S. acquires Puerto Rico, Guam and the Philippines.
1917 →	The U.S. enters World War I by declaring war on Germany and Austria-Hungary.
1920 →	The 19th Amendment to the Constitution is ratified, giving **women the right to vote.**
1929 →	The U.S. stock market crashes, and the Great Depression begins.
1933 →	President Franklin Roosevelt's economic recovery measures, known as the New Deal, are enacted by Congress.
1941 →	Japan attacks the U.S. naval base at Pearl Harbor, Hawaii, leading to the U.S.'s entry into World War II.
1945 →	Germany surrenders, marking the end of World War II in Europe. The U.S. drops two atom bombs on Japan. Japan surrenders, and World War II ends in the Pacific.
1950 →	The Korean War begins as the U.S. sends troops to defend South Korea against communist North Korea.
1953 →	The Korean War ends.
1954 →	The Supreme Court decision *Brown v. Board of Education of Topeka, Kansas,* declares that racial segregation of schools is unconstitutional.
1955 →	**Rosa Parks refuses to give up her bus seat** to a white passenger. Martin Luther King Jr. leads a black boycott of the Montgomery, Alabama, bus system.
1963 →	President John F. Kennedy is assassinated in Dallas, Texas.
1965 →	The first U.S. combat troops arrive in South Vietnam.
1968 →	Martin Luther King Jr. is assassinated in Memphis, Tennessee.
1969 →	**Astronauts Neil Armstrong and Edwin (Buzz) Aldrin Jr.** become the first men to land on the moon.
1973 →	The U.S., North Vietnam, South Vietnam and the National Liberation Front (Viet Cong) sign peace pacts in Paris. The U.S. withdraws from Vietnam.

U.S HISTORY

2001

2000

2001

2005

1974 ➡	President Nixon resigns as a result of the Watergate scandal.
1979 ➡	Iranian students storm the U.S. embassy in Tehran and hold 66 people hostage.
1981 ➡	The U.S. hostages held in Iran are released after 444 days in captivity.
1986 ➡	The space shuttle *Challenger* explodes 73 seconds after liftoff.
1991 ➡	The U.S. and its allies fight in the first Persian Gulf War, driving the Iraqis out of Kuwait.
1992 ➡	President George H. W. Bush and Russian President Boris Yeltsin formally declare an end to the cold war.
1998 ➡	The House of Representatives votes to impeach President Bill Clinton.
1999 ➡	The Senate acquits Clinton of impeachment charges.
2000 ➡	The presidential contest between Al Gore and George W. Bush is one of the closest elections in U.S. history. The U.S. Supreme Court determines the outcome, and **Bush is declared the winner.**
2001 ➡	Hijackers crash two jetliners into New York City's **World Trade Center** and another into the Pentagon. A fourth hijacked plane crashes in rural Pennsylvania. President Bush declares war on terrorism, and U.S. and British forces oust the Taliban government and attack Osama bin Laden's al-Qaeda terrorist camps in Afghanistan.
2002 ➡	A wave of corporate accounting scandals rocks the U.S. economy as Enron and several other companies are investigated by federal authorities.
2003 ➡	Seven astronauts die when the space shuttle *Columbia* explodes upon re-entry into the Earth's atmosphere. The U.S. and Britain lead a war in Iraq and topple dictator Saddam Hussein. Troops capture Hussein in December.
2004 ➡	The U.S. transfers control of Iraq to an interim Iraqi government.
2005 ➡	**Hurricane Katrina** hits the Gulf Coast, leveling entire cities in Mississippi. Parts of New Orleans are destroyed when two levees break and water submerges 80% of the city. It's the worst natural disaster in the nation's history.
2006 ➡	Democrats take control of both houses of Congress for the first time since 1994.

Coolest Inventions of 2006

Allergy-proof cats? Bike-riding robots? Drinkable water from thin air? Not long ago, these ideas might have sounded dreamlike—even a little crazy. But now they are as real as can be. Inventors came up with these and other amazing ways to improve life as we know it. Some inventions simply bring more fun to our world. See what's new on these pages. What will they think of next?

Talking Head

Mirror, mirror, on the wall, tell me who has come to call! This Magic Message Mirror looks like a normal mirror. But if someone comes to your front door, a talking head appears to let you know. For $19,995, owning it might be just a fairy tale!

Diving Dolphin

The Innespace SeaBreacher is like a real dolphin. It can jump, dive, roll and swim underwater. The craft travels up to 30 miles per hour and is 16 feet long. Joystick controllers work the robotic fins. Foot pedals move the tail. The craft will soon make a splash at exhibitions.

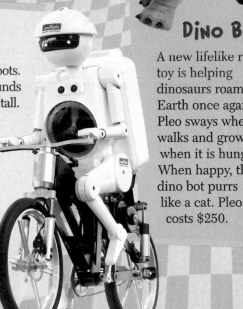

Easy Rider

Murata Boy may be smaller than most robots. He weighs just 11 pounds and is only 20 inches tall. But he does something that no other robot can do. He rides a bike. A camera in his head helps him ride in a straight line. But Murata Boy won't be pedaling into stores anytime soon.

Dino Bot

A new lifelike robot toy is helping dinosaurs roam the Earth once again. Pleo sways when it walks and growls when it is hungry. When happy, the dino bot purrs like a cat. Pleo costs $250.

Catch the Drift

Snow is fun to jump in. But clearing it takes a lot of energy and hard work. Here comes the Wovel. It's a new kind of shovel built on a 36-inch wheel. The Wovel works like a seesaw. Just push down on the handle to send scoops of snow flying. Now that's piles of fun! The Wovel costs a cool $120.

waterworks

The Aqua Sciences machine (hidden inside the blue container) can turn air into drinking water. It attracts moisture from the air. The cost: $300,000. In places that need clean water, it's worth it.

No Sneezing!

A furry friend just got friendlier. Some people are allergic to a chemical in cats' saliva, or spit. That chemical is almost all gone in this sniffle-proof kitty. Each purr-fect pal will cost $3,950.

Accidental Food Inventions

POPSICLES In 1905, 11-year-old Frank Epperson was trying to make soda pop by mixing powdered soda and water. When he left the mixture outside overnight, it froze solid, with the mixing stick standing upright. The frozen pop tasted great! Frank sold his frozen pops as Epperson icicles, which later became known as Popsicles.

CHOCOLATE CHIP COOKIES In 1930, Ruth Wakefield was baking chocolate cookies at the Toll House Inn restaurant in Whitman, Massachusetts, when she ran out of baking chocolate. Thinking fast, she broke a bar of semi-sweet chocolate into little pieces and added them to the dough. After baking the cookies, Wakefield discovered that the chips in the cookie hadn't melted but were scattered throughout the cookie. It turned out to be a tasty discovery!

POTATO CHIPS In 1853, when a customer at Moon Lake Lodge in Saratoga Springs, New York, complained that the French fries were too thick, the chef sliced the potatoes paper thin and deep fried them. These crispy chips were a big hit, but they didn't become popular until the 1920s, when Herman Lay began to sell them nationally.

ICE-CREAM CONES In 1904, an ice-cream vendor at the St. Louis World's Fair ran out of dishes. Ernest Hamwi, a nearby pastry salesman, helped him out. He rolled pastry into a cone so ice cream could fit inside—a very cool invention.

Great Inventions

1829 Braille

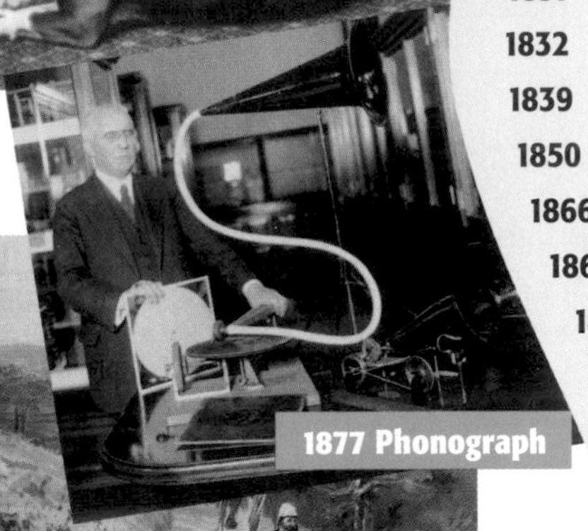

ca. 3800–3600 B.C. → Wheel
3000 B.C. → Abacus
ca. A.D. 100 → Paper
1608 → Telescope
1623 → Mechanical calculator
1709 → Piano
1752 → Lightning rod
1753 → Hot-air balloon
1783 → Steamship
1829 → Braille
1831 → Lawn mower
1832 → Matches
1839 → Rubber
1850 → Refrigerator
1866 → Dynamite
1868 → Typewriter
1869 → Vacuum cleaner
1870 → Chewing gum
1876 → Telephone
1877 → Phonograph (record player)
1885 → Bicycle
1888 → Ballpoint pen
1889 → Handheld camera
1891 → Zipper
1893 → Motion pictures (movies)
1895 → X-ray
1899 → Tape recorder
1901 → First transatlantic radio signals
       → Electric washing machine
1903 → First motorized plane
       → Windshield wipers

1877 Phonograph

1885 Bicycle

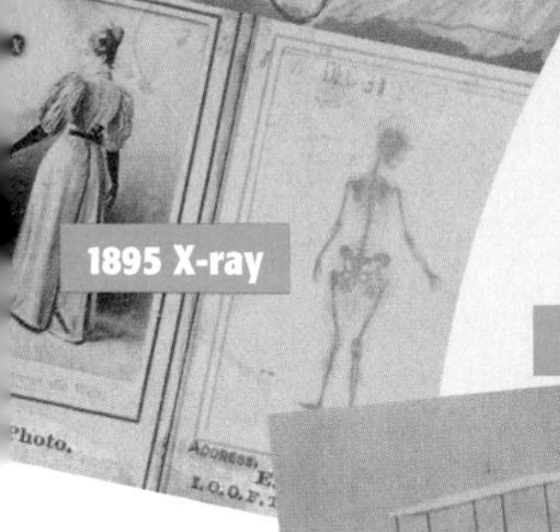

1895 X-ray

1903 First motorized plane

Alfred Nobel, a Swedish chemist and engineer, invented dynamite. He left $9 million in his will to establish the Nobel Prizes, which are awarded every year in six areas: peace, literature, physics, chemistry, physiology or medicine and economics.

On December 17, 1903, Orville and Wilbur Wright flew into history in an airplane they built themselves. Their 1903 Flyer, a double-winged plane, had a propeller and a 4-cylinder, 12-horsepower engine. Orville piloted the plane for 12 seconds while Wilbur ran alongside. The plane traveled 120 feet at 26 knots, or about 30 m.p.h. The milestone marked the beginning of the aviation era.

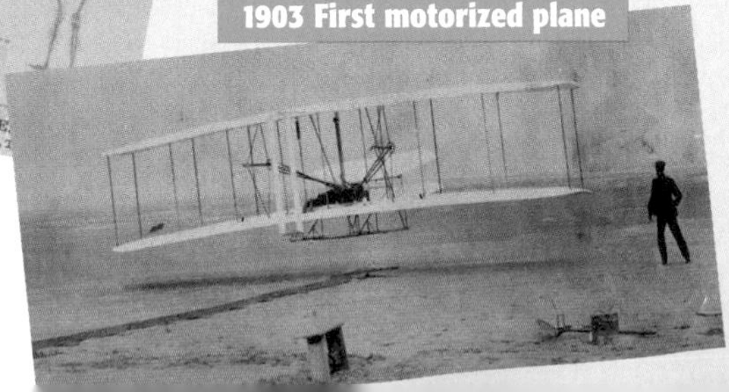

1906 → **Lightbulbs**
1907 → **Plastic**
1908 → **Ford Model T car**
1909 → **Toaster**

1909 Toaster

1911 → **Air conditioning**
1913 → **Moving assembly line**
1927 → **Television**
1928 → **Penicillin**
 → **Animated sound cartoons**
1929 → **Scotch tape**
 → **Car radio**
1930 → **Pre-sliced bread**
1933 → **FM radio**
1938 → **Helicopter**
1939 → **Jet airplane**
1940 → **Automatic dishwasher**
1945 → **Microwave oven**
1946 → **Electronic computer**
1949 → **Silly Putty**
1950 → **Disposable diaper**
1951 → **Long-distance dialing in the U.S.**
1955 → **Polio vaccine**
1957 → *Sputnik* **satellite**
1963 → **Home video recorder**
 → **Push-button telephone**
1969 → **The Internet**
1970 → **Floppy disk**
1971 → **Pocket calculator**
1972 → **Compact disk**
1975 → **Desktop computer**
1979 → **Sony Walkman**
1980 → **Rollerblades**
 → **Post-It Notes**
1981 → **Space shuttle**
1983 → **Cellular telephones**
1988 → **Facsimile (fax) machine**
1991 → **World Wide Web**
1994 → **Digital camera**
1995 → **DVD (digital video disk)**
1997 → **Dolly the sheep—the first animal made by cloning adult cells**
2000 → **Human-genome map**
2003 → **Camera phones**
2004 → **First privately built spacecraft**

Antibiotics are powerful drugs that kill bacteria that enter our bodies and make us sick. In 1928, Alexander Fleming discovered the first antibiotic, penicillin. It was made from a mold that grew in his lab. Without antibiotics, infections like strep throat could be deadly.

Did You Know?

In the 30 years following the development of antibiotics, human life expectancy increased by eight years. Prior to the discovery of antibiotics, *streptococcus pyogenes*, a common bacteria, caused half of all post-birth deaths. And *staphylococcus aureus*, bacteria that enter wounds, was fatal in 80% of infected wounds (even minor cuts and scrapes!).

1938 Helicopter

1980 Rollerblades

1981 Space shuttle

2003 Camera phones

1972 Compact disk

FROM TFK MAGAZINE

KIDS IN THE NEWS

DOLLY AKTER

For more than one billion people worldwide, safe, clean water is a luxury. Dolly Akter, 17, lives in Dhaka, Bangladesh, where poor living conditions and dirty water commonly make people sick. That is why Dolly is working with UNICEF to make sure that her neighbors learn the importance of washing their hands and drinking only water that has been boiled.

"Now that my community understands the importance of good hygiene, the people have happier lives," Dolly told TFK.

KISHAN

Kishan, 10, from Bangalore, India, is no stranger to the big screen. He has acted in 24 movies. But now, he is trying his hand at directing. *C/o [Care of] Footpath* tells the story of poor children who live on the footpaths, or streets, of India. Kishan, who also wrote and stars in the film, got the idea when he met a group of homeless kids who had to choose between working or going to school. Kishan hopes his film will shed light on child labor and help India's poor children.

So how does the young director balance his own schoolwork with the demands of show business? "I do one week of shooting, and then one week of school," he told TFK.

? TFK MYSTERY PERSON

CLUE 1: I was born in Oxford, England, in 1919. As a child, I enjoyed mythology.

CLUE 2: My great-uncle, Henry Madan, suggested Mars's moons be named Deimos and Phobos.

CLUE 3: When I was 11 years old, I came up with the name Pluto—the Greek god of the underworld—for a newly discovered planet. The Lowell Observatory officially named the planet Pluto.

WHO AM I? (See Answer Key on page 242.)

AUSTRALIA

Location → An island continent southeast of Asia, between the Indian Ocean and the South Pacific Ocean

School → Children are required to attend school from age 5 through 15. The school year is divided into four terms with a two-week break between each term. Students also get two months off during the summer. Most students wear uniforms to school.

Play → Because Australia was once a British colony, many games and sports that are popular here come from England. Cricket, a game played with a bat and ball, is a favorite. Similar to baseball, the batsman hits a ball tossed by a pitcher (bowler) after a bounce. There are four innings to a game, and hundreds of runs can be scored in a game.

Rugby is another favorite. The ball looks like an American football, and the object is to cross the goal line with the ball or kick it between the goalposts. Tackling is a big part of this brutal game, but players wear almost no protective equipment.

Family → Families in Australia resemble those in the United States. Kids live with two parents and in single-parent homes. Some mothers work, while others stay at home.

Favorite Foods → Meat is a big hit in Australia. Australians love barbecue, which they call "barbie." Favorite meats include beef, chicken, lamb and even kangaroo and water buffalo.

Vegemite, a salty, dark-brown yeast extract, is another staple of the Australian diet. It often is spread on bread and in sandwiches. It's considered Australia's national food.

Did You Know? The Aborigines were the first inhabitants of Australia. They have been living there for more than 40,000 years.

CAMBODIA

Location → Southeast Asia

School → Only about 45% of Cambodian kids finish elementary school. The figure is much lower for children who live in rural villages.

Cambodian children study math, history, geography, science, Khmer (Cambodia's official language), English and French, as well as art, music and dance. Most students wear uniforms.

Play → *Leak Kon Saeng* is a popular game in Cambodia. The game is similar to "duck duck goose," but instead of tapping a person on the head, the player who is "it" places a knotted piece of cloth behind the "goose."

Older children enjoy *ang kunh*. An *ang kunh* is an oval-shaped seed about the size of an egg. Two teams stand about 10 feet apart and place three to five *ang kunh* in a semicircle. Each team tries to knock down the other team's pieces by tossing an *ang kunh* at them.

Family → Many Cambodians live with members of their extended families. Parents, siblings, grandparents, aunts, uncles and cousins may live in the same home. The extended families often work together as well.

Cambodian parents usually give their children symbolic names that rhyme with the name of another family member.

Favorite Foods → Rice and fish! Cambodians eat rice at every meal. It is served fried, steamed or in the form of noodles. Fish is eaten fresh, dried, smoked or as a paste called *prahok* and is often spiced with hot peppers, lemon grass or mint. Cambodians even use rice in desserts. They combine it with fruit and coconut milk to create a sweet treat.

Did You Know? Thousands of tourists travel to Cambodia each year to visit the temples at Angkor Wat. The temples were built in the 12th century.

COSTA RICA

Location → Central America

School → Costa Rica takes education very seriously. It was one of the first countries in Latin America to offer free and mandatory education for all children. Children start school at age 6. They have six years of primary school and three years of secondary school. Students enter college at age 15 and attend one of Costa Rica's six universities. All students wear uniforms.

Play → *Futbol*, known in the United States as soccer, is by far the No. 1 sport in Costa Rica.

Water sports are also popular. Surfing, swimming and white-water rafting are favorite pastimes. In fact, Olympic swimmer Claudia Poll is one of Costa Rica's most famous athletes.

Family → Families typically socialize together. Most kids live with their parents until they get married, and several generations of a family often live together.

Favorite Foods → Rice and beans are staples of the Costa Rican diet. *Casado* is a favorite dish. It's made of beans, rice, meat, cabbage and plantains, which are similar to bananas.

Ceviche is a popular way of serving fish. The fish is marinated in lemon or lime juice which cooks the fish slightly.

FRANCE

Location → Western Europe

School → The school day usually runs from 8:00 a.m. to 4:00 p.m., with a two-hour lunch break. Schools close Wednesday and Sunday, and open for a half day on Saturday.

There are no uniforms in public schools. Religious dress, such as headscarves for Muslim girls or yarmulkes for Jewish boys, is banned.

Play → *Escargot* (snail), or *la marelle ronde*, is a traditional hopscotch game that uses a spiral shape and only one foot. Many traditional card games are also played.

Soccer, bicycling and tennis are favorite sports in France. In some areas, *pelote*, a traditional handball game, is popular.

Family → Most French mothers work; the majority of preschool children attend state-run day cares known as *crèches*.

France has laws about naming children. Until 1993, all names had to be chosen from an official list. Today, public prosecutors can still reject a newborn's name.

Favorite Foods → *Clafouti* is a baked dessert made of fruit, such as cherries or peaches, topped with a rich cake.

Did You Know? There are more than 350 kinds of cheese in France. French cheese may be made of cow, sheep or goat milk, or a combination of these. The average French person eats about 50 pounds of cheese per year (compared with 31 pounds per American).

Did You Know? In the 16th century, explorers mistakenly thought that the land now called Costa Rica was rich in gold. Costa Rica means "rich coast" in Spanish.

SOUTH AFRICA

Location → Southern Africa

School → Children age 7 through 15 are required to attend school. Parents must pay fees for their children to attend school, even public ones. All students wear uniforms.

Schools in South Africa are packed with kids. In fact, some schools have two or three sessions to accommodate all the students.

Play → Soccer is the most popular sport in South Africa. In 2010, South Africa will become the first African country to host the men's World Cup tournament.

South Africans of all ages play mankala, one of the oldest games in the world. It is a counting game played with a board, usually with two rows of up to 12 cups, and seeds or stones.

Family → South Africa has a large black and a smaller white population. Many of the blacks live in rural areas. Most black South Africans live in extended families, either within the same home or in separate homes clustered close together. Women usually have traditional roles. Most of the country's white population lives in cities.

Favorite Foods → *Pap* is a staple of the South African diet. Made from maize, which is like corn meal, it is eaten in the form of a porridge for breakfast with milk and sugar, or topped with a stew or gravy for dinner.

Did You Know? In 1993, South Africa repealed apartheid, a policy that legalized the separation of blacks and whites. During apartheid, whites ruled the country and discriminated against the black population.

High Scores

Here's a look at the countries that fared best on recent math and science tests.

MATH

FOURTH GRADE COUNTRY	AVERAGE SCORE	EIGHTH GRADE COUNTRY	AVERAGE SCORE
1. Singapore	594	1. Singapore	605
2. Hong Kong	575	2. South Korea	589
3. Japan	565	3. Hong Kong	586
4. Taiwan	564	4. Taiwan	585
5. Belgium	551	5. Japan	570
12. **United States**	**518**	15. **United States**	**504**
INTERNATIONAL AVERAGE	495	INTERNATIONAL AVERAGE	466

SCIENCE

FOURTH GRADE COUNTRY	AVERAGE SCORE	EIGHTH GRADE COUNTRY	AVERAGE SCORE
1. Singapore	565	1. Singapore	578
2. Taiwan	551	2. Taiwan	571
3. Japan	543	3. South Korea	558
4. Hong Kong	542	4. Hong Kong	556
5. England	540	5. Estonia	552
6. **United States**	**536**	9. **United States**	**527**
INTERNATIONAL AVERAGE	489	INTERNATIONAL AVERAGE	473

Source: International Association for the Evaluation of Educational Achievement

LANGUAGE

قف STOP

Arabic

The World's Ten Most Spoken Languages

There are more than 2,700 languages and more than 7,000 dialects spoken in the world. A dialect is a regional variety of a language that has a different pronunciation, vocabulary or meaning. These are the world's ten most popular languages.

	LANGUAGE	WHERE SPOKEN	NUMBER OF SPEAKERS
1.	Chinese (Mandarin)	China	1,075,000,000
2.	English	U.S., U.K., Canada, Australia, New Zealand	514,000,000
3.	Hindustani*	India	496,000,000
4.	Spanish	Spain, Latin America	425,000,000
5.	Russian	Russia	275,000,000
6.	Arabic	Middle East, North Africa	256,000,000
7.	Bengali	India, Bangladesh	215,000,000
8.	Portuguese	Portugal, Brazil	194,000,000
9.	Malay-Indonesian	Malaysia, Indonesia	176,000,000
10.	French	France, Belgium, Switzerland, Canada, parts of Africa	129,000,000

*Includes many dialects, including Hindi and Urdu

Source: Ethnologue

Russian

PASSAGE SURÉLEVÉ

French

ДЕЦАТА НЕМААТ СОПИРАЧКИ !

Languages Spoken in the U.S.

More than 300 languages in addition to English are spoken in the United States. These are the ten most common (after English):

1. Spanish
2. Chinese
3. French
4. German
5. Tagalog (spoken by Filipinos)
6. Vietnamese
7. Italian
8. Korean
9. Russian
10. Polish

Winning Words

Kids have participated in the National Spelling Bee since 1925. Here are some tongue-twisting words that made students into National Spelling Bee champs.

2006 winner Katharine Close

1990	fibranne	1998	chiaroscurist
1991	antipyretic	1999	logorrhea
1992	lyceum	2000	demarche
1993	kamikaze	2001	succedaneum
1994	antediluvian	2002	prospicience
1995	xanthosis	2003	pococurante
1996	vivisepulture	2004	autochthonous
1997	euonym	2005	appoggiatura
		2006	ursprache

TOP 5 TFK

Most Studied Languages in U.S. Schools

According to the U.S. Department of Education, these are the most popular languages (not including English) studied in schools.

1. Spanish
2. French
3. German
4. Italian
5. American Sign Language

Fun Language Facts

Euouae, a medieval music term, is the longest word in English that contains only vowels. It's also the word with the most consecutive vowels.

Screeched, which means to make a harsh sound, is the longest one-syllable word in English.

Unprosperousness, meaning not wealthy or profitable, is the longest word in English in which each letter is used at least two times.

The words **facetiously, abstemiously** and **arseniously** each contain all six vowels (including "y") in alphabetical order. The word **duoliteral** contains all five vowels (not including "y") in reverse alphabetical order.

At 45 letters, **pneumono-ultramicroscopicsilicovolcano-coniosis,** which refers to a lung disease, is the longest word in English. The word was invented to be the longest word in the language, and has never been used in any other context. Other, more legitimate long words include **floccinauci-nihilipilification** and **antidisestablishmentarianism.**

Floccinaucinihilipilification is the longest word in English that does not contain the letter "e."

Feedback is the shortest word in English that has the letters a, b, c, d, e and f.

There aren't any words in English that rhyme with **dangerous, discombobulate, marathon, month, ninth, orange, pint, purple, silver** or **wolf.**

"Q" is the only letter that does not occur in any of the U.S. state names.

Maine is the only U.S. state whose name is just one syllable.

Palindromes

A palindrome is a word, phrase or sentence that reads the same forward and backward. Here are some examples of palindromes:

- A Santa at NASA
- Boston did not sob.
- Civic
- Hannah
- Kayak
- Dennis and Edna sinned.
- Flee to me, remote elf.
- Ma is as selfless as I am.
- Never odd or even
- Nurses run.
- A nut for a jar of tuna
- Radar
- Not New York, Roy went on.

"Onyms"

Acronyms →→→ are words or names formed by combining the first letters of words in a phrase. For example, **SCUBA** comes from **s**elf-**c**ontained **u**nderwater **b**reathing **a**pparatus.

Antonyms →→→ are words with opposite meanings. **Hot** and **cold** are antonyms.

Eponyms →→→ are words based on or derived from a person's name. For example, the word **diesel** was named after Rudolf **Diesel,** who invented the **diesel** engine.

Heteronyms →→→ are words with identical spellings but different meanings and pronunciations. For example, **bow** and arrow, and to **bow** on stage.

Homonyms →→→ are words that sound alike (and are sometimes spelled alike) but name different things. **Die** (to stop living) and **dye** (color) are homonyms.

Pseudonyms →→→ are false names or pen names used by an author. The word comes from the Greek **pseud** (false) and **onym** (name). Mark Twain is a pseudonym for Samuel Langhorne Clemens.

Synonyms →→→ are words with the same or similar meanings. **Cranky** and **grumpy** are synonyms.

Say It in Another Language

If you want to impress your friends, try greeting them in a foreign language.

LANGUAGE	HAPPY BIRTHDAY	I LOVE YOU
German	Alles Gute zum Geburtstag!	Ich liebe Dich
Dutch	Gefeliciteerd met je verjaardag!	Ik hou van jou
Swedish	Grattis på födelsedagen!	Jag alskar dig
French	Joyeux Anniversaire!	Je t'aime
Spanish	¡Feliz Cumpleaños!	Te amo
Italian	Buon Compleanno!	Ti amo

LANGUAGE	HELLO	GOOD-BYE	YES	NO
German	hallo	auf Wiedersehen	ja	nein
Dutch	hallo	tot ziens	ja	nee
Swedish	hej	hejdå	ja	nej
French	bonjour	au revoir	oui	non
Spanish	hola	adiós	sí	no
Italian	ciao	arrivederci	si	no

Most Common Words

Here are the 50 words used most often in English.

the	his	when
of	they	we
and	at	there
a	be	can
to	this	an
in	from	your
is	I	which
you	have	their
that	or	said
it	by	if
he	one	do
for	had	will
was	not	each
on	but	about
are	what	how
as	all	up
with	were	

Idioms

If you say, "The cat's out of the bag" instead of "The secret is given away," you're using an idiom. The meaning of an idiom is different from the actual meaning of the words. Here are some popular idioms.

On cloud nine. This idiom comes from the National Weather Bureau, which ranks clouds according to their height. Since the highest ranking for a cloud is nine, people on cloud nine couldn't feel happier.

Dot the i's and cross the t's. Before typewriters and computers were invented, people hand wrote letters and other documents. It was important to write carefully, especially letters like i and t, which were easy to confuse. The idiom has come to mean to pay attention to details.

Saved by the bell. In 17th-century England, a guard at Windsor Castle was accused of falling asleep at his post. He proved that he was wrongly accused by saying he had heard the church bell chime 13 times at midnight. Townspeople supported this claim and he was not executed. The idiom means rescued at the last possible moment.

Bury the hatchet. Native Americans used to bury weapons to show that fighting had ended and enemies were at peace. Today, the idiom means to make up with someone after an argument or a fight.

A close shave. Barbers once used straight-edge razors to shave customers. Too close a shave could mean a cut or worse. Now, a close shave is a narrow escape from disaster.

Shed crocodile tears. Crocodiles have a reflex that makes their eyes tear when they open their mouths. So it looks like they are crying while devouring their prey. In fact, neither crocodiles nor people who shed "crocodile" tears feel sad.

Let Your Fingers Do the Talking

Say something with your hands. The chart at right will help you learn American Sign Language, which deaf people use to communicate. Study the hand sign for each letter of the alphabet. Then figure out TFK's warm-weather message.

A B C D E F G H I

J K L M N O P Q R

S T U V W X Y Z

We've spelled it out letter by letter. See what we have to say.

(See Answer Key on page 242.)

It's All Greek to Me

You've probably heard these foreign words and phrases used in conversation. Here's what they mean.

ad nauseam → to a sickening degree. "The politician went on *ad nauseam* about the changes he would make if elected."

au courant → up-to-date. "The shoes, the hair, the clothes—every last detail of Maya's outfit—was utterly *au courant*."

bona fide → in good faith; genuine. "Despite her modesty, it's clear that Sarah is a *bona fide* expert in her field."

bon mot → a witty remark or comment. "Jayce won over the audience by making one *bon mot* after another."

carte blanche → unrestricted power to act on one's own. "I may have *carte blanche* at

I am sorry

my grandparents' house, but my parents have strict rules."

doppelgänger → a ghostly double of a living person. "I could not shake the sense that some shadowy *doppelgänger* copied my every move."

faux pas → a social blunder. "She was so embarrassed when she realized that she'd made yet another *faux pas*."

pro bono → done or donated without charge; free. "The penniless man was lucky to find a lawyer who agreed to take his case *pro bono*."

mea culpa → I am to blame. "Drew's *mea culpa* was so sincere, I knew he felt sorry."

schadenfreude → pleasure at someone else's misfortunes. "There was a feeling of *schadenfreude* in the classroom after the teacher caught the class pet cheating."

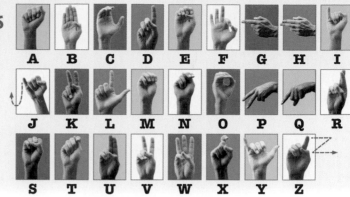

? TFK MYSTERY PERSON

CLUE 1: I was born in Feeding Hills, Massachusetts, in 1866.

CLUE 2: I graduated first in my class from the Perkins School for the Blind.

CLUE 3: The 1962 film *The Miracle Worker* was inspired by my success teaching Helen Keller how to communicate. Keller was blind, deaf and mute.

WHO AM I? (See Answer Key on page 242.)

Language

141

Metric System

Most of the world uses the metric system. The only countries not on this system are the U.S., Myanmar (formerly called Burma) and Liberia.

The metric system is based on 10s. For example, 10 decimeters make a meter.

Length

UNIT	VALUE
millimeter (mm)	0.001 meter
centimeter (cm)	0.01 meter
decimeter (dm)	0.1 meter
meter (m)	1 meter
dekameter (dam)	10 meters
hectometer (hm)	100 meters
kilometer (km)	1,000 meters

Metric Conversions

MULTIPLY	BY	TO FIND
centimeters	.3937	inches
feet	.3048	meters
gallons	3.7853	liters
grams	.0353	ounces
inches	2.54	centimeters
kilograms	2.2046	pounds
kilometers	.6214	miles
liters	1.0567	quarts
liters	.2642	gallons
meters	3.2808	feet
meters	1.0936	yards
miles	1.6093	kilometers
ounces	28.3495	grams
pounds	.4536	kilograms
quarts	.946	liters
square kilometers	.3861	square miles
square meters	1.196	square yards
square miles	2.59	square kilometers
square yards	.8361	square meters
yards	.9144	meters

Mass & Weight

UNIT	VALUE
milligram (mg)	0.001 gram
centigram (cg)	0.01 gram
decigram (dg)	0.1 gram
gram (g)	1 gram
dekagram (dag)	10 grams
hectogram (hg)	100 grams
kilogram (kg)	1,000 grams
metric ton (t)	1,000,000 grams

Capacity

UNIT	VALUE
milliliter (ml)	0.001 liter
centiliter (cl)	0.01 liter
deciliter (dl)	0.1 liter
liter (l)	1 liter
dekaliter (dal)	10 liters
hectoliter (hl)	100 liters
kiloliter (kl)	1,000 liters

go ⟶ See kids' reviews of the best math websites at timeforkids.com/math

In the United States, we use the U.S. customary system to measure things. Here are some of the units of measurement in the system.

LENGTH	WEIGHT	CAPACITY
mile (mi.)	ton (t. or tn.)	gallon (gal.)
yard (yd.)	pound (lb.)	quart (qt.)
foot (ft.)	ounce (oz.)	pint (pt.)
inch (in.)	dram (dr.)	cup (c.)

Did You Know?

A prime number is a number that can be divided, without a remainder, by only itself and by 1. Here are some examples of prime numbers: 2, 3, 5, 19, 23, 67 and 97.

Did You Know?

Troy weight is used to measure precious metals. The grain is the smallest unit in troy weight. Long ago, gold was weighed against grains or the seeds of a plant.

Measuring Length

12 inches = 1 foot

3 feet = 1 yard

5 1/2 yards = 1 rod

40 rods = 1 furlong

8 furlongs = 1 mile

Measuring Area

144 square inches = 1 square foot

9 square feet = 1 square yard

30 1/4 square yards = 1 square rod

160 square rods = 1 acre

640 acres = 1 square mile

Measuring weight

16 ounces = 1 pound

2,000 pounds = 1 ton

Measuring Liquid

2 cups = 1 pint

2 pints = 1 quart

4 quarts = 1 gallon

8 ounces = 1 cup

16 ounces = 1 pint

Cooking Measures

3 teaspoons = 1 tablespoon

4 tablespoons = 1/4 cup

5 tablespoons + 1 teaspoon = 1/3 cup

16 tablespoons = 1 cup

Multiplication Table

To find the answer to a multiplication problem, pick one number from the top of the box and one number from the left side. Follow each row into the center. The place where they meet is the answer.

X	0	1	2	3	4	5	6	7	8	9	10	11	12
0	0	0	0	0	0	0	0	0	0	0	0	0	0
1	0	1	2	3	4	5	6	7	8	9	10	11	12
2	0	2	4	6	8	10	12	14	16	18	20	22	24
3	0	3	6	9	12	15	18	21	24	27	30	33	36
4	0	4	8	12	16	20	24	28	32	36	40	44	48
5	0	5	10	15	20	25	30	35	40	45	50	55	60
6	0	6	12	18	24	30	36	42	48	54	60	66	72
7	0	7	14	21	28	35	42	49	56	63	70	77	84
8	0	8	16	24	32	40	48	56	64	72	80	88	96
9	0	9	18	27	36	45	54	63	72	81	90	99	108
10	0	10	20	30	40	50	60	70	80	90	100	110	120
11	0	11	22	33	44	55	66	77	88	99	110	121	132
12	0	12	24	36	48	60	72	84	96	108	120	132	144

More Than a Million

Numbers don't stop at the millions, billions or trillions. In fact, they go on and on and on. Here's what some really big numbers look like:

10 million	10,000,000
100 million	100,000,000
billion	1,000,000,000
trillion	1,000,000,000,000
quadrillion	1,000,000,000,000,000
quintillion	1,000,000,000,000,000,000
sextillion	1,000,000,000,000,000,000,000
septillion	1,000,000,000,000,000,000,000,000
octillion	1,000,000,000,000,000,000,000,000,000
nonillion	1,000,000,000,000,000,000,000,000,000,000
googol	1 followed by 100 zeroes
centillion	1 followed by 303 zeroes
googolplex	1 followed by a googol of zeroes

Did You Know?

To add or subtract decimals, line up the decimal points and use zeros to fill in the blanks:

$$9 - 2.67 = 9.00$$
$$-2.67$$
$$6.33$$

1,000,000,000,000

Polygons:
How Many Sides?

A geometrical figure with three or more sides is called a polygon or a polyhedron. Here are the names of some polygons.

SIDES	NAME	SHAPE
3	triangle, trigon	
4	quadrilateral, tetragon	
5	pentagon	
6	hexagon	
7	heptagon	
8	octagon	
9	nonagon, enneagon	
10	decagon	

Common Formulas

Finding Area

Area is the amount of surface within fixed lines.

SQUARE
Multiply the length of one side by itself. (For example, if the side is 6 inches long, multiply 6 x 6.)

RECTANGLE
Multiply the base by the height.

CIRCLE
Multiply the radius by itself, then multiply the product by 3.1416.

TRAPEZOID
Add the two parallel sides, multiply by the height and divide by 2.

TRIANGLE
Multiply the base by the height and then divide by 2.

Finding Circumference and Perimeter

The **circumference** of a circle is the complete distance around it. To find the circumference of a circle, multiply its diameter by 3.1416.

The **perimeter** of a geometrical figure is the complete distance around that figure. To find the perimeter, simply add up the lengths of the figure's sides.

Math

145

Roman Numerals

The ancient Romans gave us this numbering system. The year 2008 in Roman numerals is MMVIII.

One	I
Two	II
Three	III
Four	IV

Five	V
Six	VI
Seven	VII
Eight	VIII
Nine	IX
Ten	X
Eleven	XI
Twelve	XII
Thirteen	XIII
Fourteen	XIV
Fifteen	XV
Sixteen	XVI
Seventeen	XVII

Eighteen	XVIII
Nineteen	XIX
Twenty	XX
Thirty	XXX
Forty	XL
Fifty	L
Sixty	LX
Seventy	LXX
Eighty	LXXX
Ninety	XC
One hundred	C
Five hundred	D
One thousand	M

For rules on working with Roman numerals:
www.factmonster.com/romannumerals

Squares and Square Roots

A square of a number is that number times itself.

For example:

$4^2 = 16$: 4 x 4 = 16

$6^2 = 36$: 6 x 6 = 36

Finding a square root is the **inverse operation** of squaring. Inverse operations are two operations that do the opposite, such as multiplication and division.

The square root of 4 is 2, or:

$\sqrt{4}$ is 2: 2 x 2 = 4

$\sqrt{9}$ is 3: 3 x 3 = 9

Here's a table of squares and square roots for numbers from 1 to 20.

Number	Square	Square Root
1	1	1.000
2	4	1.414
3	9	1.732
4	16	2.000
5	25	2.236
6	36	2.449
7	49	2.646
8	64	2.828
9	81	3.000
10	100	3.162
11	121	3.317
12	144	3.464
13	169	3.606
14	196	3.742
15	225	3.873
16	256	4.000
17	289	4.123
18	324	4.243
19	361	4.359
20	400	4.472

To learn how to find square roots:
www.factmonster.com/findingsqroots

A Math Message

Finish Benjamin Franklin's famous quote! Do the math problem in each kite. Then use the key to match each answer to a word. Write the words in the spaces.

KEY
18 = healthy; 8 = early; 15 = rise;
20 = wealthy; 22 = wise;
12 = bed

$$\begin{array}{r} 5 \\ +7 \\ \hline \end{array}$$

$$\begin{array}{r} 18 \\ -10 \\ \hline \end{array}$$

$$\begin{array}{r} 30 \\ -15 \\ \hline \end{array}$$

$$\begin{array}{r} 9 \\ +9 \\ \hline \end{array}$$

$$\begin{array}{r} 12 \\ +8 \\ \hline \end{array}$$

$$\begin{array}{r} 27 \\ -5 \\ \hline \end{array}$$

Early to _____ and _____ to _____ makes a man _____, _____ and _____.

Numerical Prefixes

A prefix is an element at the beginning of a word. A numerical prefix lets you know how many there are of a particular thing. You can use these prefixes to figure out how many sides a figure has. For example, a **hexagon** has six sides, and a **heptagon** has seven.

Prefix	Meaning	Example
uni-	1	**unicorn:** mythical creature with one horn
mono-	1	**monorail:** train that runs on one track
bi-	2	**bicycle:** two-wheeled vehicle
tri-	3	**triceratops:** three-horned dinosaur
quadr-	4	**quadruped:** four-footed animal
quint-	5	**quintuplets:** five babies born at a single birth
penta-	5	**pentagon:** figure with five sides
hex-	6	**hexapod:** having six legs—an insect, for example
sex-	6	**sextet:** group of six musicians
hept-	7	**heptathlon:** athletic contest with seven events
sept-	7	**septuagenarian:** a person between age 70 and 79
octo-	8	**octopus:** sea creature with eight arms
nove-	9	**novena:** prayers said over nine days
deka- or deca-	10	**decade:** a period of ten years
cent-	100	**century:** a period of 100 years
hecto-	100	**hectogram:** 100 grams
milli-	1,000	**millennium:** a period of 1,000 years
kilo-	1,000	**kilogram:** 1,000 grams
mega-	1,000,000	**megaton:** 1 million tons
giga-	1,000,000,000	**gigabyte:** 1 billion bytes

Math

147

U.S. CURRENCY

MONEY

The U.S. Mint, created by Congress in 1792, makes all of the country's coins. The Bureau of Engraving and Printing (BEP), established in 1861, designs and prints U.S. bills. It also prints U.S. postage stamps. Both the Mint and the BEP are parts of the U.S. Treasury Department.

U.S. Paper Money

BILL*	PORTRAIT	DESIGN ON BACK
$1	Washington	ONE between images of the front and back of the Great Seal of the U.S.
$2 (1998)	Jefferson	The signing of the Declaration of Independence
$5 (2000)	Lincoln	Lincoln Memorial
$10 (2000)	Hamilton	U.S. Treasury Building
$20 (2003)	Jackson	White House
$50 (2004)	Grant	U.S. Capitol
$100 (1996)	Franklin	Independence Hall in Philadelphia

*Date in parentheses indicates when new versions of the bills were introduced.

→ In 1929, the size of paper money was reduced by one-third. Portraits and back designs of currency were established at this time.

→ The Bureau of Engraving and Printing produces 37 million notes a day, worth about $696 million.

→ If you had 10 billion $1 notes and spent one every second of the day, it would take 317 years to spend them all.

→ The $100 bill is the largest that is now in circulation.

→ About half the bills printed every year are $1 bills. These bills wear out in about 18 months, faster than any other.

→ The Treasury first printed paper money in 1862 during a coin shortage. The bills were issued in denominations of 1¢, 5¢, 25¢ and 50¢.

U.S. COINS

COIN	PORTRAIT	DESIGN ON BACK
Cent	Abraham Lincoln	Lincoln Memorial
Nickel	Thomas Jefferson	Commemoration of the Louisiana Purchase
Dime	Franklin Roosevelt	Torch, olive branch, oak branch
Quarter	Washington	Eagle*
Half-dollar	John F. Kennedy	Presidential coat of arms
Dollar	Sacajawea and her infant son	Eagle in flight

*The 50 State Quarters Program features new quarters with unique designs on the back. Five coins have debuted each year since 1999, and five new quarters will be released every year through 2008.

→ The U.S. Mint produces about 13 billion coins each year for general circulation.

→ During World War II, steel pennies were issued to conserve copper.

→ Lincoln is the only President on a coin who faces right.

→ In 2007, the U.S. Mint introduced the Presidential dollar coin. Four coins will be released every year, each featuring a President of the United States.

→ The dime is the only coin that does not say how much it's worth.

Richest Americans $

Here's a list of the wealthiest people in America in 2006. Net worth indicates how much money each person has and the value of what they own after their debts are factored in.

	NAME	NET WORTH	BUSINESS
1.	Bill Gates	$53 billion	cofounder of Microsoft
2.	Warren Buffett	$46 billion	chairman of Berkshire Hathaway, a company that owns and runs dozens of other companies
3.	Sheldon Adelson	$20.5 billion	chairman of Las Vegas Sands Corp., a company that owns casinos and hotels
4.	Larry Ellison	$19.5 billion	founder of Oracle software company
5.	Paul Allen	$16 billion	cofounder of Microsoft, investor

Source: *Forbes* magazine

Rising Prices

Do your parents complain about how much money they spend on food? They have good reason. Check out how food prices have changed over time.

PRODUCT	PRICE IN 1890	PRICE IN 1970	PRICE TODAY*
Half-gallon of milk	$ .14	$ .70	$2.50
Dozen eggs	$ .21	$ .61	$2.00
5 pounds of flour	$ .15	$ .59	$1.50
Pound of bacon	$ .13	$ .95	$4.00

Source: U.S. Bureau of the Census. *Approximate price.

Unequal Income

The average annual income for one person in the United States is about $42,000. Here's a look at how that compares to other countries in the world.

COUNTRY	AVERAGE ANNUAL INCOME
Argentina	$13,700
Bangladesh	$2,100
Cambodia	$2,200
Denmark	$33,400
Ecuador	$3,900
Haiti	$1,600
Guyana	$3,800
Mexico	$10,100
New Zealand	$24,200
Republic of Congo	$700
Turkey	$7,900
United States	$42,000

Did You Know?

About 3 billion people—half of the world's population—live on less than $2 a day, and about 1.3 billion people live on less than $1 a day.

A Little Goes a Long Way

Many American kids don't think twice about paying $20 for a video game or a sweatshirt. But that $20 would go a long way in third-world countries. Here's a look at what your money could buy in poor nations.

$1 covers the cost of a lifetime immunization against polio.

$5 is the cost of a mosquito net, which helps to prevent malaria.

$10 can buy a month's supply of vitamins for 48 children.

$20 buys a backpack full of school supplies for a student in Sri Lanka.

$40 pays for an entire year of school for a child in Kenya.

$50 is enough to buy a goat, which is a source of milk and cheese, for a family in Mauritania.

The HSM gang: Lucas Grabeel, Monique Coleman, Corbin Bleu, Ashley Tisdale, Zac Efron and Vanessa Anne Hudgens

THE SCOOP ON HIGH SCHOOL MUSICAL

Kid Reporter Emily Doveala talks with stars Zac Efron and Ashley Tisdale

TFK Kid Reporter Emily Doveala interviewed *High School Musical*'s Zac Efron and Ashley Tisdale in New York City. The sequel, *High School Musical 2: Sing It All or Nothing!*, began airing in spring 2007.

TFK: How long did it take to make the movie?

Zac: We had two weeks of rehearsal and then we had four weeks of principal photography.

Ashley: They had to get me in and out because I had to get back to *Suite Life* for the second season. We did a week in Los Angeles of recording, two weeks of dance rehearsal and two weeks of principal photography.

TFK: What was your favorite part about filming this movie?

Zac: Just the interaction with the cast, and making a whole bunch of new friends and singing and dancing while we were filming.

Ashley: I have to say the musical numbers were awesome. To have a movie with music videos within the movie is really cool. I think it showed up on screen that we all were having a blast. It looked like a huge party.

TFK: What was it like working with such a big cast?

Zac: It was a blast. The whole cast would hang out after every day of shooting. We'd go out and eat dinner and we just did fun stuff together.

Ashley: It was really cool getting to work with your really good friends. It was just amazing... from the costars to the extras. There were 300 extras. A lot was expected from them because they had to dance.

TFK: What was your big break?

Zac: Probably getting into a show called *Summerland*. And then probably *High School Musical* after that.

Ashley: My big break was actually *Suite Life*. I was on *Seventh Heaven*. I did *Charmed*. I did tons of TV shows, guest appearances. But *Suite Life* was my big break.

TFK: What advice would you give to kids who want to have a career in acting?

Zac: Go and sign up for the first play you can find, audition and see how you like it. If you enjoy being on stage, then I can almost guarantee that you are going to like being in front of the camera.

Ashley: Follow your dreams. If you really, really want to do it, you should definitely go for it. But you have to know that it's not all glamorous like people expect it to be.

2006 MAJOR EMMY AWARD WINNERS

Best Drama Series: *24*

Best Actor in a Drama: Kiefer Sutherland, *24*

Best Actress in a Drama: Mariska Hargitay, *Law & Order: Special Victims Unit*

Best Comedy Series: *The Office*

Best Actor in a Comedy: Tony Shalhoub, *Monk*

Best Actress in a Comedy: Julia Louis-Dreyfus, *The New Adventures of Old Christine*

The Office

Best Reality/Competition Program: *The Amazing Race*

Best Reality Program: *Extreme Makeover: Home Edition*

Best Children's Program (tie): *High School Musical* and *I Have Tourette's but Tourette's Doesn't Have Me*

Best Animated Program (one hour or more): *Before the Dinosaurs*

Best Animated Program (one hour or less): *The Simpsons*

TV FACTS AND FIGURES

→ Kids age 6 and under spend as much time in front of a TV or computer screen as they do outside.

→ The average American child sees about 200,000 acts of violence on TV by age 18.

→ 92% of all U.S. households own a VCR or DVD player.

→ On average, kids age 6 to 11 watch 20 hours, 30 minutes of TV each week.

→ The average American youth spends 1,023 hours each year watching TV and 900 hours in school.

→ On average, girls age 12 to 17 watch 22 hours of TV each week. Boys watch 21 hours, 30 minutes.

→ The average household has 2.4 TV sets.

→ 98% of all U.S. households own at least one set. 79% have more than one TV set.

→ 56% of children age 8 to 16 have a TV in their bedroom; 36% of kids age 6 and under do.

→ 40% of Americans always or often watch television while eating dinner.

Did You Know?

Reality television shows date back to 1973, when *An American Family* debuted on PBS. The show followed the real-life Loud family.

TOP 5 TFK

TV Land

The United States may be called the entertainment capital of the world, but China can claim the honor of being the television capital of the world.

COUNTRY	NUMBER OF TELEVISION SETS
1. China	400,000,000
2. United States	219,000,000
3. Japan	86,500,000
4. India	63,000,000
5. Russia	60,500,000

Source: CIA World Factbook

TFK MYSTERY PERSON

CLUE 1: I am a British actress and singer. I made my film debut in 1964 as a magical nanny named Mary Poppins.

CLUE 2: Forty years ago, I starred as Maria in *The Sound of Music*, one of the most popular movie musicals of all time.

CLUE 3: I am also an author. My books include *Mandy* and *The Last of the Really Great Whangdoodles*.

WHO AM I? (See Answer Key on page 242.)

Movies & Television

151

Top Ten Animated Films of All Time

MOVIE	MONEY EARNED IN THE U.S.*
1. Shrek 2	$436,721,703
2. Finding Nemo	339,714,978
3. The Lion King	328,539,505
4. Shrek	267,665,011
5. The Incredibles	261,437,578
6. Monsters, Inc.	255,870,172
7. Toy Story 2	245,852,179
8. Cars	244,052,771
9. Aladdin	217,350,219
10. Ice Age: The Meltdown	195,330,621

Source: Exhibitor Relations Co., Inc.
*As of January 17, 2007

Top Ten Kids Movies of 2006

MOVIE	MONEY EARNED IN THE U.S.
1. Cars	$244,052,771
2. Ice Age: The Meltdown	195,330,621
3. Night at the Museum	191,328,563
4. Happy Feet	189,409,720
5. Over the Hedge	155,019,340
6. The Santa Clause 3: The Escape Clause	84,356,631
7. Open Season	84,303,558
8. The Pink Panther	82,226,474
9. Eight Below	81,593,527
10. Charlotte's Web	73,960,555

Source: Exhibitor Relations Co., Inc.

Top Ten Kids Movies of All Time

MOVIE	MONEY EARNED IN THE U.S.*
1. Star Wars	$460,998,007
2. Shrek 2	436,471,036
3. E.T.: The Extra-Terrestrial	434,949,459
4. Star Wars Episode I— The Phantom Menace	431,088,295
5. Finding Nemo	339,714,978
6. The Lion King	328,539,505
7. Harry Potter and the Sorcerer's Stone	317,575,550
8. Star Wars Episode II— The Attack of the Clones	310,676,740
9. Return of the Jedi	309,205,079
10. The Empire Strikes Back	290,271,960

Source: Exhibitor Relations Co., Inc.
*As of January 17, 2007

Most-Rented DVDs of 2006

1. Flightplan
2. Wedding Crashers
3. Walk the Line
4. Failure to Launch
5. Fun with Dick and Jane
6. Click
7. Inside Man
8. King Kong
9. RV
10. Lord of War

Source: Rentrak Retail Essentials

Top-Selling DVDs of 2006

1. Pirates of the Caribbean: Dead Man's Chest
2. Cars
3. The Chronicles of Narnia: The Lion, the Witch and the Wardrobe
4. Harry Potter and the Goblet of Fire
5. Over the Hedge
6. King Kong
7. Wedding Crashers
8. Walk the Line
9. Ice Age: The Meltdown
10. The Little Mermaid

Source: Rentrak Retail Essentials

BiG FEAT →→

Each winter, Hollywood stars get decked out in glamorous gowns and suits for film's biggest extravaganza of the year—the Academy Awards, also known as the Oscars. Although adults dominate the list of nominees and winners, kids have made their mark in Oscar history. Check out these young Oscar contenders. (Actors whose names are in bold won an Oscar.)

ACTOR	AGE	FILM	YEAR
Justin Henry	8	*Kramer vs. Kramer*	1979
Jackie Cooper	9	*Skippy*	1931
Mary Badham	10	*To Kill a Mockingbird*	1962
Abigail Breslin	10	*Little Miss Sunshine*	2006
Quinn Cummings	10	*The Goodbye Girl*	1977
Patty McCormack	10	*The Bad Seed*	1956
Tatum O'Neal	10	*Paper Moon*	1973
Brandon De Wilde	11	*Shane*	1953
Haley Joel Osment	11	*The Sixth Sense*	1999
Anna Paquin	11	*The Piano*	1993
Keisha Castle-Hughes	13	*Whale Rider*	1999
Patty Duke	16	*The Miracle Worker*	1962
Jack Wild	16	*Oliver!*	1968

Keisha Castle-Hughes

2006 Major Oscar Winners

Jennifer Hudson

Best Picture: *The Departed*
Best Animated Picture: *Happy Feet*
Best Feature Documentary: *An Inconvenient Truth*
Best Actor: Forest Whitaker, *The Last King of Scotland*
Best Actress: Helen Mirren, *The Queen*
Best Supporting Actor: Alan Arkin, *Little Miss Sunshine*
Best Supporting Actress: Jennifer Hudson, *Dreamgirls*
Best Director: Martin Scorsese, *The Departed*
Best Song: "I Need to Wake Up," *An Inconvenient Truth*
Best Score: Gustavo Santaolalla, *Babel*

Oscar Trivia

FILMS THAT WON THE MOST OSCARS (EACH WON 11):
→ *Ben-Hur* (1959)
→ *Titanic* (1997)
→ *The Lord of the Rings: The Return of the King* (2003)

PERSON WITH MOST OSCAR WINS:
→ Walt Disney won 26 awards. Most were in short-subject categories.

MOST WINS IN THE BEST ACTOR CATEGORY (EACH WON TWO OSCARS):
→ Marlon Brando
→ Gary Cooper
→ Tom Hanks
→ Dustin Hoffman
→ Frederic March
→ Jack Nicholson
→ Spencer Tracy

MOST BEST ACTRESS AWARDS:
→ Katharine Hepburn won four Oscars.

Katharine Hepburn

→ In 1991, *Beauty and the Beast* became the first animated film nominated for a Best Picture Oscar.

→ The first Best Animated Feature award was given to *Shrek* in 2001.

→ Judi Dench won a Supporting Actress Oscar for her role as Queen Elizabeth in *Shakespeare in Love.* She appeared in the film for only eight minutes!

→ John Wayne acted in 138 films before winning an Oscar for *True Grit* in 1969.

John Wayne

→ Henry Fonda appeared in movies for 41 years before winning an Oscar for *On Golden Pond* in 1981.

→ Greer Garson, who won the Best Actress award in 1942 for her part in *Mrs. Miniver*, gave the longest speech in Oscar history. It was more than five minutes long.

MUSIC

FROM **TFK** MAGAZINE

TFK CHATS WITH THE CHEETAH GIRLS

The ladies tell all about their new film, their latest album and their upcoming nationwide tour

The Cheetah Girls are back on the prowl! In 2006, the popular singing group released the soundtrack for their new Disney Channel movie, *The Cheetah Girls 2*.

TFK: There's so much going on for you guys. Are you glad to be busy?

Adrienne: We're excited to be busy! We've been waiting for this opportunity forever, especially with all the hard work we've been putting into the movie and into the album. We love what we do.

TFK: What's the new film about?

Kiely: It is set in Barcelona, Spain, where we are competing in (a singing) competition. Along the way, we find that we have different interests, and we can all come together and still be friends. It's such a universal message that everybody can relate to.

TFK: What was it like filming in Barcelona?

Kiely: We were really excited to be together again and to do something great for our fans. But being on the streets of Barcelona and seeing all those architectural marvels was unforgettable.

TFK: What was it like working with Raven-Symone again in the film?

Sabrina: It was really fun! She is literally one of the funniest people I've ever been around. She kept me cracking up the entire shoot. It was fun to have a fourth person again too, to have someone bring a different dynamic to the group.

Adrienne: And to show girl power! Girls always get the reputation of being catty, but I think what the Cheetah Girls stand for is supporting one another and sticking together.

TFK: How is the new album different from the last soundtrack?

Sabrina: There is a huge difference. We got to go in and have discussions with different producers and have input on which direction we wanted the music to go.

Adrienne: Also, the songs fit the movie scenes perfectly. And vocally, we've all grown so much. We added a lot of our own flavors. It means a lot that the music reflects us as a singing group and not just the movie characters.

TFK: Adrienne, you got to sing in Spanish on this album.

Adrienne: It was my first time recording in Spanish. It was so much fun being able to do that. I'm very proud of my Latin heritage, and it's just exciting in this movie that we're able to share that with so many kids.

TFK: Hannah Montana's Miley Cyrus and *High School Musical*'s Vanessa Anne Hudgens are touring with you. What will that be like?

Sabrina: We are so excited. We had a chance to really get to know Miley when we were doing some Disney Channel promotions, and she is so sweet. We're already trying to think of what we're going to get her as a wrap gift.

Adrienne: We're going to sing a remake of "Girls Just Wanna Have Fun" with Miley and Vanessa. We've never had anyone on stage with us before, so it's going to be exciting.

TFK: What's up next?

Sabrina: We're hoping to do another movie, and we want to keep the Cheetah Girls alive as long as we possibly can, as long as the fans want us to.

Adrienne: We do it for them more than anything.

Kiely

Sabrina

Adrienne

iPod Playlists

Here's a sampling of songs some famous people have loaded on their iPods.

HARRY POTTER STAR DANIEL RADCLIFFE

"Hope There's Someone," Antony and the Johnsons
"Man Ray," The Futureheads
"Carrion," British Sea Power
"Buddy Holly," Weezer
"Boredom," Buzzcocks

MYSTERY WRITER LEMONY SNICKET

"Boulevard of Broken Dreams," Green Day
"Nobody's Fault but My Own," Beck
"Ramon," Laurie Anderson
"Sonata No. 9, Op. 16 'Black Mass,'" Vladimir Horowitz

ACTOR JON HEDER

"Clampdown," The Clash
"This Guy's in Love With You," Burt Bacharach
"Starchild," Jamiroquai
"Little Jeannie," Elton John
"Fat Man in the Bathtub," Little Feat

SNOWBOARDING CHAMP HANNAH TETER

"Earthquake Weather," Beck
"Dirty Harry," Gorillaz
"Sun Is Shining," Bob Marley
"Soul Meets Body," Death Cab for Cutie

RECORDING ARTIST JOJO

"Miss Murder," AFI
"Woodstock," Joni Mitchell
"Freakum Dress," Beyoncé
"Take It Easy," Eagles
"Tyrone," Erykah Badu

Pop Music Timeline

Michael Jackson

Pop music dates back to the late 1800s. In "Tin Pan Alley," an area of New York City, musicians, songwriters and pianists played their tunes for music publishers, who printed the songs. People bought sheet music so they could perform popular songs at home.

1896 → The rise of ragtime, the earliest form of jazz, marks the birth of American popular music.

1925 → Country-and-western music debuts at Nashville's Grand Ole Opry.

1935 → Benny Goodman, Glenn Miller and Artie Shaw lead popular dance bands, helping to popularize jazz.

1955 → **Elvis Presley** becomes the world's first rock star.

Elvis Presley

1959 → The National Academy of Recording Arts and Sciences presents the first Grammy Awards.

1964 → The Beatles' song "I Want to Hold Your Hand" is a sensation in the U.S., sparking the "British Invasion." The Rolling Stones soon make their mark in the United States.

1977 → The movie *Saturday Night Fever* ignites the disco inferno.

1978 → Hip hop is born in New York City. Rap follows shortly after.

1981 → MTV hits the airwaves, changing pop music forever.

1982 → **Michael Jackson** releases *Thriller,* one of the top-selling albums of all time.

1983 → The self-titled debut album from Madonna makes her an instant star. Her success paves the way for future idols like Britney Spears.

Early 1990s → Grunge rock, a combination of various rock styles, emerges in Seattle.

1996 → Napster, the music-sharing site, goes live.

2000 → Eminem's *The Marshall Mathers LP* becomes the fastest-selling hip-hop album in the country.

2002 → *American Idol* debuts and creates new pop stars.
→ **No Doubt,** Destiny's Child, and other women-led bands rise in popularity as boy bands begin to lose their fan base.

2003 → Apple Computer introduces the iTunes Music Store, allowing people to download songs for 99 cents each.

→ With Hilary Duff and the Cheetah Girls, teen pop reaches new heights.

No Doubt's Gwen Stefani

Mary J. Blige

Songs Most Downloaded in 2006

RANK	SONG	ARTIST
1.	"Bad Day"	Daniel Powter
2.	"Promiscuous"	Nelly Furtado
3.	"Sexyback"	Justin Timberlake
4.	"Crazy"	Gnarls Barkley
5.	"You're Beautiful"	James Blunt
6.	"Over My Head (Cable Car)"	Fray
7.	"How to Save a Life"	Fray
8.	"Temperature"	Sean Paul
9.	"Ridin'"	Chamillionaire
10.	"Hips Don't Lie"	Shakira featuring Wyclef Jean

Source: Nielsen SoundScan

Songs Most Played on the Radio in 2006

RANK	SONG	ARTIST
1.	"Be Without You"	Mary J. Blige
2.	"Unwritten"	Natasha Bedingfield
3.	"Temperature"	Sean Paul
4.	"Me & U"	Cassie
5.	"Hips Don't Lie"	Shakira featuring Wyclef Jean
6.	"Promiscuous"	Nelly Furtado
7.	"Bad Day"	Daniel Powter
8.	"Check On It"	Beyoncé featuring Slim Thug & Bun B
9.	"Over My Head (Cable Car)"	Fray
10.	"So Sick"	Ne-Yo

Source: Nielsen SoundScan

Top-Selling Albums of 2006

RANK	ALBUM	ARTIST
1.	*High School Musical Soundtrack*	Various
2.	*Me and My Gang*	Rascal Flatts
3.	*Some Hearts*	Carrie Underwood
4.	*All the Right Reasons*	Nickelback
5.	*FutureSex/LoveSounds*	Justin Timberlake
6.	*Back to Bedlam*	James Blunt
7.	*B'day*	Beyoncé
8.	*Hannah Montana*	Soundtrack
9.	*Taking the Long Way*	Dixie Chicks
10.	*Extreme Behavior*	Hinder

Source: Nielsen SoundScan

The Beatles

Top-Selling Albums of All Time

	ALBUM	ARTIST	NUMBER OF ALBUMS SOLD (IN MILLIONS)
1.	*Eagles/Their Greatest Hits 1971–1975*	Eagles	29
2.	*Thriller*	Michael Jackson	27
3.	*Led Zeppelin IV*	Led Zeppelin	23
4.	*The Wall*	Pink Floyd	23
5.	*Back in Black*	AC/DC	21
6.	*Greatest Hits Volume I & Volume II*	Billy Joel	21
7.	*Double Live*	Garth Brooks	20
8.	*Come On Over*	Shania Twain	20
9.	*The Beatles*	The Beatles	19
10.	*Rumours*	Fleetwood Mac	19

Source: Recording Industry Association of America

Big Hits

These musicians and bands have sold the most albums in the United States.

	ARTIST	NUMBER OF ALBUMS SOLD (IN MILLIONS)
1.	The Beatles	169.0
2.	Elvis Presley	118.5
3.	Garth Brooks	116.0
4.	Led Zeppelin	109.5
5.	Eagles	91.0
6.	Billy Joel	79.5
7.	Pink Floyd	73.5
8.	Barbra Streisand	71.0
9.	Elton John	69.0
10.	AC/DC	68.0

Source: Recording Industry Association of America

2006 MTV Video Music Awards

Video of the Year: Panic! at the Disco, "I Write Sins Not Tragedies"

Best Male Video: James Blunt, "You're Beautiful"

Best Female Video: Kelly Clarkson, "Because of You"

Best Group Video: All-American Rejects, "Move Along"

Best Rap Video: Chamillionaire featuring Krayzie Bone, "Ridin'"

Best R&B Video: Beyoncé featuring Slim Thug & Bun B, "Check On It (Pink Panther)"

Best Hip-Hop Video: Black Eyed Peas, "My Humps"

Best Dance Video: Pussycat Dolls featuring Snoop Dogg, "Buttons"

Best Rock Video: AFI, "Miss Murder"

Best Pop Video: Pink, "Stupid Girls"

Best New Artist in a Video: Avenged Sevenfold, "Bat Country"

Viewer's Choice: Fall Out Boy, "Dance, Dance"

Chamillionaire

The Black Eyed Peas

American Idols

Several top performers on the hit TV show *American Idol* have gone on to become, well, American idols. Here's a look at the most successful *AI* alumni.

QUINTUPLE PLATINUM (sold 5 million copies)
→ *Breakaway*, Kelly Clarkson (winner, season 1)

TRIPLE PLATINUM (sold 3 million copies)
→ *Some Hearts*, Carrie Underwood (winner, season 4)

DOUBLE PLATINUM (sold 2 million copies)
→ *Thankful*, Kelly Clarkson
→ *Measure of a Man*, Clay Aiken (runner-up, season 2)

PLATINUM (sold 1 million copies)
→ *Soulful*, Ruben Studdard (winner, season 2)
→ *Merry Christmas with Love*, Clay Aiken
→ *Free Yourself*, Fantasia (winner, season 3)

GOLD (sold 500,000 copies)
→ *I Need an Angel*, Ruben Studdard
→ *Josh Gracin*, Josh Gracin (4th place, season 2)
→ *The Real Thing*, Bo Bice (runner-up, season 4)

Major Grammy Award Winners 2006

Album of the Year: *Taking the Long Way*, Dixie Chicks

Record of the Year: "Not Ready to Make Nice," Dixie Chicks

Song of the Year: "Not Ready to Make Nice," Martie Maguire, Natalie Maines, Emily Robison and Dan Wilson (Dixie Chicks)

New Artist: Carrie Underwood

Pop Vocal Album: *Continuum*, John Mayer

Country Album: *Taking the Long Way*, Dixie Chicks

Rap Album: *Release Therapy*, Ludacris

Rock Album: *Stadium Arcadium*, Red Hot Chili Peppers

R&B Album: *The Breakthrough*, Mary J. Blige

Alternative Music Album: *St. Elsewhere*, Gnarls Barkley

Electronic/Dance Album: *Confessions on a Dance Floor*, Madonna

TFK MYSTERY PERSON

CLUE 1: I was born in 1928 in New Orleans, Louisiana. I am a legendary rhythm-and-blues singer, songwriter and pianist.

CLUE 2: I have sold more records than any other recording artist from the 1950s except Elvis Presley.

CLUE 3: During Hurricane Katrina, I was rescued from my flooded home in New Orleans.

WHO AM I? (See Answer Key on page 242.)

Music

THE OLYMPIAN GODS AND GODDESSES

In Greek mythology, 12 gods and goddesses ruled the universe from atop Greece's Mount Olympus. All the Olympians are related to one another. The Romans adopted most of these gods and goddesses, but with new names (given below in parentheses).

The most powerful of all was Zeus (Jupiter), god of the sky and the king of Olympus. His temper affected the weather; he threw thunderbolts when he was unhappy. He was married to Hera.

Hera (Juno) was the goddess of marriage and the queen of Olympus. She was Zeus's wife and sister. Many myths describe how she got back at Zeus for his many insults.

Poseidon (Neptune) was the god of the sea. He was the most powerful god after his brother, Zeus. He lived in a beautiful palace under the sea and caused earthquakes when he was in a rage.

Hades (Pluto) was king of the dead. He lived in the underworld, the heavily guarded land that he ruled. He was married to Persephone (daughter of the goddess Demeter), whom he kidnapped.

Aphrodite (Venus) was the goddess of love and beauty. Some people believed she was a daughter of Zeus. Others believed she rose from the sea.

Apollo (same Roman name) was the god of music and healing. He was also an archer and hunted with a silver bow.

Ares (Mars) was the god of war. He was both cruel and a coward. Ares was the son of Zeus and Hera, but neither of his parents liked him.

Hephaestus (Vulcan) was the god of fire and the forge (a furnace in which metal is heated). Although he made armor and weapons for the gods, he loved peace.

Artemis (Diana) was the goddess of the hunt and the protector of women in childbirth. She loved all wild animals.

Poseidon

Hades

Ares

Athena (Minerva) was the goddess of wisdom. She was also skilled in the art of war. Athena sprang full-grown from the forehead of Zeus and became his favorite child.

Hestia (Vesta) was the goddess of the hearth (a fireplace at the center of the home). She was the oldest Olympian.

Hermes (Mercury) was the messenger god, a trickster and a friend to thieves. He was the son of Zeus. The speediest of all gods, he wore winged sandals and a winged hat.

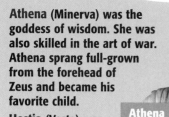
Athena

THESE OLYMPIANS ARE SOMETIMES INCLUDED IN THE LIST OF RULERS:

Demeter (Ceres) was the goddess of the harvest. The word "cereal" comes from her Roman name.

Dionysus (Bacchus) was the god of wine. In ancient Greece, he was honored with springtime festivals that centered on theater.

Hermes

A Greek Family Tree

Zeus was the son of Cronus and Rhea. These two Titans ruled the universe before being overthrown by their children, the Olympians. Zeus was the king of Olympus, and Hera was the queen. Zeus was the father of many gods with his wife, Hera, and with other women. Here's the genealogy, or family tree, of the Greek gods. A plus sign (+) means that the two gods produced children. For example, Zeus + Leto indicates that they were the parents of Apollo and Artemis.

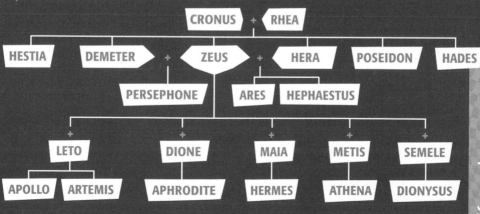

CRONUS + RHEA

HESTIA   DEMETER + ZEUS + HERA   POSEIDON   HADES

PERSEPHONE   ARES   HEPHAESTUS

+ LETO   + DIONE   + MAIA   + METIS   + SEMELE

APOLLO   ARTEMIS   APHRODITE   HERMES   ATHENA   DIONYSUS

GODS AND GODDESSES AROUND THE WORLD

Loki

EGYPTIAN

➜ **Ra** was the supreme god and the god of the Sun. The early pharaohs claimed to be descended from him. He sometimes took the form of a hawk or a lion.

➜ **Nut** represented the heavens and helped to put the world in order. She had the ability to swallow stars and the pharaohs and cause them to be born again. She existed before all else had been created.

➜ **Osiris** was the god of the underworld and the judge of the dead. He was associated with the cycle of life and was often shown wearing mummy wrappings.

➜ **Isis** invented agriculture. She was the goddess of law, healing, motherhood and fertility. She came to be seen as a Mother Earth figure.

➜ **Horus** was a sky god who loved goodness and light. The son of Osiris and Isis, he was often shown as a young child.

➜ **Thoth** was the god of wisdom and magic. He was believed to have invented writing, astronomy and other arts, and served as a scribe, or writer, to the gods.

➜ **Nephthys** was the goddess of the dead. She was a kind friend to the newly dead as well as to those left behind.

Thoth

NORSE

➜ **Odin** was the supreme god and, along with his brothers Vili and Ve, the creator of the world. He was also the ruler of war and wisdom.

➜ **Frigg** was the goddess of the sky, marriage and motherhood. It was believed that she knew the fate of each person, but she kept it a close secret.

➜ **Loki** was the god of mischief and death. He liked to invent horrible ways to harm the other gods. His nastiness and trickery earned him many enemies.

➜ **Freyja** was the goddess of love and fertility. She was very beautiful and enjoyed music and song. Fairies were among her most beloved companions.

➜ **Balder** was the god of light, peace and joy. A kind and gentle god, he was slain in a plot hatched by Loki. He was greatly mourned, especially by his parents, Odin and Frigg.

MAYAN

➜ **Hunahpu** was the god of the Sun and the father of the first humans. A great hero, with his brother, he defeated the forces of death and went on to rule in the heavens.

➜ **Hurankan** was the god of the storms and winds. When the first humans made him angry, he swept them away in a violent flood. The word "hurricane" comes from his name.

➜ **Ixchel** was the goddess of the moon and the protector of pregnant women. She was often shown as an old woman wearing a full skirt and holding a serpent.

➜ **Chac** was the god of agriculture and a great friend of humans. He brought them rain and used his huge tail and fangs to protect planted fields.

➜ **Itzamma** was the official god of the Mayan empire and the founder of its people. Corn, chocolate, writing and calendars were among his many gifts to them.

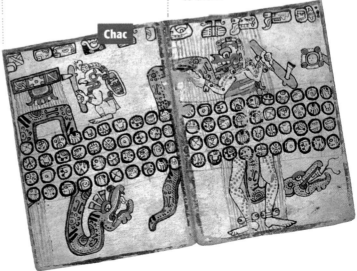

Chac

Monsters in Greek Mythology

ARGUS
Argus may have had as many as 100 eyes, which were located all over his body. Hera employed him as a guard. After he was killed by Hermes, Hera put his eyes in the tail of the peacock, her favorite bird.

GORGONS
The Gorgons were horrifyingly ugly monsters who lived at the edge of the world. Their hair was made of serpents, and one look from a Gorgon's eyes would turn a man to stone. Perseus killed the Gorgon Medusa by beheading her while looking at her reflection in a mirror.

MINOTAUR
The Minotaur was a man-eating monster with the head of a bull. King Minos kept it hidden in a labyrinth (a maze) in Knossos, on the island of Crete, where he used it to frighten his enemies. Theseus killed the Minotaur.

SCYLLA AND CHARYBDIS
The powerful monsters Scylla and Charybdis lived together in a sea cave. Scylla had many fierce dog heads and ate sailors alive. Charybdis created whirlpools by sucking in and spitting out seawater.

CERBERUS
Cerberus was a huge and powerful three-headed dog. He was owned by Hades, god of the dead, who used the fearsome hound to guard the entrance to the underworld. In his final labor, Hercules went to the underworld and kidnapped Cerberus.

SIRENS
The Sirens were giant, winged creatures with the heads of women. They lived on rocks in the sea, where their beautiful singing lured sailors to shipwreck. Odysseus filled his sailors' ears with wax so that they would not fall victim to the Sirens.

HYDRA
The Hydra was a massive, poisonous serpent with nine heads. Every time one head was injured, another two grew in its place. Hercules sought out the monster in its dark marsh and destroyed it.

CYCLOPS
Each of the Cyclops was gigantic and had a single eye in the middle of its forehead. The Cyclops made lightning and thunderbolts for Zeus. The brutal Polyphemus, a Cyclops and a son of Poseidon, was blinded by Odysseus.

GEORGE WASHINGTON (SERVED 1789–1797)
1
Born: Feb. 22, 1732, in Virginia; died: Dec. 14, 1799
Political Party: None (first term), Federalist
Vice President: John Adams
DID YOU KNOW? **Washington was the only President unanimously elected. He received all 69 electoral votes.**
FIRST LADY: **Martha Dandridge Custis**

JOHN ADAMS (SERVED 1797–1801)
2
Born: Oct. 30, 1735, in Massachusetts; died: July 4, 1826
Political Party: Federalist
Vice President: Thomas Jefferson
DID YOU KNOW? **Adams was the first President to live in the White House.**
FIRST LADY: **Abigail Smith**

THOMAS JEFFERSON (SERVED 1801–1809)
3
Born: April 13, 1743, in Virginia; died: July 4, 1826
Political Party: Democratic-Republican
Vice Presidents: Aaron Burr, George Clinton
DID YOU KNOW? **In signing the 1803 Louisiana Purchase, Jefferson nearly doubled the size of the United States.**
FIRST LADY: **Wife Martha Wayles Skelton died before he became president.**

JAMES MADISON (SERVED 1809–1817)
4
Born: March 16, 1751, in Virginia; died: June 28, 1836
Political Party: Democratic-Republican
Vice Presidents: George Clinton, Elbridge Gerry
DID YOU KNOW? **Madison was the only President to have two Vice Presidents die in office. Clinton died in 1812 and Gerry died in 1814.**
FIRST LADY: **Dorothy "Dolley" Payne Todd**

JAMES MONROE (SERVED 1817–1825)
5
Born: April 28, 1758, in Virginia; died: July 4, 1831
Political Party: Democratic-Republican
Vice President: Daniel D. Tompkins
DID YOU KNOW? **The Monroe Doctrine forbade foreign countries like Spain and Russia from expanding into North and South America.**
FIRST LADY: **Elizabeth "Eliza" Kortright**

For biographies of the Presidents:
www.factmonster.com/presidents

6

JOHN QUINCY ADAMS (SERVED 1825–1829)
Born: July 11, 1767, in Massachusetts; died: Feb. 23, 1848
Political Party: Democratic-Republican
Vice President: John C. Calhoun
DID YOU KNOW? In 1843, Adams became the first President to have his photograph taken.
FIRST LADY: Louisa Catherine Johnson

7

ANDREW JACKSON (SERVED 1829–1837)
Born: March 15, 1767, in South Carolina; died: June 8, 1845
Political Party: Democratic
Vice Presidents: John C. Calhoun, Martin Van Buren
DID YOU KNOW? Jackson took several bullets while fighting in duels—an activity for which he was famous.
FIRST LADY: Wife Rachel Donelson died before he became president.

8

MARTIN VAN BUREN (SERVED 1837–1841)
Born: Dec. 5, 1782, in New York; died: July 24, 1862
Political Party: Democratic
Vice President: Richard M. Johnson
DID YOU KNOW? Van Buren was the first President born a U.S. citizen rather than a British subject.
FIRST LADY: Wife Hannah Hoes died before he became president.

9

WILLIAM HENRY HARRISON (SERVED 1841)
Born: Feb. 9, 1773, in Virginia; died: April 4, 1841
Political Party: Whig
Vice President: John Tyler
DID YOU KNOW? Harrison had the shortest presidency: he died after only a month in office.
FIRST LADY: Anna Tuthill Symmes

10

JOHN TYLER (SERVED 1841–1845)
Born: March 29, 1790, in Virginia; died: Jan. 18, 1862
Political Party: Whig
Vice President: None
DID YOU KNOW? Tyler was the first President to marry in office. He was also the President with the most children (15).
FIRST LADY: Letitia Christian (d. 1842); Julia Gardiner

11

JAMES KNOX POLK (SERVED 1845–1849)
Born: Nov. 2, 1795, in North Carolina; died: June 15, 1849
Political Party: Democratic
Vice President: George M. Dallas
DID YOU KNOW? Polk's inauguration was the first one to be reported by telegraph.
FIRST LADY: Sarah Childress

ZACHARY TAYLOR (SERVED 1849–1850)
Born: Nov. 24, 1784, in Virginia; died: July 9, 1850
Political Party: Whig
Vice President: Millard Fillmore
DID YOU KNOW? Taylor did not vote until he was 62 years old.
FIRST LADY: Margaret Mackall Smith

12

MILLARD FILLMORE (SERVED 1850–1853)
Born: Jan. 7, 1800, in New York; died: March 8, 1874
Political Party: Whig
Vice President: None
DID YOU KNOW? Fillmore and his first wife, Abigail, started the White House Library.
FIRST LADY: Abigail Powers

13

FRANKLIN PIERCE (SERVED 1853–1857)
Born: Nov. 23, 1804, in New Hampshire; died: Oct. 8, 1869
Political Party: Democratic
Vice President: William R. King
DID YOU KNOW? Pierce was the only elected President not re-nominated by his party for a second term.
FIRST LADY: Jane Means Appleton

14

JAMES BUCHANAN (SERVED 1857–1861)
Born: April 23, 1791, in Pennsylvania; died: June 1, 1868
Political Party: Democratic
Vice President: John C. Breckinridge
DID YOU KNOW? Buchanan was the only President to never marry.
FIRST LADY: None. His niece, Harriet Lane Johnston, served as his First Lady.

15

ABRAHAM LINCOLN (SERVED 1861–1865)
Born: Feb. 12, 1809, in Kentucky; died: April 15, 1865
Political Party: Republican
Vice Presidents: Hannibal Hamlin, Andrew Johnson
DID YOU KNOW? Lincoln's Gettysburg Address and Second Inaugural Address are among the greatest presidential speeches.
FIRST LADY: Mary Todd

16

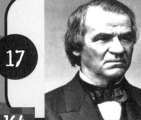

ANDREW JOHNSON (SERVED 1865–1869)
Born: Dec. 29, 1808, in North Carolina; died: July 31, 1875
Political Parties: Union, Democratic
Vice President: None
DID YOU KNOW? Johnson was the first President to be impeached. The Senate found him not guilty, however, and he remained President.
FIRST LADY: Eliza McCardle

17

18

ULYSSES S. GRANT (SERVED 1869–1877)
Born: April 27, 1822, in Ohio; died: July 23, 1885
Political Party: Republican
Vice Presidents: Schuyler Colfax, Henry Wilson

DID YOU KNOW? Grant's much-praised *Memoirs* has been in print since 1885.

FIRST LADY: Julia Boggs Dent

19

RUTHERFORD B. HAYES (SERVED 1877–1881)
Born: Oct. 4, 1822, in Ohio; died: Jan. 17, 1893
Political Party: Republican
Vice President: William A. Wheeler

DID YOU KNOW? The first telephone was installed in the White House while Hayes was President.

FIRST LADY: Lucy Ware Webb

20

JAMES A. GARFIELD (SERVED 1881)
Born: Nov. 19, 1831, in Ohio; died: Sept. 19, 1881
Political Party: Republican
Vice President: Chester A. Arthur

DID YOU KNOW? Garfield was the first President who campaigned in two languages—English and German.

FIRST LADY: Lucretia Rudolph

21

CHESTER A. ARTHUR (SERVED 1881–1885)
Born: Oct. 5, 1829, in Vermont; died: Nov. 18, 1886
Political Party: Republican
Vice President: None

DID YOU KNOW? A stylish dresser, Arthur was nicknamed "Gentleman Boss" and "Elegant Arthur."

FIRST LADY: Wife Ellen Lewis Herndon died before he became president.

22

GROVER CLEVELAND (SERVED 1885–1889)
Born: March 18, 1837, in New Jersey; died: June 24, 1908
Political Party: Democratic
Vice President: Thomas A. Hendricks

DID YOU KNOW? Cleveland was the only President to be married in the White House.

FIRST LADY: Frances Folsom

23

BENJAMIN HARRISON (SERVED 1889–1893)
Born: Aug. 20, 1833, in Ohio; died: March 13, 1901
Political Party: Republican
Vice President: Levi P. Morton

DID YOU KNOW? Benjamin Harrison was the only President who was a grandson of a President (William Henry Harrison).

FIRST LADY: Caroline Lavina Scott (d. 1892); Mary Scott Lord Dimmick

Presidents

24

GROVER CLEVELAND (SERVED 1893–1897)
Born: March 18, 1837, in New Jersey; died: June 24, 1908
Political Party: Democratic
Vice President: Adlai E. Stevenson
DID YOU KNOW? **Cleveland was the only President to be defeated and then re-elected, serving two non-consecutive terms.**
FIRST LADY: **Frances Folsom**

25

WILLIAM McKINLEY (SERVED 1897–1901)
Born: Jan. 29, 1843, in Ohio; died: Sept. 14, 1901
Political Party: Republican
Vice Presidents: Garret A. Hobart, Theodore Roosevelt
DID YOU KNOW? **During his presidency, Hawaii was annexed and the Philippines, Guam and Puerto Rico became U.S. territories.**
FIRST LADY: **Ida Saxton**

26

THEODORE ROOSEVELT (SERVED 1901–1909)
Born: Oct. 27, 1858, in New York; died: Jan. 6, 1919
Political Party: Republican
Vice President: Charles W. Fairbanks
DID YOU KNOW? **Theodore Roosevelt was the first President to ride in an airplane and a submarine.**
FIRST LADY: **Edith Kermit Carow**

27

WILLIAM H. TAFT (SERVED 1909–1913)
Born: Sept. 15, 1857, in Ohio; died: March 8, 1930
Political Party: Republican
Vice President: James S. Sherman
DID YOU KNOW? **Taft was the only President who went on to serve as the Chief Justice of the Supreme Court.**
FIRST LADY: **Helen Herron**

28

WOODROW WILSON (SERVED 1913–1921)
Born: Dec. 28, 1856, in Virginia; died: Feb. 3, 1924
Political Party: Democratic
Vice President: Thomas R. Marshall
DID YOU KNOW? **Wilson was the first President to hold a news conference. About 125 members of the press attended the event on March 15, 1913.**
FIRST LADY: **Ellen Louise Axson (d. 1914); Edith Bolling Galt**

29

WARREN G. HARDING (SERVED 1921–1923)
Born: Nov. 2, 1865, in Ohio; died: Aug. 2, 1923
Political Party: Republican
Vice President: Calvin Coolidge
DID YOU KNOW? **Harding was a newspaper publisher before he was President.**
FIRST LADY: **Florence King**

go ▸ Learn fun facts about Theodore Roosevelt at timeforkids.com/bio/troosevelt

30

CALVIN COOLIDGE (SERVED 1923–1929)
Born: July 4, 1872, in Vermont; died: Jan. 5, 1933
Political Party: Republican
Vice President: Charles G. Dawes
DID YOU KNOW? Coolidge was the first President to be sworn in by his father who was a justice of the peace.
FIRST LADY: Grace Anna Goodhue

31

HERBERT C. HOOVER (SERVED 1929–1933)
Born: Aug. 10, 1874, in Iowa; died: Oct. 20, 1964
Political Party: Republican
Vice President: Charles Curtis
DID YOU KNOW? An asteroid, Hooveria, was named for Hoover.
FIRST LADY: Lou Henry

32

FRANKLIN D. ROOSEVELT (SERVED 1933–1945)
Born: Jan. 30, 1882, in New York; died: April 12, 1945
Political Party: Democratic
Vice Presidents: John Garner, Henry Wallace, Harry S Truman
DID YOU KNOW? Franklin D. Roosevelt was the only President elected to four terms.
FIRST LADY: Anna Eleanor Roosevelt

33

HARRY S TRUMAN (SERVED 1945–1953)
Born: May 8, 1884, in Missouri; died: Dec. 26, 1972
Political Party: Democratic
Vice President: Alben W. Barkley
DID YOU KNOW? Truman was a farmer, a hatmaker and a judge before entering politics.
FIRST LADY: Elizabeth "Bess" Virginia Wallace

34

DWIGHT D. EISENHOWER (SERVED 1953–1961)
Born: Oct. 14, 1890, in Texas; died: March 28, 1969
Political Party: Republican
Vice President: Richard M. Nixon
DID YOU KNOW? Eisenhower was a five-star general in World War II before becoming President.
FIRST LADY: Marie "Mamie" Geneva Doud

35

JOHN F. KENNEDY (SERVED 1961–1963)
Born: May 29, 1917, in Massachusetts; died: Nov. 22, 1963
Political Party: Democratic
Vice President: Lyndon B. Johnson
DID YOU KNOW? Kennedy was the first Roman Catholic President.
FIRST LADY: Jacqueline Lee Bouvier

go Read an article on Franklin D. Roosevelt at timeforkids.com/bio/fdr

LYNDON B. JOHNSON (SERVED 1963–1969)

Born: Aug. 27, 1908, in Texas; died: Jan. 22, 1973
Political Party: Democratic
Vice President: Hubert H. Humphrey
DID YOU KNOW? **Lyndon Johnson was the first person to take the oath of office on an airplane. It was the presidential jet.**
FIRST LADY: **Claudia Alta "Lady Bird" Taylor**

36

RICHARD M. NIXON (SERVED 1969–1974)

Born: Jan. 9, 1913, in California; died: April 22, 1994
Political Party: Republican
Vice Presidents: Spiro T. Agnew, Gerald R. Ford
DID YOU KNOW? **Nixon was the only President to resign.**
FIRST LADY: **Thelma Catherine "Pat" Ryan**

37

GERALD R. FORD (SERVED 1974–1977)

Born: July 14, 1913, in Nebraska; died: Dec. 26, 2006
Political Party: Republican
Vice President: Nelson A. Rockefeller
DID YOU KNOW? **Ford was the first President not to be elected as either President or Vice President by a popular vote.**
FIRST LADY: **Elizabeth "Betty" Anne Bloomer Warren**

38

JIMMY CARTER (SERVED 1977–1981)

Born: Oct. 1, 1924, in Georgia
Political Party: Democratic
Vice President: Walter F. Mondale
DID YOU KNOW? **Carter won the Nobel Peace Prize in October 2002.**
FIRST LADY: **Rosalynn Smith**

39

RONALD W. REAGAN (SERVED 1981–1989)

Born: Feb. 6, 1911, in Illinois; died: June 5, 2004
Political Party: Republican
Vice President: George H. W. Bush
DID YOU KNOW? **Reagan worked for nearly 30 years as a Hollywood actor.**
FIRST LADY: **Nancy Davis**

40

GEORGE H.W. BUSH (SERVED 1989–1993)

Born: June 12, 1924, in Massachusetts
Political Party: Republican
Vice President: J. Danforth Quayle
DID YOU KNOW? **Bush was the first President to spend a holiday with troops overseas: Thanksgiving in Saudi Arabia.**
FIRST LADY: **Barbara Pierce**

41

WILLIAM J. CLINTON (SERVED 1993–2001)

42

Born: Aug. 19, 1946, in Arkansas
Political Party: Democratic
Vice President: Albert Gore Jr.
DID YOU KNOW? Clinton was the second of two Presidents to be impeached. The Senate acquitted him.
FIRST LADY: Hillary Rodham

GEORGE W. BUSH (SERVED 2001–)

43

Born: July 6, 1946, in Connecticut
Political Party: Republican
Vice President: Richard B. Cheney
DID YOU KNOW? George W. Bush was an owner of the Texas Rangers baseball team from the late 1980s until 1998.
FIRST LADY: Laura Welch

First Pets

Teddy Roosevelt watching his son on a horse

Animals have been loyal sidekicks to Presidents since the days of George Washington. He had a parrot, 36 hounds and a horse! Take a look at the creatures that have called the White House home.

First Lady Grace Coolidge with her pet raccoon, Rebecca

PRESIDENT	PETS
Thomas Jefferson	a mockingbird; two bear cubs, which were gifts from Lewis and Clark
John Quincy Adams	an alligator, silkworms
Abraham Lincoln	a turkey, goats, cats, dogs, pigs, a white rabbit
Theodore Roosevelt	dogs, cats, a badger, a pony, 12 horses, a macaw, a piebald rat, a garter snake, five bears, five guinea pigs, two kangaroo rats, lizards, roosters, an owl, a flying squirrel, a raccoon, a coyote, a lion, a hyena, a zebra
Calvin Coolidge	dogs, cats, canaries, raccoons, a donkey, a bobcat, a thrush, a goose, a bear, an antelope, a wallaby, a pygmy hippo, lion cubs
John F. Kennedy	dogs, a cat, a canary, a rabbit, a horse, ponies, hamsters

? TFK MYSTERY PERSON

CLUE 1: I was born in 1890 in Denison, Texas.

CLUE 2: I was in the U.S. military for 41 years and earned the high rank of five-star general. I became the 34th President of the United States in 1953 and served two terms.

CLUE 3: In 1954, I signed a bill that made November 11 Veterans Day, a national salute to former members of the military.

WHO AM I? (See Answer Key on page 242.)

Presidents

FIVE MAJOR FAITHS

	JUDAISM	CHRISTIANITY
FOUNDER	The Hebrew leader **Abraham** founded Judaism around 2000 B.C. **Moses** gave the Jews the **Torah** around 1250 B.C.	**Jesus Christ**, who was crucified around A.D. 30 in Jerusalem
HOW MANY GODS	One	One
HOLY WRITINGS	The most important are the **Torah**, or the five books of Moses. Others include Judaism's oral tradition, which is known as the **Talmud** when it is written down.	The **Bible** is the main sacred text of Christianity.
BELIEFS	Jews believe in the laws of God and the words of the prophets. Judaism introduced **monotheism**, the belief in one god. In Judaism, however, actions are more important than beliefs.	Jesus taught love of God and neighbor and a concern for justice.
TYPES	The three main types are **Orthodox, Conservative** and **Reform**. Orthodox Jews strictly follow the traditions of Judaism. Conservative Jews follow most traditional practices, but less strictly than the Orthodox. Reform Jews are the least traditional.	In 1054, Christians separated into the Eastern Orthodox Church and the Roman Catholic Church. In the early 1500s, the major Protestant groups (Lutheran, Presbyterian and Episcopalian) came into being. Dozens of other groups have since developed.
WHERE	There are large Jewish populations in **Israel** and in the **United States**.	Through its missionary activity, Christianity has spread to most parts of the globe.

Jesus

A boy holds the Torah at his Bar Mitzvah.

Holy Places

Throughout the world there are places of special significance to different religious groups. Here's a sampling of some of the world's most sacred spots.

→ **THE HOLY LAND,** a collective name for Israel, Jordan and Egypt, is a place of pilgrimage for Muslims, Jews and Christians.

→ **THE GANGES RIVER** in India is sacred to Hindus. They drink its water, bathe in it and scatter the ashes of their dead in it.

ISLAM	HINDUISM	BUDDHISM
Muhammad, who was born in A.D. 570 at Mecca, in Saudi Arabia	Hinduism has no founder. The oldest religion, it may date to prehistoric times.	Siddhartha Gautama, called the Buddha, in the 4th or 5th century B.C. in India
One	Many	None, but there are enlightened beings (Buddhas)
The Koran is the sacred book of Islam.	The most ancient are the four Vedas.	The most important are the Tripitaka, the Mahayana Sutras, Tantra and Zen texts.
The Five Pillars, or main duties, are: 1. Profession of faith 2. Prayer 3. Charitable giving 4. Fasting during the month of Ramadan 5. Pilgrimage to Mecca (called a *hajj*) at least once	Reincarnation is the belief that all living things are in a cycle of death and rebirth. Life is ruled by the laws of karma, in which rebirth depends on moral behavior.	The Four Noble Truths: 1. All beings suffer. 2. Desire for possessions, power and so on causes suffering. 3. Desire can be overcome. 4. The path that leads away from desire is the Eightfold Path (the Middle Way).
Almost 90% of Muslims are Sunnis. Shiites are the second largest group. The Shiites split from the Sunnis in 632, when Muhammad died.	No single belief system unites Hindus. A Hindu can believe in only one god, in many or in none.	Theravada (Way of the Elders) and Mahayana (Greater Vehicle) are the two main types.
Islam is the main religion of the Middle East, Asia and North Africa.	Hinduism is practiced by more than 80% of India's population.	Buddhism is the main religion in many Asian countries.

Muslims praying

Hindu god Shiva

Buddha

→ **THE BLACK HILLS** of South Dakota are a holy place for some Native American people, who travel there in "vision quests"—searches for peace and oneness with the universe.

→ **MOUNT FAI SHAN** is China's sacred mountain. It is thought to be a center of living energy—a holy place for Buddhists.

→ **THE SACRED MOSQUE** in Mecca, Saudi Arabia, is cherished by Muslims. Muslims around the world face in the direction of Mecca five times a day to pray.

Religious Holidays

Christian Holidays 2008

Ash Wednesday: February 6
The first day of Lent

Easter: March 23
The resurrection of Jesus

Pentecost: May 11
The feast of the Holy Spirit

First Sunday in Advent: November 30
The start of the Christmas season

Christmas: December 25
The birth of Jesus

Jewish Holidays 2008

All Jewish holidays begin at sundown the day before the dates listed here.

Purim: March 21
The feast of the lots

Passover: April 20
The feast of unleavened bread

Shavuot: June 9
The feast of first fruits

Rosh Hashanah: September 30
The Jewish New Year

Yom Kippur: October 9
The day of atonement

Sukkot: October 14
The feast of the tabernacles

Simchat Torah: October 21
The rejoicing of the law

Hanukkah: December 22
The beginning of the festival of lights

Muslim Holidays 2008

All Muslim holidays begin at sundown the day before the dates listed here.

Muharram: January 10
The Muslim New Year

Mawlid al-Nabi: March 20
The prophet Muhammad's birthday

Ramadan: September 2
The month of fasting

Eid al-Adha: December 9
The festival of sacrifice

Pakistani women and children praying during Ramadan

Religious Dress

People from many religions use dress as a sign of their faith. Sometimes a special type of dress is required by religion, while other times it is a matter of custom.

→ Islam requires both men and women to be modest not only in behavior but also in dress. Some Muslim women wear a *hijab* that covers most of the head and body.

→ Sikhs—followers of Sikhism, a religion from India—also keep their heads covered. Sikh men wrap their heads in cotton turbans, while Sikh women may wear turbans or headscarves.

→ Orthodox Jewish men wear *yarmulkes* (skullcaps), *payos* (sideburns) and *tzitzit* (fringed shawls) at all times. Conservative Jewish men usually wear *yarmulkes* while praying or at religious events.

→ Buddhist nuns and monks wear robes in a variety of colors, from gray to orange, depending on their region and their tradition. In many cases, both nuns and monks in the Buddhist tradition shave their heads.

→ "Plain people" such as the Amish and Mennonites dress in simple clothing that reflects a devotion to traditional ways. Men often wear plain hats and long coats, and women wear simple dresses and aprons.

Women in American Religion

Even though it is only recently that women have been permitted to hold official roles in many religions, they have always been important parts of American religious life. Here are some firsts in the history of women and American religion.

FIRST COMMUNITY OF NUNS IN THE THIRTEEN COLONIES: A Carmelite convent near Port Tobacco, Maryland, established by Mother Bernardina Matthews, in 1790.

FIRST WOMAN MINISTER IN A RECOGNIZED DENOMINATION: Antoinette (Brown) Blackwell, in 1853. She was ordained in the Congregational Church but later became a Unitarian.

FIRST MAJOR RELIGION FOUNDED BY AN AMERICAN WOMAN: The Church of Christ, Scientist, established by Mary Baker Eddy, in 1879.

FIRST U.S. CITIZEN TO BECOME A SAINT: Mother Maria Frances Cabrini, in 1946. She was born in Italy in 1850.

FIRST NATIVE-BORN AMERICAN WOMAN TO BECOME A SAINT: Elizabeth Ann Seton, in 1975. She had established the first American community of the Sisters of Charity, in Maryland in 1809.

FIRST WOMAN RABBI: Sally Priesand, in 1972. She was ordained at Hebrew Union College in Cincinnati.

FIRST WOMAN BISHOP OF THE EPISCOPAL CHURCH: Katharine Jefferts Schori, in 2006.

Bishop Katharine Jefferts Schori

The Seven Deadly Sins

In Christianity, the seven deadly sins are considered "deadly" because it is believed that they can do terrible damage to the soul. The now-famous list does not appear in the Bible and may have been put together by Gregory the Great (540–604). The deadly sins, sometimes known as "capital" or "cardinal" sins, are:

pride greed lust envy gluttony anger sloth

Top Ten Organized Religions in the World

Hindu god Ganesh

RANK	RELIGION	MEMBERS
1.	Christianity	2.1 billion
2.	Islam	1.3 billion
3.	Hinduism	851 million
4.	Buddhism	375 million
5.	Sikhism	25 million
6.	Judaism	15 million
7.	Baha'ism	7.5 million
8.	Confucianism	6.4 million
9.	Jainism	4.5 million
10.	Shintoism	2.8 million

Source: *Encyclopaedia Britannica*

Did You Know?

An atheist does not believe in God. An agnostic believes that it is not known whether God exists. About 7% of Americans say they are atheist or agnostic.

FROM **TFK** MAGAZINE

SCIENTISTS FIND A BIG BAD BIRD

An artist's drawing of the giant bird

Millions of years ago, a giant meat-eating bird roamed an area in what is today Argentina. Scientists recently announced that they had identified the skull and foot bones of that bird. It is the largest bird ever discovered. The 15-million-year-old fossil was unearthed by a high school student in 2004, in the Patagonia region of Argentina.

"The animal was bigger than an ostrich and had a head as big as a horse's," Luis Chiappe, director of the Dinosaur Institute in Los Angeles, California, told TFK. Chiappe has studied the fossil.

The flightless bird, which was about 10 feet tall and weighed about 400 pounds, belonged to the phorusrhacid (for-rus-rah-kid), or "terror bird," family. It had a beak much like an eagle's and ate mostly small animals.

Paleontologists once believed that large terror birds were heavy and slow, but this discovery shows the opposite. These big birds were fleet-footed creatures. "[They were] gigantic and yet their feet and legs were slender, showing that they were fast runners," says Chiappe. He believes that the big bird lived in open forest areas in South America between 60 million and 2 million years ago.

–BY CLAUDIA ATTICOT

Sculptor Richard Webber created a model of the "terror bird."

Fish fossil

How Fossils Form

Fossils are the remains or imprints of prehistoric plants or animals. They are found in sedimentary rock (rock formed from sand and mud), coal, tar, volcanic ash or hardened tree sap. Usually only the hard parts of plants and animals, such as bones and teeth, become fossils.

Most animals that became fossils either lived in water or were washed into a body of water. After an animal died, its soft parts, such as its fur, skin, muscle and organs, decomposed. The hard parts that remained were buried under moist layers of mud or sand, where there was no oxygen or bacteria to cause them to decay. Over time, many of these bodies of water dried up.

The sediment that covered the bones eventually turned into solid rock. Over millions of years, minerals in the surrounding rock replaced the original animal material, forming a fossil.

Sometimes, water seeped into the rocks and dissolved the animal tissue. When this happened, the outline of the fossil remained intact between the layers of rock, leaving a fossil in the form of a natural mold.

Paleontologists, scientists who study forms of life from earlier geologic periods, use the fossils to learn about the creatures that roamed Earth millions of years ago.

THE BRANCHES OF SCIENCE

THE PHYSICAL SCIENCES

Physics The study of matter and energy and the interactions between them. Physicists study such subjects as gravity, light and time.

Chemistry The science that deals with the composition, properties, reactions and structure of matter.

Astronomy The study of the universe beyond Earth's atmosphere. Polish astronomer Nicolaus Copernicus was the first scientist to theorize that the Sun is at the center of the solar system.

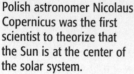

Chemist

THE EARTH SCIENCES

Geography The science that deals with Earth's surface and how it relates to climate, the population, land use, industry and vegetation

Geology The science of the origin, history and structure of Earth, and the physical, chemical and biological changes that it has experienced or is experiencing

Oceanography The exploration and study of the oceans

Paleontology The science of the forms of life that existed in prehistoric or geologic periods as known from fossil remains

Meteorology The science that deals with the atmosphere and its phenomena, such as weather and climate

Botanist

THE LIFE SCIENCES (BIOLOGY)

Anatomy The science that deals with the structure of the human body

Botany The study of plants

Ecology The science that studies the relationship between organisms and their environment

Genetics The study of heredity

Medicine The science of diagnosing, treating and preventing illness, disease and injury

Zoology The science of animals and animal life

Types of Scientists

→ An **agronomist** specializes in soil and crops.

→ An **astronomer** studies stars, planets and galaxies.

→ A **botanist** specializes in plants.

→ A **cytologist** specializes in the study of cells.

→ An **epidemiologist** studies the spread of diseases.

→ A **geneticist** studies how traits are inherited.

→ A **geologist** specializes in the history of Earth.

→ A **geographer** studies Earth's surface.

→ A **marine biologist** studies ocean plants and animals.

→ A **meteorologist** studies weather and climate.

← A **microbiologist** studies microscopic plants and animals.

→ A **paleontologist** specializes in fossils.

→ A **physicist** studies matter and energy and how they are related.

→ A **seismologist** studies earthquakes.

The Code of Life

DNA (deoxyribonucleic acid), found in living cells, is a long molecule shaped like a twisted ladder. It contains an almost endless variety of chemical patterns that create instructions for the human body to follow. Our genes are made of DNA and determine things like what color hair and eyes we'll have. James Watson of the United States and Francis Crick of England discovered DNA in 1953. They were awarded the Nobel Prize for their work. The discovery has helped doctors understand diseases and may someday prevent some illnesses such as heart disease and cancer.

Science

FIVE KINGDOMS OF LIFE

Every living creature on Earth belongs to a kingdom. Scientists debate how many kingdoms there are, but most agree there are five. Here is how the FIVE KINGDOMS are organized.

MONERA

are single-celled organisms that don't have a nucleus. Bacteria make up the entire kingdom. There are more forms of bacteria than any other organism on Earth. Some bacteria are beneficial to us, such as the ones found in yogurt. Others can cause us to get sick.

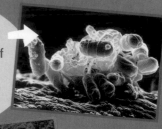

PROTISTS

are mostly single-celled organisms that have a nucleus. They usually live in water. Some protists move around, while others stay in one place. Examples of protists include some algae, paramecium and amoeba.

FUNGI

are usually motionless organisms that absorb nutrients for survival. They include mushrooms, molds and yeasts.

PLANTS

contain chlorophyll, a green pigment necessary for photosynthesis, a process in which plants convert energy from sunlight into food. Their cell walls are made sturdy by a material called cellulose. Plants are fixed in one place. They are divided into two groups: flower- and fruit-producing plants and those that don't produce flowers or fruits. They include garden flowers, agricultural crops, grasses, shrubs, ferns, mosses and conifers.

ANIMALS

are the most complex organisms on Earth. Animals are multi-celled organisms, eat food for survival and have nervous systems. They are divided into vertebrates and invertebrates and include mammals, amphibians, reptiles, birds and fish.

THE ELEMENTS

Elements are the building blocks of nature. Water, for example, is created from two basic ingredients: the element hydrogen and the element oxygen. Each element is a substance made up of only one type of **atom.** For example, all the atoms in a bar of pure gold are the same. Elements cannot be split up into any simpler substances. (When elements combine, they form substances called **compounds.** Water is a compound.)

Atom

An atom, however, is made up of even smaller particles. These are known as subatomic particles. The most important are:

→ **PROTONS,** which have positive electrical charges.

→ **ELECTRONS,** which have negative electrical charges.

→ **NEUTRONS,** which are electrically neutral.

The **atomic number** of an element is the number of protons in one atom of the element. Each element has a different atomic number. For example, the atomic number of hydrogen is 1, and the atomic number of oxygen is 8.

Ammonia is made up of one nitrogen atom and three hydrogen atoms (NH_3).

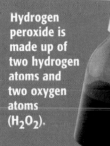

Hydrogen peroxide is made up of two hydrogen atoms and two oxygen atoms (H_2O_2).

Table salt is made up of one sodium atom and one chlorine atom (NaCl).

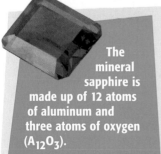

The mineral sapphire is made up of 12 atoms of aluminum and three atoms of oxygen ($A_{12}O_3$).

A water molecule is made up of two hydrogen atoms and one oxygen atom (H_2O).

Did You Know?

The Periodic Table is based on the 1869 Periodic Law proposed by Russian chemist Dmitry Mendeleyev. He had noticed that when arranged by atomic weight, the chemical elements lined up to form groups with similar properties. He was able to use this to predict the existence of undiscovered elements and note errors in atomic weights. In 1913, Henry Moseley of England rearranged the elements of the table by their atomic number.

Did You Know?

The air we breathe is made up of several gases. Here's a breakdown:

GAS	PERCENTAGE
nitrogen	78%
oxygen	20%
carbon dioxide	about 1%
inert gases, called noble gases	about 1%

For the entire Periodic Table of the Elements:
www.factmonster.com/periodictable

Science

AMAZING ADVANCES IN SCIENCE

Isaac Newton, an English mathematician and physicist, is considered the greatest scientist of all time. Among his many discoveries, the most important may be his law of universal gravitation. In 1664, Newton figured out that **gravity** is the force that draws objects toward each other. It explained why things fall down and why the planets orbit the Sun.

Communications satellites make it possible for us to send email, access hundreds of TV and radio stations, use cell phones and determine our exact location from just about any place in the word. These satellites orbit hundreds to thousands of miles above Earth's surface. They send and receive radio signals through computers, satellite phones, Global Positioning Systems (GPS) and other devices, making available an endless amount of information and technology. In 1962, Telstar, owned by AT&T, became the first active communications satellite launched into orbit.

Before French chemist **Louis Pasteur** began experimenting with bacteria in the 1860s, people did not know **what caused disease.** He not only discovered that disease came from microorganisms, but he also realized that bacteria could be killed by heat and disinfectant. This idea led doctors to wash their hands and sterilize their instruments, which has saved millions of lives.

The $2 billion **Hubble Space Telescope,** which was lifted into orbit in 1990, is the most complex and sensitive space observatory ever built. Astronomers use the telescope to explore the universe. The telescope has detected the oldest known planet, Methuselah, which is an astonishing 12.7 billion years old; helped astronomers prove the existence of black holes; peeked farther and deeper into space than any other device; and helped to confirm the age of the universe. The giant telescope is about the same size as a school bus and weighs some 25,500 pounds.

The **theory of special relativity,** which **Albert Einstein** published in 1905, explains the relationships between speed, time and distance. The complicated theory states that the speed of light always remains the same—186,000 miles/second—regardless of how fast someone or something is moving toward or away from the light's source. This theory became the foundation for much of modern science.

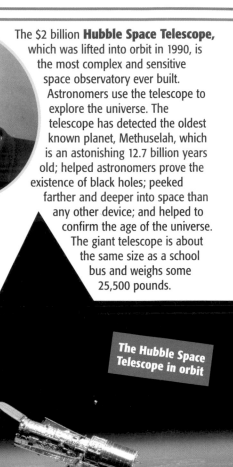

The Hubble Space Telescope in orbit

Science FAQs

→ What are stem cells?

Stem cells, the building blocks of human development, are sometimes called "magic seeds." That's because they can regenerate different kinds of human tissue. The use of stem cells is controversial because the best source for the cells is human embryos. Stem cells form four to five days after an egg is fertilized. These embryos must be destroyed to harvest the cells, and some people say this is the same as taking human life. Others think that an embryo that is just a few days old is simply a tiny cluster of cells and not the same as a human life. They maintain that stem cells could someday save human lives. Stem cells show promise of being able to treat and cure many illnesses and diseases, such as Alzheimer's, diabetes and Parkinson's disease.

→ What is evolution?

Evolution is a theory, developed in 1859 by British naturalist Charles Darwin, that says all organisms evolve, or change, very slowly over time. These changes are adaptations that allow a species to survive in its environment. These adaptations happen by chance. When successful, the adaptations help organisms survive, reproduce and raise offspring. If a species doesn't adapt, it may become extinct. Darwin called this process natural selection, but it is often called "the survival of the fittest."

→ What causes a rainbow?

Although light looks colorless, it's made up of many colors— red, orange, yellow, green, blue, indigo and violet. These colors are known as the spectrum. When light shines into water, the rays of light refract, or bend, at different angles. Different colors bend at different angles—red bends the least and violet the most. When light passes through a raindrop at a certain angle, the rays separate into the colors of the spectrum—and you see a beautiful rainbow.

→ Why do I feel dizzy when I spin?

Inside your ears are tubes that are filled with liquid. The liquid moves when you move, telling your brain what position your body is in. When you spin, the liquid also spins. The liquid continues to spin after you stop, and your brain thinks you're still spinning. You continue to feel that everything is going in circles until the liquid stops moving.

→ What causes lightning?

When air rises and falls within a thunderstorm, positive and negative charges form in the storm cloud. The bottom of the thundercloud has a negative charge, and the top has a positive charge. A flash of lightning can happen inside a cloud, moving between the positively and negatively charged areas. Lightning also takes place when a charge becomes so strong that the air can't stop it from jumping from the cloud to the ground, which has a positive charge. The average flash of lightning could light a 100-watt light bulb for more than three months. The air near a lightning strike is five times hotter than the surface of the Sun. The intense heat causes the air to expand faster than the speed of sound, creating thunder.

Rocks

Rocks are everywhere. Beach sand, mountains and soil are all made of rock. Rocks are classified into three categories, based on how they are formed.

Molten rock

IGNEOUS ROCKS are formed when molten rock (magma) from within the Earth cools and solidifies. There are two kinds: intrusive igneous rocks solidify beneath Earth's surface; extrusive igneous rocks solidify at the surface. Examples: **granite, basalt, obsidian**

SEDIMENTARY ROCKS are formed when sediment (bits of rock plus material such as shells and sand) gets packed together. These rocks can take millions of years to form. Most rocks that you see on the ground are sedimentary.
Examples: **sandstone, coal, limestone**

Sandstone

METAMORPHIC ROCKS are sedimentary or igneous rocks that have been transformed by heat, pressure or both. Metamorphic rocks are usually formed deep within Earth, during a process like mountain building.
Examples: **schist, marble, slate**

Minerals and Gems

Diamond

Minerals are solid, inorganic (not living) substances that are found in and on Earth. Most are chemical compounds, which means they are made up of two or more elements. For example, the mineral sapphire is made up of aluminum and oxygen. A few minerals, such as gold, silver and copper, are made from a single element. Minerals are considered the building blocks of rocks.

Many minerals, such as gold and platinum, are very valuable because they are beautiful and rare. Quartz is the most common mineral.

Gems are minerals or other substances that have been cut and polished. Valuable gems include diamonds, rubies and emeralds.

JOURNEY TO THE CENTER OF THE EARTH

INNER CORE: The center of Earth. About 800 miles thick, it is made of solid iron and nickel.

MANTLE: The mantle is about 1,800 miles thick and extends nearly to the surface of Earth. It's made up of rock.

CRUST: The outer layer of Earth, made up mostly of rock, the crust measures between 5 miles and 25 miles thick. It is thinnest under the oceans.

OUTER CORE: The outer core surrounds the inner core. It's composed mostly of liquid iron and nickel and is about 1,400 miles thick.

CREATE YOUR OWN GREENHOUSE EFFECT

You've probably heard a lot about global warming and the greenhouse effect. Here's an experiment to show the greenhouse effect at work.

MATERIALS

▶ two glasses or glass jars that are exactly the same size
▶ 4 cups cold water
▶ 8 ice cubes
▶ a clear plastic bag or clear plastic wrap
▶ 2 thermometers

WHAT TO DO

1. Pour 2 cups of cold water into each jar.
2. Put 4 ice cubes in each jar.
3. Cover one jar with the plastic bag or plastic wrap.
4. Leave both jars in the sun for one hour.
5. Remove the plastic wrap from the jar.
6. Place the thermometers in each jar.
7. Once the mercury stops moving up, record the temperatures of the water in each glass.

WHAT HAPPENED

The temperature of the water in the covered jar will be higher. That's because the covered jar—the greenhouse jar— trapped the heat and some of the Sun's energy inside the glass, making the water temperature rise. Some of the heat escaped from the uncovered jar, causing that water to cool.

Plant Hall of Fame

Biggest Flower: *Rafflesia arnoldii.* Each bloom can be up to 3 feet wide and weigh as much as 24 pounds. Found in Southeast Asia, the reddish-brown flower gives off an incredibly stinky odor.

Most Massive Living Thing: The giant sequoia. One tree found in California's Sierra Nevada is almost 275 feet tall with a circumference of 103 feet at the base. It is estimated to weigh nearly 1,400 tons and contains enough timber to build 120 average-size houses. It is believed to be around 2,100 years old.

Giant sequoia

Biggest Leaves: Raffia palm. Native to tropical Africa, its huge leaves can grow as long as 80 feet.

Oldest Trees: Bristlecone pines. These trees are found in California, Nevada and Utah. The oldest-known living bristlecone pine is more than 4,700 years old.

Biggest fungus: *Armillaria ostoyae,* or the honey mushroom. Not only is this the largest fungus, but it's also probably the biggest living organism in the world. Located in Malheur National Forest in eastern Oregon, the fungus lives 3 feet underground and spans 3.5 miles.

Deadliest: The castor-bean plant. The source of castor oil, it also contains ricin, which is lethal to humans (but the oil is not). A single castor-bean seed can kill.

Carnivorous Plants

Some plants grow in places where the soil is thin or lacking in nutrients, like bogs and rocky areas, and these plants must get some of their nutrients by trapping and digesting animals, usually insects. More than 600 species and subspecies of carnivorous plants have been identified, although some are now extinct. The Venus flytrap is probably the most famous.

Carnivorous plants use different strategies to attract their prey. Some are sweetly scented, others are brightly colored, still others have parts that are sticky or slippery or designed in a way that makes it hard for prey to escape. Once they have attracted their dinner, carnivorous plants use five basic trapping strategies:

In pitfall traps (pitcher plants, for example), the prey falls into a rolled leaf that contains a pool of digestive enzymes and/or bacteria at the bottom.

Flypaper traps (sundews, for example) use a glue-like substance to hold onto unsuspecting insects.

Snap traps (Venus flytrap, for example) has leaves that actually snap shut to create a plant prison.

Bladder traps use a bladder to suck in aquatic creatures.

Lobster-pot traps use inward-pointing hairs to force prey toward digestive enzymes.

Venus flytrap

FROM
TFK
MAGAZINE

EIGHT IS ENOUGH

Poor, puny Pluto. After it was discovered in 1930, it basked in the glory of being named the ninth planet in the solar system. But in the years since, astronomers have debated whether Pluto truly is a planet. After all, it is smaller than the other planets, has a strange tilt and travels in an odd orbit. In 2006, about 2,500 astronomers from 75 countries met in Prague, Czech Republic, to decide Pluto's fate. The International Astronomical Union voted on guidelines that define a planet. The result: Pluto is not a planet.

Some scientists proposed expanding the number of planets to 12. Pluto, its moon Charon, and two other objects, Eris and Ceres, would be planets. In the end, the astronomers decided that only Mercury, Venus, Earth, Mars, Jupiter, Saturn, Uranus and Neptune fit the definition of "classical planets." They are celestial bodies in orbit around the Sun. They are massive enough to be nearly round and to have either incorporated or repelled most other objects in their orbits.

All is not lost for Pluto. It has been reclassified a "dwarf planet." And that's good news for planet hunters. "Many more Plutos wait to be discovered," says Richard Binzel, a professor at the Massachusetts Institute of Technology in Cambridge.

This artist's drawing shows Pluto's size in relation to Earth, the Moon and two planet-like objects called Sedna and Quaoar, which are located beyond Pluto.

Sedna
800–1,100 miles
in diameter

Quaoar
(800 miles)

Pluto
(1,400 miles)

Moon
(2,100 miles)

Earth
(8,000 miles)

Our Solar System

The Sun

The solar system is made up of the Sun (*solar means related to the Sun*) at its center, eight planets and the various moons, asteroids, comets and meteors controlled primarily by the Sun's gravitational pull. The Sun, our closest star, is thought to be about 4.6 billion years old. This fiery ball measures 870,000 miles (1,392,000 km) across, and its temperature is estimated to be more than 27,000,000°F (15,000,000°C) at its core. More than a million Earth-size planets could fit inside it. The Sun's great mass exerts a powerful gravitational pull on everything in our solar system, including Earth.

The Sun

Mercury

Venus

Moon

Earth

Mars

Jupiter

Saturn

Neptune

Uranus

The Planets

Our solar system has eight planets: Mercury, Venus, Earth, Mars, Jupiter, Saturn, Uranus and Neptune. The planets travel around the Sun in an oval-shaped path called an orbit. One revolution around the Sun is called a year. As each planet orbits the Sun, it also spins on its axis.

The Moon

The Moon travels around Earth in an oval orbit at 22,900 miles (36,800 km) per hour. Temperatures range from -299°F (-184°C) during its night to 417°F (214°C) during its day, except at the poles, where the temperature is a constant -141°F (-96°C). The Moon's gravity affects our planet's ocean tides. The closer the Moon is to Earth, the greater the effect. The time between high tides is about 12 hours 25 minutes.

Earth

The Moon

The Milky Way

Galaxies

Astronomers think that the universe could contain 40 billion to 50 billion galaxies—huge systems with billions of stars. Our own galaxy is the Milky Way. It contains about 200 billion stars.

The Planets

MERCURY

Named for a Roman god (a winged messenger), this planet zooms around the Sun at 30 miles per second!

SIZE
Two-fifths the size of Earth

DIAMETER
3,032.4 miles (4,880 km)

SURFACE
The surface's plains, cliffs and craters are covered by a dusty layer of minerals.

ATMOSPHERE
A thin mixture of helium (95%) and hydrogen

TEMPERATURE
The sunlit side reaches 950°F (510°C). The dark side drops to -346°F (-210°C).

MEAN DISTANCE FROM THE SUN
36 million miles (57.9 million km)

REVOLUTION TIME (IN EARTH DAYS OR YEARS)
88 Earth days

**MOONS: 0
RINGS: 0**

VENUS

Named after the Roman goddess of love and beauty, Venus is also known as the morning star and evening star since it is visible at these times.

SIZE
Slightly smaller than Earth

DIAMETER
7,519 miles (12,100 km)

SURFACE
A rocky, dusty expanse of mountains, canyons and plains, with a 200-mile river of hardened lava

ATMOSPHERE
Carbon dioxide (95%), nitrogen, sulfuric acid and traces of other elements

TEMPERATURE
Ranges from 55°F (13°C) to 396°F (202°C) at the surface

MEAN DISTANCE FROM THE SUN
67.24 million miles (108.2 million km)

REVOLUTION TIME (IN EARTH DAYS OR YEARS)
243.1 Earth days

**MOONS: 0
RINGS: 0**

EARTH

Our planet is not perfectly round. It bulges at the equator and is flatter at the poles.

SIZE
Four planets in our solar system are larger and three are smaller than Earth.

DIAMETER
7,926.2 miles (12,756 km)

SURFACE
Earth is made up of water (70%) and solid ground.

ATMOSPHERE
Nitrogen (78%), oxygen (20%), other gases

TEMPERATURE
Averages 59°F (15°C) at sea level

MEAN DISTANCE FROM THE SUN
92.9 million miles (149.6 million km)

REVOLUTION TIME (IN EARTH DAYS OR YEARS)
365 days, 5 hours, 48 minutes

**MOONS: 1
RINGS: 0**

THE GREAT RED SPOT Jupiter's Great Red Spot is a raging storm of gases, mainly red phosphorus. The storm is larger in size than Earth and has continued for centuries with no sign of dying down.

MARS

JUPITER

SATURN

Because of its blood-red color (which comes from iron-rich dust), this planet was named for the Roman god of war.

The largest planet in our solar system was named for the most important Roman god.

Named for the Roman god of farming, the second largest planet has many majestic rings surrounding it.

SIZE
About one-half the size of Earth

SIZE
11 times the diameter of Earth

SIZE
About 10 times larger than Earth

DIAMETER
4,194 miles (6,794 km)

DIAMETER
88,736 miles (142,800 km)

DIAMETER
74,978 miles (120,660 km)

SURFACE
Canyons, dunes, volcanoes and polar caps of water ice and carbon dioxide ice

SURFACE
A ball of gas and liquid

SURFACE
Liquid and gas

ATMOSPHERE
Carbon dioxide (95%)

ATMOSPHERE
Whirling clouds of colored dust, hydrogen, helium, methane, water and ammonia

ATMOSPHERE
Hydrogen and helium

TEMPERATURE
Between 80°F and -199°F (27°C and -128°C)

TEMPERATURE
-234°F (-148°C) average

TEMPERATURE
-288°F (-178°C) average

MEAN DISTANCE FROM THE SUN
141.71 million miles (227.9 million km)

MEAN DISTANCE FROM THE SUN
483.88 million miles (778.3 million km)

MEAN DISTANCE FROM THE SUN
887.14 million miles (1,427 million km)

REVOLUTION TIME (IN EARTH DAYS OR YEARS)
687 Earth days

REVOLUTION TIME (IN EARTH DAYS OR YEARS)
11.9 Earth years

REVOLUTION TIME (IN EARTH DAYS OR YEARS)
29.5 Earth years

MOONS: 2
RINGS: 0

MOONS: 63
RINGS: 3

MOONS: 56
RINGS: ABOUT 1,000

TURN THE PAGE FOR MORE PLANETS

Space

(CONTINUED)

URANUS

This greenish-blue planet is named for an ancient Greek sky god.

SIZE
About four times larger than Earth

DIAMETER
32,193 miles (51,810 km)

SURFACE
Little is known.

ATMOSPHERE
Hydrogen, helium and methane

TEMPERATURE
Uniform temperature of -353°F (-214°C)

MEAN DISTANCE FROM THE SUN
1,783,980,000 miles (2,870,000,000 km)

REVOLUTION TIME (IN EARTH DAYS OR YEARS)
84 Earth years

MOONS: 27
RINGS: 11

NEPTUNE

This stormy blue planet is named for an ancient Roman sea god.

SIZE
About four times the size of Earth

DIAMETER
30,775 miles (49,528 km)

SURFACE
A liquid layer covered with thick clouds and raging storms

ATMOSPHERE
Hydrogen, helium, methane and ammonia

TEMPERATURE
-353°F (-214°C)

MEAN DISTANCE FROM THE SUN
2,796,460,000 miles (4,497,000,000 km)

REVOLUTION TIME (IN EARTH DAYS OR YEARS)
164.8 Earth years

MOONS: 13
RINGS: 4

DAYS

A day is measured by how long it takes Earth to rotate on its axis once—24 hours. The names of the days are based on seven celestial bodies—the Sun (Sunday), the Moon (Monday), Mars (Tuesday), Mercury (Wednesday), Jupiter (Thursday), Venus (Friday) and Saturn (Saturday). The ancient Romans believed these bodies revolved around Earth and influenced its events.

The surface of Mercury

 Click through an interactive space suit at timeforkids.com/spacesuit

MONTHS

Months are based roughly on the cycles of the Moon. A lunar (Moon) month is 29½ days, or the time from one new Moon to the next.

But 12 lunar months add up to just 354 days—11 days fewer than are in our calendar year. To even things out, these 11 days are added to months during the year. As a result, most months have 30 or 31 days.

YEARS

The calendar most Americans use is called the Gregorian calendar. In an ordinary year this calendar has 365 days, which is about the amount of time it takes the Earth to make one trip around the Sun.

Earth's journey actually takes slightly more than a year. It takes 365 days, 5 hours, 48 minutes and 46 seconds. Every fourth year these extra hours, minutes and seconds are added up to make another day. When this happens, the year has 366 days and is called a **leap year.**

Famous Stargazers

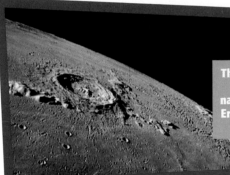

There are craters on the Moon named after both Eratosthenes and Copernicus.

ERATOSTHENES
→ **(276–195 B.C.)** This Greek astronomer was the first to accurately measure the size of Earth.

PTOLEMY
→ **(A.D. 120–189)** The ancient Greek astronomer Ptolemy theorized that Earth is the center of the universe, and the Sun, Moon, planets and stars revolve around it.

NICOLAUS COPERNICUS
→ **(1473–1543)** Polish astronomer Copernicus was the first to theorize that the Sun, not Earth, is the center of our universe—a controversial idea that was at first strongly rejected.

JOHANNES KEPLER
→ **(1571–1630)** The German astronomer Kepler discovered that the orbits of the planets are elliptical (oval) rather than round.

GALILEO GALILEI
→ **(1564–1642)** The Italian astronomer Galileo is considered the first astronomer to use the telescope. With it he discovered the craters on our Moon and proved that the planets circle the Sun.

SIR ISAAC NEWTON
→ **(1643–1727)** This British astronomer discovered the principle of gravity. He used the theory of gravity to explain how the Moon is held in its orbit around Earth.

EDMOND HALLEY
→ **(1656–1742)** This British astronomer was the first to calculate the orbit of a comet. The comet named for him, Halley's comet, passes close enough to Earth to be seen about every 76 years.

EDWIN HUBBLE
→ **(1889–1953)** The American astronomer Hubble classified the different types of galaxies in the universe and developed the theory that the universe is expanding. This theory is called Hubble's Law.

Constellations

For more than 5,000 years, people have looked into the night sky and seen the same stars we see today. They noticed groups of stars that stayed in the same shape and connected them with imaginary lines.

These groups are known as **constellations.** They help astronomers quickly locate other objects in the sky. There are 88 recognized constellations. Here are some well-known ones as they appear in the sky and in art.

Hercules

Orion

Aquarius

Gemini

This map of the skies was drawn in 1790.

The Zodiac

As Earth revolves around the Sun, a different part of the sky becomes visible. The dates below show when the constellations can be seen on the horizon in North America.

CONSTELLATION	ENGLISH NAME	DATES
Aquarius	Water bearer	Jan. 20–Feb. 19
Pisces	Fish	Feb. 20–March 20
Aries	Ram	March 21–April 19
Taurus	Bull	April 20–May 20
Gemini	Twins	May 21–June 20
Cancer	Crab	June 21–July 22
Leo	Lion	July 23–Aug. 22
Virgo	Virgin	Aug. 23–Sept. 22
Libra	Scales	Sept. 23–Oct. 22
Scorpio	Scorpion	Oct. 23–Nov. 21
Sagittarius	Archer	Nov. 22–Dec. 21
Capricorn	Sea goat	Dec. 22–Jan. 19

FROM TFK MAGAZINE

TEAM PLAYERS

Football brothers Tiki and Ronde Barber take a time-out to chat with TFK

Ronde and Tiki Barber

Tiki Barber is a running back for the New York Giants. His brother, Ronde, is a defensive back for the Tampa Bay Buccaneers. The Barber brothers sat down with TFK to talk about their new kids' book *Teammates.*

TFK: How do you maintain the Barber bond while playing for different teams?

Tiki: It's very easy because I think at heart we still feel like teammates, so the same things we used to get on each other about—being accountable, attention to detail—we still do now. I still root for him even though we're playing against each other.

Ronde: There's no team other than mine that I root harder for than [Tiki's]. That's just the nature of us growing up as teammates. You just can't take that out of us.

Tiki: Now the only time we can be teammates is if we both make the Pro Bowl.

Ronde: Which is a good thing. That happened the last two years.

TFK: What makes a good teammate?

Ronde: Somebody who can see past himself and understand that the greater good is in the team accomplishment.

Tiki: Someone who tries to make those around him better. The way I've mostly done it is by example, by showing them that everything matters, even little things, and if that example wears off on someone, I think collectively we all get better.

TFK: How has your brother made you a better teammate?

Ronde: The constructive criticism that we've always given each other. When you know someone who cares about you and is looking out for your best interest, you hear what you need to hear not what you want to hear.

Tiki: He shows me what I do right, and he shows me what I do wrong.

TFK: Did your competitive nature ever cause problems when you were kids?

Tiki: Till we hurt each other, yes. We used to fight all the time, especially on opposing pickup teams. When we were about 14 or 15, I punched him in the stomach, and I broke my wrist. That was the last time we fought.

Ronde: That's going to be the next book, *Fighting My Brother* (laughs).

Tiki: I think our competitive nature is what made us who we are because we never directly competed. He played defense, I played offense. In high school, he was national champ in the hurdles, and I was like, "I'm not going to play second fiddle to that." It pushed me. The same is still true today—he has a Super Bowl ring and I don't. That's what my drive is.

TFK: What is your most memorable sports moment as teammates?

Ronde: This picture [on the back of their book] is. We were playing a Little League championship game, and we beat this team that we probably shouldn't have. But we did because we played a great game. At the end they played [the song] "We are the Champions." The moment has stayed with me ever since. It was our first championship.

Tiki: My only championship.

Both (laughing): We were terrible in high school.

TFK: What do you hope kids learn from you?

Tiki: The importance of family.

Ronde: Yeah, family first. Never give up. Obviously, we all know that we're going to fail. A lot of kids don't know how to express that or deal with that, so by seeing the example of people who have been successful but who have also dealt with failure, I think it could be encouraging.

Tiki: It's the tough times that make you appreciate your success. The bottom line is, there are messages in sports and I think as role models, we are great vehicles to tell those.

PRO FOOTBALL

Originally a game played by colleges, **professional football** became popular in America in the 1920s. The National Football League (NFL) was established in 1922 and merged with the American Football League in 1970 to form a 26-team league. With the addition of the Houston Texans in 2002, the NFL now consists of 32 teams.

Peyton Manning

Super Stories

Super Bowl XLI will go down in the history books as a game of many firsts. Indianapolis Colts coach Tony Dungy and Chicago Bears coach Lovie Smith generated lots of pre-game buzz as the first African American head coaches to lead their teams to the championship game. At game time, Mother Nature delivered another twist. A steady downpour made "41" the first Super Bowl played in the rain. On the opening kickoff, Kevin Hester of the Bears ran the return all the way down the field for a touchdown—another Super Bowl first. Play then turned sloppy, with eight combined turnovers. The Colts pulled away in the second half, and Peyton Manning and the Colts captured—you guessed it—their first ever Lombardi Trophy, beating the Bears 29–17.

COLLEGE FOOTBALL

Top Dog

The **Heisman Trophy** is an annual award given since 1935 to an outstanding college-football player. Several Heisman winners have gone on to success in the NFL and been elected to the Pro Football Hall of Fame after retiring. Current NFL players Reggie Bush (2005) and Matt Leinart (2003) are recent winners. In 2006, quarterback Troy Smith of the Ohio State Buckeyes won the Heisman with 1,662 votes. O. J. Simpson, with 1,750 votes in 1968, is the only player who earned more votes than Troy did.

Other 2007 Bowl Games

ROSE BOWL *(Pasadena, California)*
Southern California 32, Michigan 18

ORANGE BOWL *(Miami, Florida)*
Louisville 24, Wake Forest 13

FIESTA BOWL *(Glendale, Arizona)*
Boise State 43, Oklahoma 42

SUGAR BOWL *(New Orleans, Louisiana)*
Louisiana State 41, Notre Dame 14

COTTON BOWL *(Dallas, Texas)*
Auburn 17, Nebraska 14

GATOR BOWL *(Jacksonville, Florida)*
West Virginia 38, Georgia Tech 35

OUTBACK BOWL *(Tampa, Florida)*
Penn State 20, Tennessee 10

Florida quarterback Chris Leak

Gators Got It

The University of Florida Gators chomped the top-ranked Ohio State Buckeyes 41–14 in the BCS (Bowl Championship Series) national championship game held January 8, 2007, in Glendale, Arizona. Ohio was the first to score in the first quarter, but Florida had two touchdowns in the same quarter to take a lead it never gave up. The Gators were crowned national champs with the win. Before 1998, polls of writers and coaches named the unofficial champ. The BCS combines polls and computer averages to rank the teams and decide which ones advance to the bowl games. The 2007 bowl season introduced the BCS National Championship Game with the two top-ranked teams fighting for the title. Other high-ranking teams played earlier in the Rose, Orange, Fiesta and Sugar Bowls.

BASEBALL

Ryan Howard

Many people believe that baseball was invented in 1839 by Abner Doubleday at Cooperstown, New York, the site of the National Baseball Hall of Fame and Museum. But research has proved that a game called "base ball" was played in the United States and in England before 1839. In fact, Jane Austen mentioned the game in her 1817 novel *Northanger Abbey*.

The first baseball game as we know it was played at Elysian Fields, Hoboken, New Jersey, on June 19, 1846, between the Knickerbockers and the New York Nine.

Johan Santana

Top Players of 2006

MOST VALUABLE PLAYER
A.L.→ Justin Morneau, Minneapolis Twins
N.L.→ Ryan Howard, Philadelphia Phillies

CY YOUNG AWARD (BEST PITCHER)
A.L.→ Johan Santana, Minneapolis Twins
N.L.→ Brandon Webb, Arizona Diamondbacks

ROOKIE OF THE YEAR
A.L.→ Justin Verlander, Detroit Tigers
N.L.→ Hanley Ramirez, Florida Marlins

HOME-RUN CHAMPIONS
A.L.→ David Ortiz, Boston Red Sox, 54 home runs
N.L.→ Ryan Howard, Philadelphia Phillies, 58 home runs

BATTING CHAMPIONS
A.L.→ Joe Mauer, Minnesota Twins, .347 batting average
N.L.→ Freddy Sanchez, Pittsburgh Pirates, .344 batting average

World Series

The Cardinals celebrate.

The 2006 World Series was a Midwest matchup between the St. Louis Cardinals and the Detroit Tigers. This was the third time the two teams had faced off for the crown—in 1934 the Cards were victorious and in 1968 the Tigers took home the trophy. Neither St. Louis nor Detroit was expected to make it to the World Series. At the end of the 2006 regular season, a New York subway series looked probable—the Mets and the Yankees had the best records of the season—but the underdog Tigers and Cardinals battled their way to the fall classic. St. Louis then defeated Detroit 4 games to 1. The Cardinals last won the World Series in 1982.

Did You Know?

In 1929, the players of the New York Yankees became the first in professional baseball to wear numbers on their jerseys. The numbers represented their batting order.

The Little League World Series

Cody Walker

The Little League World Series—the sport's annual world-championship tournament—has been played in Williamsport, Pennsylvania, every year since 1947. In 2006, Columbus (Georgia) Northern Little League defeated Kawaguchi Little League of Japan, 2–1. Cody Walker's 2-run homer was backed up by pitcher Kyle Carter's 3-hit, 11-strikeout performance on the mound. Kyle made Little League World Series history by being the only pitcher to win four games in one series. The Kawaguchi pitcher Go Matsumota also had an excellent day, allowing only three hits and striking out nine batters.

BASKETBALL

In 1891, Dr. James Naismith invented basketball in Springfield, Massachusetts. The game was originally played with a soccer ball and two peach bushel baskets, which is how the game got its name. Twelve of the 13 rules Naismith created are still part of the game. One thing has changed: Originally there were nine players on each team; now there are only five. The Basketball Hall of Fame is named in Naismith's honor.

Diana Taurasi

WNBA Hot Shots—2006 Scoring Leaders

	GAMES	POINTS	AVERAGE
Diana Taurasi, Phoenix	34	860	25.3
Seimone Augustus, Minnesota	34	744	21.9
Lisa Leslie, Los Angeles	34	680	20.0

2006 NBA Scoring Leaders

	GAMES	POINTS	AVERAGE
Kobe Bryant, Los Angeles	80	2,832	35.4
Allen Iverson, Philadelphia	72	2,377	33.0
LeBron James, Cleveland	79	2,478	31.4

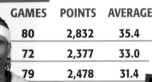
Allen Iverson

2006 Basketball Championships

NBA	The Miami Heat defeated the Dallas Mavericks, 4 games to 2
WNBA	The Detroit Shock beat the Sacramento Monarchs, 3 games to 2

Did You Know?

Philadelphia basketball center Wilt Chamberlain scored a whopping 100 points against the New York Knicks on March 2, 1962. No other player has scored 100 points in one game.

Dwyane Wade and Shaquille O'Neal of the Miami Heat

UCLA's Josh Shipp

March Madness

Fans describe the end of college-basketball season as March Madness. That's because the men's and women's championship tournaments are held in March and feature more than 100 of the best teams in the country.

Tennessee holds the most women's titles (six), but the 2004 women's champ, the University of Connecticut, is catching up, with five titles. UCLA has won the most men's championships (11).

SOCCER

Soccer is the world's most popular sport. Known as football throughout the rest of the world, soccer is played by boys, girls, men and women of nearly all ages. Hundreds of millions of people play the game.

The World Cup

The world's biggest soccer tournament is called the World Cup. It's played every four years by teams made up of each country's best players.

The 2006 World Cup took place in 12 cities across Germany. More than 30 billion people around the world watched from June 9 to July 9. The final match pitted Italy against France. Italy won 5–3 on penalties after a 1–1 tie. French star Zinédine Zidane was ejected late in the game for head-butting Italian defender Marco Materazzi.

Germany won the women's 2003 World Cup, held in the United States. China will host the 2007 women's World Cup. The 2010 men's tournament will be played in South Africa, the first time it will be held on the African continent.

World-Cup Champions

MEN	WOMEN
1930 Uruguay	1991 U.S.A.
1934 Italy	1995 Norway
1938 Italy	1999 U.S.A.
1942, 1946 not held	2003 Germany
1950 Uruguay	
1954 West Germany	
1958 Brazil	
1962 Brazil	
1966 England	
1970 Brazil	
1974 West Germany	
1978 Argentina	
1982 Italy	
1986 Argentina	
1990 West Germany	
1994 Brazil	
1998 France	
2002 Brazil	
2006 Italy	

U.S.A. vs. Mexico

HOCKEY

Ice hockey, by birth and upbringing a Canadian game, is an offshoot of field hockey. Some historians say the first ice hockey game was played in Montreal in December 1879 between two teams composed almost exclusively of McGill University students. In that game, there were 15 players on a side. The players used an assortment of sticks to keep the puck in motion. Early rules allowed nine men on a side, but the number was reduced to seven in 1886 and later to six.

In the winter of 1894–1895, a group of college students from the United States visited Canada and saw hockey played. Enthusiastic about the game, they introduced it as a winter sport when they returned home.

→ All-Time Career Point Scorers

PLAYER	GOALS	ASSISTS	POINTS
1. Wayne Gretzky	894	1,963	2,857
2. Mark Messier	694	1,193	1,887
3. Gordie Howe	801	1,049	1,850
4. Ron Francis	549	1,249	1,798
5. Marcel Dionne	731	1,040	1,771

→ Top Goalies

These goaltenders have won the most games.

PLAYER	GAMES	WINS	LOSSES	TIES
1. Patrick Roy	1,029	551	315	131
2. Ed Belfour	905	457	303	111
3. Terry Sawchuk	971	447	330	172
4. Martin Brodeur	813	446	240	105
5. Jacques Plante	837	435	247	146

Carolina Hurricane Rod Brind'Amour

The Stanley Cup

Each player on the team that wins the NHL championship gets his name engraved on the Stanley Cup, along with all the previous winners. The original cup was only seven inches high; now it stands more than three feet tall. The Montreal Canadiens have won the most titles with 23. The Carolina Hurricanes won the 2006 Stanley Cup.

OLYMPICS

The first Olympic Games were held in Olympia, Greece, around 777 B.C. Only men were allowed to compete. Events included boxing, wrestling and chariot racing. No medals were awarded. Instead, winners received a crown of olive leaves. The Games went on for more than 1,000 years, but were cancelled in A.D. 393.

In 1894, French educator Pierre de Coubertin proposed a revival of the ancient Games. He believed that a modern Olympics with competitors from around the world would promote peace and understanding among nations.

Li Ya

That year, Coubertin formed the International Olympic Committee to help bring back the Games.

The modern Olympics premiered in Athens, Greece, in 1896. Only summer events were included. Figure skating was part of the Summer Olympics in 1908. The sport later became part of the Winter Games, which started in Chamonix, France, in 1924.

The spirit of the ancient Olympics is still alive today. The Games are a source of national pride and peaceful competition for countries all over the world.

Upcoming Olympic Games

2008 (summer) Beijing, China

2010 (winter) Vancouver, British Columbia

2012 (summer) London, England

Cecile Alzina

Sasha Cohen, Shizuka Arakawa and Irina Slutskaya

Fun Facts About the Olympics

→ Host Greece won the most medals (47) at the first modern Olympic Summer Games in 1896.

→ Norway has won the most medals—280—at the Winter Games. The United States has won the most—2,190—at the Summer Games.

→ The five Olympic rings represent the five major regions of the world: Africa, the Americas, Asia, Europe and Oceania. Every national flag in the world includes one of the five colors of the rings, which are (from left to right) blue, yellow, black, green and red.

→ No country in the Southern Hemisphere has ever hosted a Winter Games.

→ Three continents—Africa, South America and Antarctica—have never hosted an Olympics.

→ Speed skater Bonnie Blair won six medals at the Olympic Winter Games. That's more than any other American athlete.

→ No one has won more medals at the Winter Games than cross-country skier Bjorn Dählie of Norway, who has 12.

→ Larissa Latynina, a gymnast from the former Soviet Union, finished her Summer Olympic Games career with 18 total medals—the most in history.

Monique Hennagan

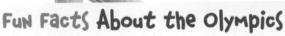

Shani Davis

Andreas Ditter and Martin Marinov

AUTO RACING

Automobile racing originated in France in 1894 and appeared in the U.S. the next year.

Jimmie Johnson

What Do the Flags Mean?

Race officials use flags to instruct drivers during a race. Here's what they mean.

GREEN → Go!

YELLOW → Caution. There is a problem on the track, and drivers must go slow and not pass.

RED → Stop. Something has made the track unusable (maybe an accident or bad weather).

WHITE → Last lap.

CHECKERED → Finish. The race is over.

Who's Who in Pit Row

When a car pulls off the track for a pit stop, it might look like chaos, but it is actually a precise routine. Here's a list of the key pit-crew men and women.

JACK MAN → the crew "quarterback" is in charge of jacking up the car so its tires can be changed.

GAS MAN → refills the gas tank with a giant gas can that can weigh 90 pounds when full. Most pit stops require two cans.

CATCH-CAN MAN → catches overflow gas in a special canister and lets the jack man know when fueling is complete.

FRONT/REAR TIRE CARRIER → carries new tires to the car and carries old ones back over the wall. Tires can weigh 75 pounds each and are extremely hot.

FRONT/REAR TIRE CHANGER → takes off the five lug nuts holding each tire in place with an air gun in less than two seconds and secures the new tires.

Our Need for Speed

The biggest and oldest race held in the U.S. is the Indianapolis 500. It's held every year at the oval-shaped Indianapolis Motor Speedway in Indiana. Sam Hornish Jr. was the 2006 Indy 500 winner.

NASCAR

The National Association for Stock Car Auto Racing's Nextel Cup Series is the most popular auto-racing series in the United States. The NASCAR season runs from February to November. The biggest Nextel Cup race of the year is the Daytona 500. Kevin Harvick won the 2007 Daytona 500. Jimmie Johnson was the 2006 NASCAR Nextel points champion.

Formula One world Champions

Germany's Michael Schumacher won his seventh Formula One World Championship in 2004, giving him two more titles than his nearest competitor on the all-time list, Argentina's Juan-Manuel Fangio. Fernando Alonso of Spain won the championship in 2005 and 2006.

Fernando Alonso

TOP TITLE WINNERS

7—Michael Schumacher (Germany)

5—Juan-Manuel Fangio (Argentina)

4—Alain Prost (France)

Off the Beaten Sports Track

Everyone has heard of basketball, baseball and tennis, but what about snow-snake or kite fighting? These are two of the many exotic sports that are played around the world.

Foot tennis In Malaysia, this game is often played between two teams of two players each. A net is stretched at no particular height across the middle of a playing area, and a wicker ball about the size of a soccer ball is used. Players try to pass the ball back and forth over the net using only their feet, knees and thighs. Each time the ball drops, the other team gets a point.

Kite fighting Kite fighting is a highly competitive sport played in Afghanistan, Pakistan, India, Thailand and South America. Each player hopes to get his or her kite to fly highest. The players try to cut their opponents' kite strings with sharp objects embedded in their kites. The kite that flies highest and longest wins.

Octopush This underwater hockey game was first played in South Africa in the 1960s. The players wear skin-diving equipment, such as masks, flippers and snorkels, in a swimming pool. With miniature hockey sticks and an ice hockey puck, the players follow all the rules of ice hockey—but on the floor of the pool.

Snow-snake This age-old Native American sport is still played today. The "snake" is a polished wooden rod whose front end is shaped like a snake's head. It slides at speeds of up to 100 m.p.h. down a long, curved trail in the snow. Each team gets four chances to throw the snake. The team whose snake goes the farthest wins.

Cycling

American Floyd Landis won the 2006 Tour de France, covering the 2,237-mile course in 89 hours, 39 minutes and 30 seconds. Oscar Pereiro of Spain came in just 57 seconds behind him. Landis's title was tainted, however, as he was charged with using drugs that may have helped his performance during the race.

Favorite Sports All Over the World

Soccer is the world's most popular sport. It is played by millions of people in more than 140 countries. Here is a list of the favorite sports in several countries.

COUNTRY	MOST POPULAR SPORT
Canada	Ice hockey
Germany	Soccer
Japan	Baseball
The Netherlands	Ice skating
Norway	Skiing
Philippines	Basketball
Scotland	Golf
Thailand	Kite fighting
U.S.	Baseball

Floyd Landis

Sports

SKIING AND SNOWBOARDING

Alpine Skiing

Renate Götschl

The Norwegians, Swedes and Lapps (people from Finland) used skis for many centuries before skiing became a sport. Emigrants from these countries introduced skis to the United States. The first skier of record in the U.S. was a Norwegian mailman named "Snowshoe" Thompson, who moved to the U.S. around 1850 and used skis when carrying mail.

Ski clubs sprang up in the U.S. more than 100 years ago in Wisconsin and Minnesota, and ski contests were held there in 1886. In 1936, Franz Pfnur and Christl Cranz, both of Germany, won the first alpine-skiing Olympic gold medals.

These are the events held in most present-day alpine competitions:

Downhill features the longest course and is the fastest of the alpine events. Skiers can reach speeds of more than 90 miles per hour as they race down the slope. Downhill racing includes turns, jumps and gliding stages.

In the **slalom,** the shortest race, single poles, called gates, are placed closely together on the course. It's the most technically challenging event, as skiers must make quick, sharp turns through the gates.

On a **giant slalom** course, gates span the length of the run. They are spaced more widely apart than the slalom gates. This makes for a faster run with wider turns than the slalom. Each gate is made of two poles connected by a piece of fabric.

Super giant slalom, the newest alpine event, was introduced into competitions in 1987. It has a much longer course than either the slalom or giant slalom and the gates are the most widely spaced of the slaloms. Super giant slalom skiers "tuck" into a low, scrunched position to get the most speed from their run.

Jasey Jay Anderson

Snowboarding

Sherman Poppen is generally considered to be the inventor of the snowboard. In 1965, he fastened two skis together so his daughter could "surf" down a snow-covered slope near their Michigan home. He called the sport snurfing, a combination of snow and surfing.

Early snowboarders, mostly male teens, were often viewed as rebels. Now, males and females of all ages are seen cruising down the slopes on snowboards.

Snowboarding debuted as an Olympic sport in 1998. Men and women compete in **halfpipe, parallel giant slalom** and **snowboard cross** events. The halfpipe is a U-shaped course carved into a mountain. Competitors are scored for their technique. In the parallel giant slalom, snowboarders race against each other on separate slalom courses. Snowboard cross features a long course with turns and jumps.

Extreme Sports

The X Games were dreamed up by the sports television network ESPN. They debuted during the summer of 1994 in Newport and Providence, Rhode Island. The games were supposed to take place every two years. But the first games were so popular, organizers made it an annual competition.

The summer games include bicycle stunts, Moto X, skateboarding, surfing, inline skating and wakeboarding. Probably the most famous "extreme" athlete is skateboarder Tony Hawk. He was the first skateboarder to land a 900 trick in the halfpipe competition. A 900 is two and a half complete midair rotations on the skateboard. It's called a 900 because one complete spin is 360° around (like a circle) and 2.5 x 360 = 900.

The winter games include snowboarding, skiing and snowmobiling. At the 2007 games, superstar snowboarder Shaun White came up short in two events he has dominated for the past several years: superpipe and slopestyle. Norway's Andreas Wiig took home gold in slopestyle, and Steve Fisher won the top honor in the superpipe. Jamie Anderson, 16, won the women's snowboard slopestyle title, becoming the youngest athlete to medal in the games. Skier Tanner Hall won his sixth gold medal in the men's superpipe, leaving his rival Simon Dumont with the silver medal.

Laura Perkins

Chris Burandt

Winter X Games 11

JANUARY 25–28, 2007
BUTTERMILK MOUNTAIN, ASPEN/SNOWMASS, COLORADO

SNOWBOARDING: Torah Bright (women's superpipe), Joanie Anderson (women's snowboarder X), Jamie Anderson (women's slopestyle), Steve Fisher (men's superpipe), Nate Holland (men's snowboarder X), Andreas Wiig (men's slopestyle), Andreas Wiig (best trick)

SKIING: Tanner Hall (men's superpipe), Casey Puckett (men's skier X), Candide Thovex (men's slopestyle), Sarah Burke (women's superpipe), Ophelie David (women's skier X), Tyler Walker (monoskier X)

SNOWMOBILING: Chris Burandt (freestyle), Tucker Hibbert (SnoCross)

TENNIS

Amelie Mauresmo

Roger Federer

Tennis Champions

AUSTRALIAN OPEN (2007)
MEN: Roger Federer
WOMEN: Serena Williams

FRENCH OPEN (2006)
MEN: Rafael Nadal
WOMEN: Justine Henin-Hardenne

WIMBLEDON (2006)
MEN: Roger Federer
WOMEN: Amelie Mauresmo

U.S. OPEN (2006)
MEN: Roger Federer
WOMEN: Maria Sharapova

Official Number of Players on a Team

SPORT	NUMBER
Baseball	9
Basketball	5
Field hockey	11
Football (American)	11
Ice hockey	6
Soccer	11
Softball (fast pitch)	9
Softball (slow pitch)	10
Volleyball	6

GYMNASTICS

Alexander Artemev

Alicia Sacramone

Gymnastics is one of the most physically demanding sports, not to mention one of the most popular at the Summer Olympics.

The Fédération Internationale de Gymnastique (FIG) is the organization that oversees gymnastics throughout the world. The FIG recognizes seven gymnastic areas: men's artistic gymnastics, women's artistic gymnastics, rhythmic gymnastics, trampoline, sports aerobics, sports acrobatics and noncompetitive general gymnastics.

Gymnastic Stars

→ OLGA KORBUT, a Soviet gymnast, inspired many girls to take up gymnastics after she won three gold medals at the 1972 Olympics in Munich. At the 1976 summer games in Montreal, Canada, Romanian gymnast NADIA COMANECI became the first woman to score a perfect 10.

→ KERRI STRUG provided one of the most exciting events of the 1996 Olympics—and gymnastics history—when she nailed her vault on an injured ankle to ensure a gold medal for the U.S. team.

→ At the 2004 Olympics in Athens, PAUL HAMM and CARLY PATTERSON of the United States earned gold in the all-around competition. The U.S. team won a total of nine gymnastic medals in Athens.

2006 World Championships

The U.S. women's gymnastics team made a respectable showing at the 2006 World Championship held in Aarhus, Denmark, in October. The team took the silver medal, right behind China's gold. Jana Bieger won individual silver medals in floor exercise and all-around. Alicia Sacramone earned silver in the vault and Anastasia Liukin also won silver on the uneven bars. For the men, Alexander Artemev, with a bronze in the pommel horse, was the only American medal winner.

GOLF

It may be that golf originated in Holland—historians believe it did—but certainly Scotland developed the game and is famous for it. Formal competition began in 1860 with the British Open Championship.

Sherri Steinhauer

Tee Time

The four major events in men's professional golf (the Grand Slam) are:
→ THE MASTERS
→ BRITISH OPEN
→ U.S. OPEN
→ PGA CHAMPIONSHIP

The four major events in women's professional golf (the Women's Grand Slam) are:
→ LPGA CHAMPIONSHIP
→ U.S. WOMEN'S OPEN
→ KRAFT NABISCO CHAMPIONSHIP
→ WOMEN'S BRITISH OPEN

The RYDER CUP is the most prestigious team golf event in the world. It is played every two years between a team of American golfers and a team of European golfers. Team Europe won the 2006 Ryder Cup.

The SOLHEIM CUP is the women's version of the Ryder Cup and will take place in Sweden in 2007.

Winners of Majors in 2006

MEN:
The Masters: Phil Mickelson
British Open: Tiger Woods
U.S. Open: Geoff Ogilvy
PGA Championship: Tiger Woods
U.S. Amateur Champion: Richie Ramsay

WOMEN:
LPGA Championship: Se Ri Pak
U.S. Women's Open: Annika Sorenstam
Kraft Nabisco Championship: Karrie Webb
Women's British Open: Sherri Steinhauer
U.S. Amateur Champion: Kimberly Kim

Kimberly Kim, 14, is the youngest person to win the U.S. Women's Amateur Championship. She didn't even know that the tournament was an important one until she saw a commercial for it on television.

Animal Sports

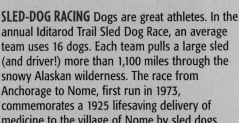

The Iditarod

HORSE RACING

Animals are a big part of the sports world, and horses in particular play a large role. The history of horse racing can be traced to ancient Egypt and Greece, where horse-and-chariot races were part of the Olympic Games. It is often called the "sport of kings" because breeding and racing horses was a popular hobby of the royal family in England during the 12th century.

Preakness Stakes

SLED-DOG RACING Dogs are great athletes. In the annual Iditarod Trail Sled Dog Race, an average team uses 16 dogs. Each team pulls a large sled (and driver!) more than 1,100 miles through the snowy Alaskan wilderness. The race from Anchorage to Nome, first run in 1973, commemorates a 1925 lifesaving delivery of medicine to the village of Nome by sled dogs.

Triple Crown

Horse racing in the United States reaches its peak each spring with the running of the Triple Crown. The Triple Crown is a series of three races starting with the Kentucky Derby, which is held each year on the first Saturday in May at Churchill Downs in Louisville, Kentucky. The next race is the Preakness Stakes, followed by the Belmont Stakes.

Here is a list of the 11 horses that have won the Triple Crown—that is, won all three races in the same year. Notice that it hasn't been done in 30 years!

YEAR	HORSE
1919	Sir Barton
1930	Gallant Fox
1935	Omaha
1937	War Admiral
1941	Whirlaway
1943	Count Fleet
1946	Assault
1948	Citation
1973	Secretariat
1977	Seattle Slew
1978	Affirmed

Sports Superstitions

Players and fans alike have their ways of trying to avoid bad luck. Some sports superstitions are stranger than others. Here are a few.

BASEBALL

→ Spitting into your hand before picking up the bat is said to bring good luck.

→ A wad of gum stuck on a player's hat brings good luck.

→ It is bad luck if a dog walks across the diamond before the first pitch.

→ Lending a bat to a fellow player is a serious jinx.

BASKETBALL

→ The last person to shoot a basket during the warm-up will have a good game.

→ Wiping the soles of your sneakers brings good luck.

→ Bouncing the ball before taking a foul shot is said to be good luck.

FOOTBALL

→ Double numbers on a player's uniform brings good luck.

→ It's bad luck for a professional football player to take a new number when he is traded to another team.

ICE HOCKEY

→ It's bad luck for hockey sticks to lie crossed.

→ It is bad luck to say "shutout" in the locker room before a game.

→ Players believe they'll win the game if they tap the goalie on the shin pads before a game.

→ Many players put their pads and skates on in the same order every day.

TENNIS

→ It's bad luck to hold more than two balls at a time when serving.

→ Players think it's bad luck to wear the color yellow.

→ Players walk around the outside of the court when switching sides for good luck.

FROM TFK MAGAZINE

POPULATION BOOM!

300 million...and counting!

Our nation is growing quickly. A new American is born every 11 seconds! In October 2006, the official number of people in the United States reached 300 million.

The U.S. Census Bureau counts the nation's population. It is not an easy job. Every 10 years, the Census Bureau does an official count. In other years, the Census Bureau uses a special math formula to count the people.

Some say that the formula does not include all of the people who live in the U.S. They believe the population reached 300 million earlier than announced. But "we are confident that we're somewhat close," says Howard Hogan, of the Census Bureau.

My, How We've Grown

The U.S. population has exploded in recent years. There will likely be 400 million Americans in the year 2043. Many of these new Americans will have come from other countries.

Only China and India have more people than the U.S. As America grows, the world grows too. More people must share food, water and space. People are thinking about ways to make life better for everyone on the planet.

In 1915, there were 100 million Americans. In 1967, there were 200 million. In 2006, we hit 300 million. Take a look at the chart to see how the U.S. has grown and changed.

Here We Grow!

Many people born in other countries are becoming American citizens. Experts say the numbers will climb.

–BY ANDREA DELBANCO

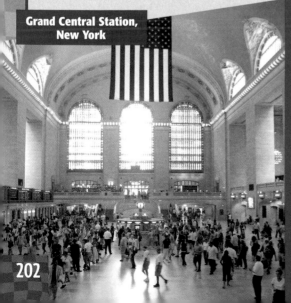

Grand Central Station, New York

A Look Back at the U.S. Population

The figures do not include overseas armed forces.

Year	Population
1790	3,929,214
1800	5,308,483
1820	9,638,453
1850	23,191,876
1880	50,155,783
1900	75,994,575
1920	105,710,620
1950	150,697,361
1980	226,545,805
1990	248,709,873

New York's Fifth Avenue

A LOOK AT THE U.S. POPULATION*

MALES: 138,053,563   (49.1% of population)

FEMALES: 143,368,343   (50.9% of population)

NUMBER OF KIDS AGE 5 TO 9: 20,549,505

NUMBER OF KIDS AGE 10 TO 14: 20,528,072

AVERAGE FAMILY SIZE: 3.14 people

MEDIAN AGE OF THE POPULATION: 35.3

2006: 300,000,000

RACE*

75.1% of Americans are white.

12.5% are of Hispanic origin (they may be of any race).

12.3% are black.

3.6% are Asian, Native Hawaiian or Pacific Islander.

0.9% are Native American or Alaskan Native.

*Figures are based on Census 2000

ANCESTRY OF THE U.S. POPULATION

The United States is indeed a big melting pot, made up of people of different ethnicities and cultures. Here are the top ancestries of U.S. citizens, according to the U.S. Census Bureau.

1. German
2. Irish
3. African American
4. English
5. American
6. Mexican
7. Italian
8. Polish
9. French
10. American Indian

FOREIGN-BORN AMERICANS

The term "foreign-born" refers to Americans who were not born in this country. Below is a list of the top ten places where these Americans were born.

1. Mexico
2. China
3. Philippines
4. India
5. Cuba
6. Vietnam
7. El Salvador
8. Korea
9. Dominican Republic
10. Canada

Source: Immigration and Naturalization Service

American Indians

There are more than 550 federally recognized American Indian tribes in the United States, including 223 village groups in Alaska. "Federally recognized" means these tribes and groups have a special legal relationship with the U.S. government.

Largest American Indian Tribes

TRIBE NAME	POPULATION
1. Cherokee	729,533
2. Navajo	298,197
3. Latin American Indian	180,940
4. Choctaw	158,774
5. Sioux	153,360
6. Chippewa	149,669
7. Apache	96,833
8. Blackfoot	85,750
9. Iroquois	80,822
10. Pueblo	74,085

Source: U.S. Census Bureau

American Indian Population by State

Here are the states with the highest American Indian populations.

STATE	POPULATION
1. Oklahoma	252,420
2. California	242,164
3. Arizona	203,527
4. New Mexico	134,355
5. Washington	81,483
6. North Carolina	80,155
7. Texas	65,877
8. New York	62,651
9. Michigan	55,638
10. South Dakota	50,575

Source: U.S. Census Bureau

SYMBOLS OF THE UNITED STATES

THE GREAT SEAL

Benjamin Franklin, John Adams and Thomas Jefferson began designing the Great Seal in 1776. The Great Seal is printed on the back of the $1 bill and is used on certain government documents, such as foreign treaties.

The bald eagle, our national bird, is at the center of the seal. It holds a banner in its beak. The motto says *E pluribus unum*, which is Latin for "out of many, one." This refers to the colonies that united to make a nation. In one claw, the eagle holds an olive branch for peace; in the other claw, it carries arrows for war.

THE PLEDGE OF ALLEGIANCE TO THE FLAG

The original pledge was published in the September 8, 1892, issue of *The Youth's Companion* in Boston. For years, there was a dispute over who should get credit for writing the pledge, James B. Upham or Francis Bellamy, both members of the magazine's staff. In 1939, the United States Flag Association decided that Bellamy deserved the credit. Here's the original version of the pledge:

I pledge allegiance to my Flag
and the Republic for which it
stands—one nation
indivisible—with liberty
and justice for all.

THE U.S. FLAG

In 1777, the Continental Congress decided that the flag would have 13 alternating red and white stripes, for the 13 colonies, and 13 white stars on a blue background. A new star has been added for every new state. Today the flag (shown above) has 50 stars.

LIBERTY BELL

The Liberty Bell was cast in England in 1752 for the Pennsylvania Statehouse (now named Independence Hall) in Philadelphia. It arrived in Philadelphia with a crack, and it was recast in 1753. The bell, which weighs about 2,000 pounds, is inscribed with a passage from Leviticus (a book of the Bible): "Proclaim liberty throughout all the land unto all the inhabitants thereof." The bell was rung on July 8, 1776, for the first public reading of the Declaration of Independence. The bell cracked again on July 8, 1835, while tolling the death of Chief Justice John Marshall. It has not been rung since.

OTHER SYMBOLS

The **bald eagle** has been our national bird since 1782. The Founding Fathers had been unable to agree on which native bird should have the honor—Benjamin Franklin strongly preferred the turkey! Besides appearing on the Great Seal, the bald eagle is also pictured on coins, the $1 bill, all official U.S. seals and the President's flag.

The image of **Uncle Sam,** with his white hair and top hat, first became famous on World War I recruiting posters. The artist, James Montgomery Flagg, used himself as a model. But the term dates back to the War of 1812, when a meat-packer nicknamed Uncle Sam supplied beef to the troops. The initials for his nickname were quite appropriate!

Largest Cities in the U.S.

New York City

	CITY	POPULATION*
1.	New York, New York	8,008,278
2.	Los Angeles, California	3,694,820
3.	Chicago, Illinois	2,896,016
4.	Houston, Texas	1,953,631
5.	Philadelphia, Pennsylvania	1,517,550
6.	Phoenix, Arizona	1,321,045
7.	San Diego, California	1,223,400
8.	Dallas, Texas	1,188,580
9.	San Antonio, Texas	1,144,646
10.	Detroit, Michigan	951,270

*Figures are based on Census 2000.

MOST COMMON FIRST NAMES IN THE UNITED STATES

Is your name Jacob or Michael, Emily or Olivia? If it is, you have one of the most popular names in the country! Here's a list of the most popular first names.

GIRLS

1. Emily
2. Emma
3. Madison
4. Abigail
5. Olivia
6. Isabella
7. Hannah
8. Samantha
9. Ava
10. Ashley

BOYS

1. Jacob
2. Michael
3. Joshua
4. Matthew
5. Ethan
6. Andrew
7. Daniel
8. Anthony
9. Christopher
10. Joseph

TWINS

1. Jacob, Joshua
2. Matthew, Michael
3. Daniel, David
4. Faith, Hope
5. Ethan, Evan
6. Taylor, Tyler
7. Isaac, Isaiah
8. Joseph, Joshua
9. Nathan, Nicholas
10. Madison, Mason

TOURIST TRAPS

Millions of foreigners visit the United States each year. Here's a look at their favorite destinations.

STATE	CITY
1. New York	1. New York
2. Florida	2. Los Angeles
3. California	3. Miami
4. Hawaii	4. Orlando
5. Nevada	5. San Francisco

Smartest States in America

1. Vermont
2. Massachusetts
3. Connecticut
4. New Jersey
5. Maine
6. Virginia
7. Montana
8. Wisconsin
9. Iowa
10. Pennsylvania

Source: Morgan Quitno's annual reference book, *Education State Rankings, 2006–2007*

Seattle

Denver

City Nicknames

CITY	NICKNAME
Boston	Beantown
Chicago	Windy City
Denver	Mile-High City
New York	Big Apple
Philadelphia	City of Brotherly Love
San Francisco	City by the Bay
Seattle	Emerald City

San Francisco

Philadelphia

FAMOUS FIRSTS IN THE U.S.

FAMOUS FIRST	NAME, LOCATION	DATE
Aquarium	New York Aquarium, New York, New York	1896
Bank	First Bank of the United States, Philadelphia, Pennsylvania	1781
Baseball stadium	Forbes Field, Pittsburgh, Pennsylvania	1909
College	Harvard, Cambridge, Massachusetts	1636
Daily newspaper	Pennsylvania Packet and Daily Advertiser, Philadelphia	1784
Ferris wheel	Chicago, Illinois	1893
Hospital	Pennsylvania Hospital, Philadelphia	1752
Lighthouse	Boston Light, Boston, Massachusetts	1716
Movie theater	Electric Theater, Los Angeles, California	1902
Parking meter	Oklahoma City, Oklahoma	1935
Public museum	Charleston Museum, Charleston, South Carolina	1773
Public school	Boston Latin, Boston	1635
Public TV station	KUHT or HoustonPBS, Houston, Texas	1953
Skyscraper	Home Insurance Building, Chicago, Illinois	1885
Subway	Green Line, Boston	1914

State Regions

The states in these regions often have similar climate, geography, traditions and history.

New England Connecticut, Maine, Massachusetts, New Hampshire, Rhode Island, Vermont

Middle Atlantic Delaware, Maryland, New Jersey, New York, Pennsylvania

South Alabama, Arkansas, Florida, Georgia, Kentucky, Louisiana, Mississippi, Missouri, North Carolina, South Carolina, Tennessee, Virginia, West Virginia

Midwest Illinois, Indiana, Iowa, Kansas, Michigan, Minnesota, Nebraska, North Dakota, Ohio, South Dakota, Wisconsin

Southwest Arizona, New Mexico, Oklahoma, Texas

West Alaska, California, Colorado, Hawaii, Idaho, Montana, Nevada, Oregon, Utah, Washington, Wyoming

Sizing Up the States

Largest: **Alaska, 570,374 square miles**
Smallest: **Rhode Island, 1,045 square miles**
Most populous: **California, 35,893,799 residents**
Least populous: **Wyoming, 506,529 residents**

EXTREME POINTS OF THE U.S.

EXTREME POINTS	LATITUDE	LONGITUDE	DISTANCE (from the geographic center of the U.S. in Castle Rock, South Dakota)
NORTHERNMOST: Point Barrow, Alaska	71°23' N	156°29' W	2,507 miles (4,034 km)
EASTERNMOST: West Quoddy Head, Maine	44°49' N	66°57' W	1,788 miles (2,997 km)
SOUTHERNMOST: Ka Lae (South Cape), Hawaii	18°55' N	155°41' W	3,463 miles (5,573 km)
WESTERNMOST: Cape Wrangell, Alaska (Attu Island)	52°55' N	172°27' E	3,625 miles (5,833 km)

Degrees | Minutes | Direction

NATIONAL PARK SYSTEM

On August 25, 1916, President Woodrow Wilson signed an act that established the National Park Service. Tens of millions of people visit the national parks every year. Here are some interesting facts about our nation's treasures.

→ Yellowstone National Park is the oldest national park in the world.

→ Delaware is the only state that does not contain an area in the National Park System.

→ About 89,000 people across the U.S. volunteer in the parks each year.

→ The largest area in the system is Wrangell–St. Elias National Park and Preserve in Alaska. At 13,200,000 acres (including the park and preserve), it makes up 16.3% of the entire system.

→ The smallest area is the Thaddeus Kosciuszko National Memorial, in Pennsylvania, at 0.02 acres. It commemorates the life and work of this Polish patriot and hero of the American Revolution.

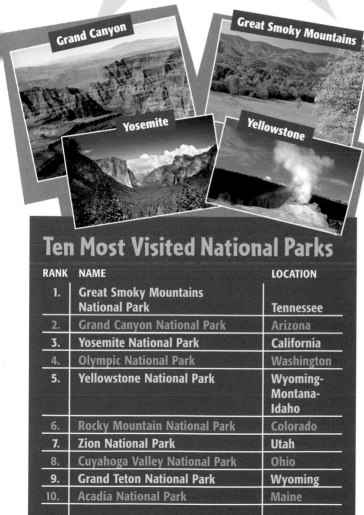

Grand Canyon

Great Smoky Mountains

Yosemite

Yellowstone

Ten Most Visited National Parks

RANK	NAME	LOCATION
1.	Great Smoky Mountains National Park	Tennessee
2.	Grand Canyon National Park	Arizona
3.	Yosemite National Park	California
4.	Olympic National Park	Washington
5.	Yellowstone National Park	Wyoming-Montana-Idaho
6.	Rocky Mountain National Park	Colorado
7.	Zion National Park	Utah
8.	Cuyahoga Valley National Park	Ohio
9.	Grand Teton National Park	Wyoming
10.	Acadia National Park	Maine

Source: National Park Service

Offbeat National Parks

There are 388 parks, monuments and recreation areas in the National Park System. Here are a few sites that are less well known but fascinating.

HAWAII VOLCANOES NATIONAL PARK NEAR HILO, HAWAII
Visitors will find the Earth's most massive volcano, 13,677-foot Mauna Loa, and watch bubbling lava flow from the world's most active volcano, Kilauea.

ALCATRAZ ISLAND SAN FRANCISCO, CALIFORNIA
In the middle of San Francisco Bay, "the Rock" was America's most famous federal prison.

***BROWN V. BOARD OF EDUCATION* NATIONAL HISTORIC SITE TOPEKA, KANSAS**
The Supreme Court case that ended segregation in public schools originated in Topeka, Kansas. This site, located in an elementary school once reserved for African American kids, honors the decision.

United States

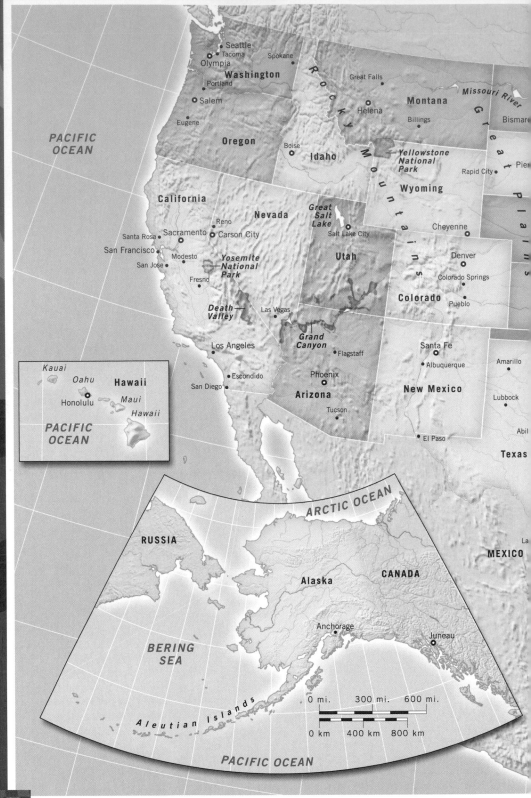

PACIFIC
OCEAN

Seattle
Tacoma
Olympia
Washington
Portland
Salem
Eugene

Spokane

Great Falls

Montana
Helena
Billings

Missouri River

Bismar

Oregon

Boise
Idaho

Rocky Mountains

Yellowstone
National
Park

Wyoming

Rapid City

Pier

G r e a t   P l a i n s

California

Reno
Santa Rosa
Sacramento   Carson City
San Francisco
San Jose   Modesto
Fresno

Nevada

Yosemite
National
Park

Death
Valley

Great
Salt
Lake

Salt Lake City

Utah

Cheyenne

Denver
Colorado Springs
Pueblo

Colorado

Los Angeles

Las Vegas

Grand
Canyon

Flagstaff

Santa Fe
Albuquerque

Amarillo

San Diego

Escondido

Phoenix

Arizona

Tucson

New Mexico

Lubbock

Abil

El Paso

Texas

Kauai
Oahu
Honolulu

Hawaii
Maui
Hawaii

PACIFIC
OCEAN

RUSSIA

ARCTIC OCEAN

La

MEXICO

Alaska

CANADA

BERING
SEA

Anchorage

Juneau

Aleutian Islands

0 mi.   300 mi.   600 mi.

0 km   400 km   800 km

PACIFIC OCEAN

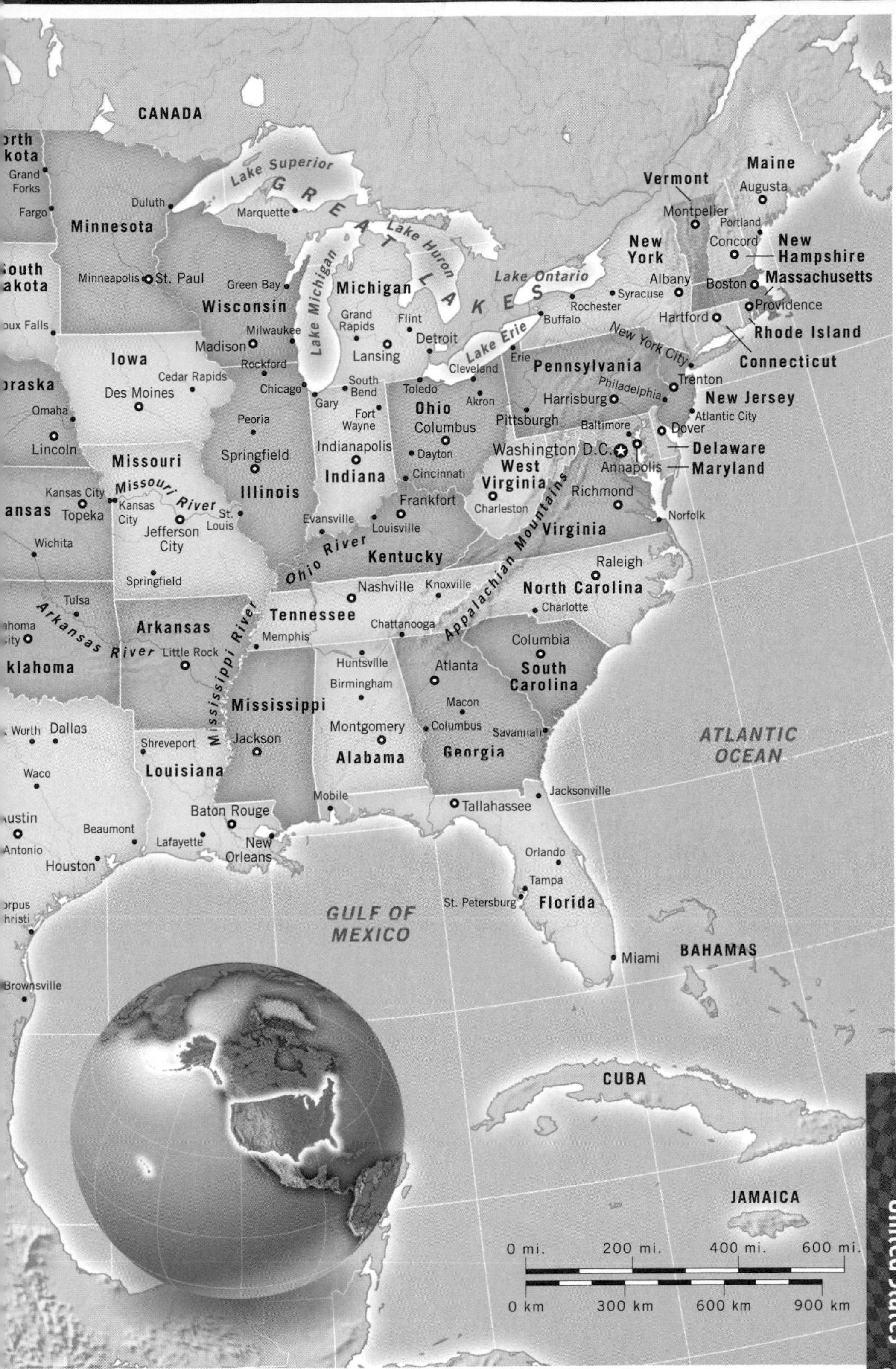

CANADA

NORTH DAKOTA
Grand Forks
Fargo

Lake Superior
Duluth
Marquette

G R E A T

Lake Huron

Lake Ontario

MAINE
Augusta

VERMONT
Montpelier
Portland

Minnesota

SOUTH DAKOTA
Sioux Falls

Minneapolis • St. Paul

Green Bay

Wisconsin

Grand Rapids

Flint

MICHIGAN

Lake Michigan

L A K E S

Concord

NEW HAMPSHIRE

NEW YORK
Albany

Boston

MASSACHUSETTS

Syracuse

Rochester

Providence

NEBRASKA
Omaha
Lincoln

Madison
Milwaukee

Rockford

IOWA
Des Moines

Cedar Rapids

Chicago

Peoria

Lansing

South Bend

Gary

Fort Wayne

Detroit

Lake Erie

Cleveland

Erie

Toledo

Akron

OHIO

Columbus

Buffalo

New York City

Hartford

RHODE ISLAND

CONNECTICUT

Trenton

PENNSYLVANIA

Harrisburg

Philadelphia

NEW JERSEY

Atlantic City

MISSOURI

Springfield

Indianapolis

Dayton

INDIANA

Cincinnati

Pittsburgh

Baltimore

Dover

DELAWARE

Washington D.C.

Annapolis

MARYLAND

KANSAS
Kansas City
Topeka

Missouri River

Kansas City

St. Louis

Jefferson City

ILLINOIS

Evansville

Frankfort

Louisville

WEST VIRGINIA

Richmond

Charleston

VIRGINIA

Norfolk

Springfield

Ohio River

KENTUCKY

Nashville

Knoxville

Raleigh

Wichita

Appalachian Mountains

NORTH CAROLINA

Charlotte

OKLAHOMA
Oklahoma City

Arkansas River

ARKANSAS

TENNESSEE

Chattanooga

Little Rock

Memphis

Columbia

SOUTH CAROLINA

Tulsa

Huntsville

Atlanta

Fort Worth
Dallas

Waco

Mississippi River

Shreveport

MISSISSIPPI

Jackson

Birmingham

Montgomery

ALABAMA

Macon

Columbus

GEORGIA

Savannah

ATLANTIC OCEAN

Austin
San Antonio
Houston

Beaumont

Lafayette

LOUISIANA

Baton Rouge

New Orleans

Mobile

Tallahassee

Jacksonville

Corpus Christi

GULF OF MEXICO

Orlando

Tampa

St. Petersburg

FLORIDA

BAHAMAS

Brownsville

Miami

CUBA

JAMAICA

0 mi.   200 mi.   400 mi.   600 mi.

0 km   300 km   600 km   900 km

ALABAMA

→ CAPITAL: **Montgomery**
→ LARGEST CITY: **Birmingham**
→ ABBREVIATION: **Ala.**
→ POSTAL CODE: **AL**

ORIGIN OF NAME: May come from a Choctaw word meaning "thicket-clearers"

ENTERED UNION (RANK): December 14, 1819 (22)

MOTTO: *Audemus jura nostra defendere* (We dare defend our rights)

TREE: Southern longleaf pine

FLOWER: Camellia

BIRD: Yellowhammer (yellow-shafted flicker)

OTHER: Dance: square dance; nut: pecan

SONG: "Alabama"

NICKNAME: Yellowhammer State

RESIDENTS: Alabamian, Alabaman

LAND AREA: 50,750 square miles (131,443 sq km)

POPULATION (2006): 4,599,030

HOME OF: George Washington Carver, who discovered more than 300 uses for peanuts

DiD YOU KNOW?
The Confederacy was founded in Montgomery in 1861.

ALASKA

→ CAPITAL: **Juneau**
→ LARGEST CITY: **Anchorage**
→ ABBREVIATION: **Alaska**
→ POSTAL CODE: **AK**

ORIGIN OF NAME: From an Aleut word meaning "great land" or "that which the sea breaks against"

ENTERED UNION (RANK): January 3, 1959 (49)

MOTTO: North to the future

TREE: Sitka spruce

FLOWER: Forget-me-not

BIRD: Willow ptarmigan

OTHER: Sport: dog mushing

SONG: "Alaska's Flag"

NICKNAMES: The Last Frontier and Land of the Midnight Sun

RESIDENTS: Alaskan

LAND AREA: 570,374 square miles (1,477,267 sq km)

POPULATION (2006): 670,053

HOME OF: The longest coastline in the U.S., 6,640 miles, which is greater than that of all other states combined

Anchorage

Juneau

DiD YOU KNOW?
When it was purchased for about 2¢ an acre in 1867, Alaska was called "Seward's Folly."

ARIZONA

→ **CAPITAL:** Phoenix
→ **LARGEST CITY:** Phoenix
→ **ABBREVIATION:** Ariz.
→ **POSTAL CODE:** AZ

Phoenix

ORIGIN OF NAME: From the Native American *Arizonac,* meaning "little spring"
ENTERED UNION (RANK): February 14, 1912 (48)
MOTTO: *Ditat deus* (God enriches)

TREE: Palo verde
FLOWER: Flower of saguaro cactus
BIRD: Cactus wren
OTHER: Gemstone: turquoise; neckwear: bolo tie
SONG: "Arizona"
NICKNAME: Grand Canyon State
RESIDENTS: Arizonan, Arizonian
LAND AREA: 113,642 square miles (296,400 sq km)
POPULATION (2006): 6,166,318
HOME OF: The most telescopes in the world, in Tucson

DiD YOU KNOW?
London Bridge was shipped to Lake Havasu City and rebuilt there stone by stone.

ARKANSAS

→ **CAPITAL:** Little Rock
→ **LARGEST CITY:** Little Rock
→ **ABBREVIATION:** Ark.
→ **POSTAL CODE:** AR

Little Rock

ORIGIN OF NAME: From the Quapaw Indians
ENTERED UNION (RANK): June 15, 1836 (25)
MOTTO: *Regnat populus* (The people rule)

TREE: Pine
FLOWER: Apple blossom
BIRD: Mockingbird
OTHER: Fruit and vegetable: pink tomato; insect: honeybee
SONG: "Arkansas"
NICKNAME: Natural State
RESIDENTS: Arkansan
LAND AREA: 52,075 square miles (134,874 sq km)
POPULATION (2006): 2,810,872
HOME OF: The only active diamond mine in the U.S.

DiD YOU KNOW?
Arkansas's Hattie Caraway was the first woman elected to the U.S. Senate.

CALIFORNIA

→ **CAPITAL:** Sacramento
→ **LARGEST CITY:** Los Angeles
→ **ABBREVIATION:** Calif.
→ **POSTAL CODE:** CA

CALIFORNIA REPUBLIC

ORIGIN OF NAME: From a book, *Las Sergas de Esplandián,* by Garcia Ordóñez de Montalvo, circa 1500

ENTERED UNION (RANK): September 9, 1850 (31)

MOTTO: *Eureka* (I have found it)

TREE: California redwood

FLOWER: Golden poppy

BIRD: California valley quail

OTHER: Dance: West Coast swing; prehistoric artifact: chipped-stone bear

SONG: "I Love You, California"

NICKNAME: Golden State

RESIDENTS: Californian

LAND AREA: 155,973 square miles (403,970 sq km)

POPULATION (2006): 336,457,549

HOME OF: General Sherman, a 2,500-year-old sequoia

Sacramento

Los Angeles

DiD YOU KNOW?
More immigrants settle in California than in any other state.

COLORADO

→ **CAPITAL:** Denver
→ **LARGEST CITY:** Denver
→ **ABBREVIATION:** Colo.
→ **POSTAL CODE:** CO

ORIGIN OF NAME: From the Spanish, "ruddy" or "red"

ENTERED UNION (RANK): August 1, 1876 (38)

MOTTO: *Nil sine numine* (Nothing without providence)

TREE: Colorado blue spruce

FLOWER: Rocky Mountain columbine

BIRD: Lark bunting

OTHER: Fossil: *Stegosaurus;* gemstone: aquamarine

SONG: "Where the Columbines Grow"

NICKNAME: Centennial State

RESIDENTS: Coloradan, Coloradoan

LAND AREA: 103,730 square miles (268,660 sq km)

POPULATION (2006): 4,753,377

HOME OF: The world's largest silver nugget (1,840 pounds), found in 1894 near Aspen

Denver

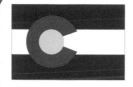

DiD YOU KNOW?
There are 54 peaks in the Rocky Mountains that rise above 14,000 feet.

CONNECTICUT

→ **CAPITAL:** Hartford
→ **LARGEST CITY:** Bridgeport
→ **ABBREVIATION:** Conn.
→ **POSTAL CODE:** CT

ORIGIN OF NAME: From the Mohegan Indian word *Quinnehtukqut,* meaning "beside the long tidal river"

ENTERED UNION (RANK): January 9, 1788 (5)

MOTTO: *Qui transtulit sustinet*
(He who transplanted still sustains)

TREE: White oak

FLOWER: Mountain laurel

BIRD: American robin

OTHER: Hero: Nathan Hale; heroine: Prudence Crandall

SONG: "Yankee Doodle"

NICKNAME: Constitution State or Nutmeg State

RESIDENTS: Nutmegger

LAND AREA: 4,845 square miles (12,550 sq km)

POPULATION (2006): 3,504,809

HOME OF: The first American cookbook—*American Cookery* by Amelia Simmons—published in Hartford in 1796

Hartford
Bridgeport

DID YOU KNOW?
The U.S. Constitution was modeled after Connecticut's colonial laws.

DELAWARE

→ **CAPITAL:** Dover
→ **LARGEST CITY:** Wilmington
→ **ABBREVIATION:** Del.
→ **POSTAL CODE:** DE

DECEMBER 7, 1787

ORIGIN OF NAME: From Delaware River and Bay, named for Sir Thomas West, Baron De La Warr

ENTERED UNION (RANK):
December 7, 1787 (1)

MOTTO: Liberty and independence

TREE: American holly

FLOWER: Peach blossom

BIRD: Blue hen chicken

OTHER: Colors: colonial blue and buff; insect: ladybug

SONG: "Our Delaware"

NICKNAMES: Diamond State, First State and Small Wonder

RESIDENTS: Delawarean

LAND AREA: 1,955 square miles (5,153 sq km)

POPULATION (2006): 853,476

HOME OF: The first log cabins in North America, built in 1683 by Swedish immigrants

Wilmington
Dover

DID YOU KNOW?
Delaware was the first of the original 13 colonies to ratify the U.S. Constitution.

United States

213

FLORIDA

Tallahassee

Jacksonville

ORIGIN OF NAME:
From the Spanish,
meaning "feast of flowers"

ENTERED UNION (RANK): March 3, 1845 (27)

MOTTO: In God we trust

TREE: Sabal palm

FLOWER: Orange blossom

BIRD: Mockingbird

OTHER: Shell: horse conch;
soil: Myakka fine sand

SONG: "The Sewanee River"

NICKNAME: Sunshine State

RESIDENTS: Floridian, Floridan

LAND AREA: 54,153 square miles (140,256 sq km)

POPULATION (2006): 18,089,888

HOME OF: U.S. spacecraft launchings from Cape Canaveral, formerly Cape Kennedy

**DiD YOU
KNOW?**
There are two rivers in
Florida with the name
Withlacoochee.

GEORGIA

ORIGIN OF NAME: In honor
of George II of England

ENTERED UNION (RANK):
January 2, 1788 (4)

MOTTO: Wisdom, justice
and moderation

TREE: Live oak

FLOWER: Cherokee rose

BIRD: Brown thrasher

OTHER: Crop: peanut; fossil:
shark tooth

SONG: "Georgia on My Mind"

NICKNAMES: Peach State and
Empire State of the South

RESIDENTS: Georgian

LAND AREA: 57,919 square miles (150,010 sq km)

POPULATION (2006): 9,363,941

HOME OF: One of the world's largest college campuses,
Berry College, in Rome

★ Atlanta

DiD YOU KNOW?
During the Civil War,
Atlanta was burned and
nearly destroyed by
Union troops.

HAWAII

Honolulu

ORIGIN OF NAME: Probably from a Polynesian word meaning "ancestral home"

ENTERED UNION (RANK): August 21, 1959 (50)

MOTTO: *Ua mau ke ea o ka aina i ka pono* (The life of the land is perpetuated in righteousness)

TREE: Kukui (candlenut)

FLOWER: Yellow hibiscus

BIRD: Nene (Hawaiian goose)

OTHER: Gem: black coral; marine mammal: humpback whale

SONG: "Hawaii Ponoi"

NICKNAME: Aloha State

RESIDENTS: Hawaiian

LAND AREA: 6,423 square miles (16,637 sq km)

POPULATION (2006): 1,285,498

HOME OF: The only royal palace in the U.S. (Iolani)

DID YOU KNOW?
Hawaii was formed by undersea volcanoes.

IDAHO

ORIGIN OF NAME: Although popularly believed to be a Native American word, it is an invented name whose meaning is unknown.

ENTERED UNION (RANK): July 3, 1890 (43)

MOTTO: *Esto perpetua* (It is forever)

TREE: White pine

FLOWER: Lilac

BIRD: Mountain bluebird

OTHER: Fish: cutthroat trout; horse: Appaloosa

SONG: "Here We Have Idaho"

NICKNAME: Gem State

RESIDENTS: Idahoan

LAND AREA: 82,751 square miles (214,325 sq km)

POPULATION (2006): 1,466,465

HOME OF: The longest Main Street in America, 33 miles, in Island Park

DID YOU KNOW?
Idaho produces about 25% of the country's potato crop.

Boise

United States

ILLINOIS

→ **CAPITAL:** Springfield
→ **LARGEST CITY:** Chicago
→ **ABBREVIATION:** Ill.
→ **POSTAL CODE:** IL

ILLINOIS

ORIGIN OF NAME: Algonquian for "tribe of superior men"
ENTERED UNION (RANK): December 3, 1818 (21)
MOTTO: State sovereignty, national union

TREE: White oak
FLOWER: Violet
BIRD: Cardinal
OTHER: Animal: white-tailed deer; prairie grass: big bluestem
SONG: "Illinois"
NICKNAME: Prairie State
RESIDENTS: Illinoisan
LAND AREA: 55,593 square miles (143,987 sq km)
POPULATION (2006): 12,831,970
HOME OF: The tallest building in the country, the Sears Tower, in Chicago

DiD YOU KNOW?
The country's first skyscraper was built in Chicago in 1885.

INDIANA

→ **CAPITAL:** Indianapolis
→ **LARGEST CITY:** Indianapolis
→ **ABBREVIATION:** Ind.
→ **POSTAL CODE:** IN

ORIGIN OF NAME: Means "land of Indians"
ENTERED UNION (RANK): December 11, 1816 (19)
MOTTO: The crossroads of America
TREE: Tulip tree

FLOWER: Peony
BIRD: Cardinal
OTHER: River: Wabash; stone: limestone
SONG: "On the Banks of the Wabash, Far Away"
NICKNAME: Hoosier State
RESIDENTS: Indianan, Indianian
LAND AREA: 35,870 sq miles (92,904 sq km)
POPULATION (2006): 6,313,520
HOME OF: The famous car race, the Indianapolis 500

DiD YOU KNOW?
Wabash, Indiana, was the first U.S. city to be lighted by electricity.

IOWA

ORIGIN OF NAME: Probably from an Indian word meaning "this is the place"

ENTERED UNION (RANK): December 28, 1846 (29)

MOTTO: Our liberties we prize and our rights we will maintain

TREE: Oak

FLOWER: Wild rose

BIRD: Eastern goldfinch

OTHER: Fossil: crinoid; rock: geode

SONG: "Song of Iowa"

NICKNAME: Hawkeye State

RESIDENTS: Iowan

LAND AREA: 55,875 square miles (144,716 sq km)

POPULATION (2006): 2,982,085

HOME OF: The shortest and steepest railroad in the U.S., in Dubuque: 296 feet long, 60° incline

Des Moines ★

DID YOU KNOW?
The Eskimo Pie, the first chocolate-covered ice-cream bar, was invented in Onawa in 1921.

KANSAS

ORIGIN OF NAME: From a Sioux word meaning "people of the south wind"

ENTERED UNION (RANK): January 29, 1861 (34)

MOTTO: *Ad astra per aspera* (To the stars through difficulties)

TREE: Cottonwood

FLOWER: Sunflower

BIRD: Western meadowlark

OTHER: Animal: buffalo; reptile: ornate box turtle

SONG: "Home on the Range"

NICKNAMES: Sunflower State and Jayhawk State

RESIDENTS: Kansan

LAND AREA: 81,823 square miles (211,922 sq km)

POPULATION (2006): 2,764,075

HOME OF: Helium, discovered by scientists in 1905 at the University of Kansas

Topeka ★

● Wichita

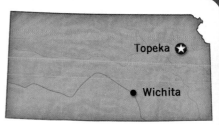

DID YOU KNOW?
The world's largest ball of twine is in Cawker City.

United States

217

→ **CAPITAL: Frankfort**
→ **LARGEST CITY: Louisville**
→ **ABBREVIATION: Ky.**
→ **POSTAL CODE: KY**

ORIGIN OF NAME: From an Iroquoian word (*Kentahten*) meaning "land of tomorrow"

ENTERED UNION (RANK): June 1, 1792 (15)

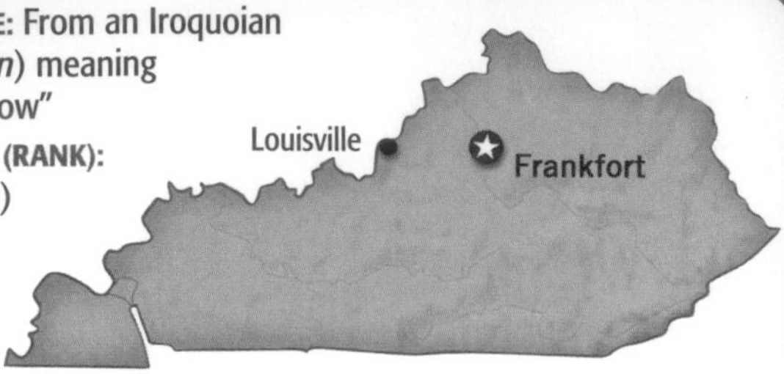

MOTTO: United we stand, divided we fall

TREE: Tulip poplar

FLOWER: Goldenrod

BIRD: Kentucky cardinal

OTHER: Bluegrass song: "Blue Moon of Kentucky"; horse: thoroughbred

SONG: "My Old Kentucky Home"

NICKNAME: Bluegrass State

RESIDENTS: Kentuckian

LAND AREA: 39,732 square miles (102,907 sq km)

POPULATION (2006): 4,206,074

HOME OF: The largest underground cave in the world, the Mammoth-Flint Cave system, over 300 miles long

Louisville ⭐ Frankfort

DID YOU KNOW?
"Happy Birthday to You" was written by two Louisville teachers.

→ **CAPITAL: Baton Rouge**
→ **LARGEST CITY: New Orleans**
→ **ABBREVIATION: La.**
→ **POSTAL CODE: LA**

ORIGIN OF NAME: In honor of Louis XIV of France

ENTERED UNION (RANK): April 30, 1812 (18)

MOTTO: Union, justice and confidence

TREE: Bald cypress

FLOWER: Magnolia

BIRD: Eastern brown pelican

OTHER: Crustacean: crawfish; dog: Catahoula leopard hound

SONGS: "Give Me Louisiana" and "You Are My Sunshine"

NICKNAME: Pelican State

RESIDENTS: Louisianan, Louisianian

LAND AREA: 43,566 square miles (112,836 sq km)

POPULATION (2006): 4,287,768

HOME OF: About 98% of the world's crawfish

New Orleans

Baton Rouge ⭐

DID YOU KNOW?
Tourists have been flocking to New Orleans for Mardi Gras since 1838.

MAINE

ORIGIN OF NAME: First used to distinguish the mainland from the coastal islands

ENTERED UNION (RANK): March 15, 1820 (23)

MOTTO: *Dirigo* (I lead)

TREE: White pine

FLOWER: White pine cone and tassel

BIRD: Chickadee

OTHER: Animal: moose; cat: Maine coon cat

SONG: "State of Maine Song"

NICKNAME: Pine Tree State

RESIDENTS: Mainer

LAND AREA: 30,865 square miles (79,939 sq km)

POPULATION (2006): 1,321,574

HOME OF: The most easterly point in the U.S., West Quoddy Head

Augusta

Portland

DID YOU KNOW?

Maine is the world's largest producer of blueberries.

MARYLAND

ORIGIN OF NAME: In honor of Henrietta Maria (Queen of Charles I of England)

ENTERED UNION (RANK): April 28, 1788 (7)

MOTTO: *Fatti maschii, parole femine* (Manly deeds, womanly words)

TREE: White oak

FLOWER: Black-eyed Susan

BIRD: Baltimore oriole

OTHER: Crustacean: Maryland blue crab; sport: jousting

SONG: "Maryland! My Maryland!"

NICKNAMES: Free State and Old Line State

RESIDENTS: Marylander

LAND AREA: 9,775 square miles (25,316 sq km)

POPULATION (2006): 5,615,727

HOME OF: The first umbrella factory in the U.S., opened in 1828, in Baltimore

Baltimore

Annapolis

DID YOU KNOW?

During the Civil War, Maryland was a slave state but part of the Union.

MASSACHUSETTS

→ **CAPITAL:** Boston
→ **LARGEST CITY:** Boston
→ **ABBREVIATION:** Mass.
→ **POSTAL CODE:** MA

Boston ⭐

ORIGIN OF NAME: From the Massachusett Indian tribe, meaning "at or about the great hill"

ENTERED UNION (RANK): February 6, 1788 (6)

MOTTO: *Ense petit placidam sub libertate quietem* (By the sword we seek peace, but peace only under liberty)

TREE: American elm

FLOWER: Mayflower

BIRD: Chickadee

OTHER: Beverage: cranberry juice; dessert: Boston cream pie

SONG: "All Hail to Massachusetts"

NICKNAMES: Bay State and Old Colony State

RESIDENTS: Bay Stater

LAND AREA: 7,838 square miles (20,300 sq km)

POPULATION (2006): 6,437,193

HOME OF: The first World Series, played between the Boston Pilgrims and the Pittsburgh Pirates in 1903

DID YOU KNOW?
The first basketball game was played in Springfield, Massachusetts, in 1891.

MICHIGAN

→ **CAPITAL:** Lansing
→ **LARGEST CITY:** Detroit
→ **ABBREVIATION:** Mich.
→ **POSTAL CODE:** MI

ORIGIN OF NAME: From an Indian word (*Michigana*) meaning "great or large lake"

ENTERED UNION (RANK): January 26, 1837 (26)

MOTTO: *Si quaeris peninsulam amoenam circumspice* (If you seek a pleasant peninsula, look around you)

TREE: White pine

FLOWER: Apple blossom

BIRD: Robin

OTHER: Reptile: painted turtle; wildflower: dwarf lake iris

SONG: "Michigan, My Michigan"

NICKNAME: Wolverine State

RESIDENTS: Michigander, Michiganian

LAND AREA: 56,809 square miles (147,135 sq km)

POPULATION (2006): 10,095,643

HOME OF: Battle Creek, "Cereal City," maker of most of the breakfast cereal in the U.S.

Lansing ⭐

Detroit

DID YOU KNOW?
Michigan is the country's top producer of automobiles and auto parts.

MINNESOTA

→ **CAPITAL:** St. Paul
→ **LARGEST CITY:** Minneapolis
→ **ABBREVIATION:** Minn.
→ **POSTAL CODE:** MN

ORIGIN OF NAME: From a Dakota Indian word meaning "sky-tinted water"

ENTERED UNION (RANK): May 11, 1858 (32)

MOTTO: *L'Étoile du nord* (The north star)

TREE: Red (or Norway) pine

FLOWER: Lady slipper

BIRD: Common loon

OTHER: Drink: milk; mushroom: morel

SONG: "Hail Minnesota"

NICKNAMES: North Star State, Gopher State and Land of 10,000 Lakes

RESIDENTS: Minnesotan

LAND AREA: 79,617 square miles (206,207 sq km)

POPULATION (2006): 5,167,101

HOME OF: One of the world's oldest rocks, 3.8 billion years old

Minneapolis
St. Paul

DiD YOU KNOW?
Although it's called "Land of 10,000 Lakes," Minnesota has more than 15,000 lakes.

MISSISSIPPI

→ **CAPITAL:** Jackson
→ **LARGEST CITY:** Jackson
→ **ABBREVIATION:** Miss.
→ **POSTAL CODE:** MS

ORIGIN OF NAME: From an Indian word meaning "Father of Waters"

ENTERED UNION (RANK): December 10, 1817 (20)

MOTTO: *Virtute et armis* (By valor and arms)

TREE: Magnolia

FLOWER: Magnolia

BIRD: Mockingbird

OTHER: Stone: petrified wood; water mammal: bottlenose dolphin

SONG: "Go, Mississippi"

NICKNAME: Magnolia State

RESIDENTS: Mississippian

LAND AREA: 46,914 square miles (121,506 sq km)

POPULATION (2006): 2,910,540

HOME OF: Coca-Cola, first bottled in 1894 in Vicksburg

Jackson

DiD YOU KNOW?
Hernando de Soto explored the Mississippi River in 1540.

United States

221

MISSOURI

→ CAPITAL: **Jefferson City**
→ LARGEST CITY: **Kansas City**
→ ABBREVIATION: **Mo.**
→ POSTAL CODE: **MO**

ORIGIN OF NAME: Named after the Missouri Indian tribe; means "town of the large canoes"

ENTERED UNION (RANK): August 10, 1821 (24)

MOTTO: *Salus populi suprema lex esto* (The welfare of the people shall be the supreme law)

TREE: Flowering dogwood

FLOWER: Hawthorn

BIRD: Bluebird

OTHER: Musical instrument: fiddle; tree nut: eastern black walnut

SONG: "Missouri Waltz"

NICKNAME: Show-Me State

RESIDENTS: Missourian

LAND AREA: 68,898 square miles (178,446 sq km)

POPULATION (2006): 5,842,713

HOME OF: Mark Twain and some of his characters, such as Tom Sawyer and Huckleberry Finn

DiD YOU KNOW?
The strongest earthquake in U.S. history was centered in New Madrid in 1811.

MONTANA

→ CAPITAL: **Helena**
→ LARGEST CITY: **Billings**
→ ABBREVIATION: **Mont.**
→ POSTAL CODE: **MT**

ORIGIN OF NAME: The Latin form of a Spanish word meaning "mountainous"

ENTERED UNION (RANK): November 8, 1889 (41)

MOTTO: *Oro y plata* (Gold and silver)

TREE: Ponderosa pine

FLOWER: Bitterroot

BIRD: Western meadowlark

OTHER: Animal: grizzly bear; stones: sapphire and agate

SONG: "Montana"

NICKNAME: Treasure State

RESIDENTS: Montanan

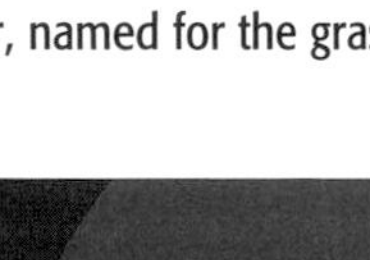

LAND AREA: 145,556 square miles (376,991 sq km)

POPULATION (2006): 944,632

HOME OF: Grasshopper Glacier, named for the grasshoppers that can be seen frozen in ice

DiD YOU KNOW?
Glacier National Park has 60 glaciers, 200 lakes and countless streams.

NEBRASKA

ORIGIN OF NAME: From an Oto Indian word meaning "flat water"

ENTERED UNION (RANK): March 1, 1867 (37)

MOTTO: Equality before the law

TREE: Cottonwood

FLOWER: Goldenrod

BIRD: Western meadowlark

OTHER: Ballad: "A Place Like Nebraska"; soft drink: Kool-Aid

SONG: "Beautiful Nebraska"

NICKNAMES: Cornhusker State and Beef State

RESIDENTS: Nebraskan

LAND AREA: 76,878 square miles (199,113 sq km)

POPULATION (2006): 1,768,331

HOME OF: The only roller-skating museum in the world, in Lincoln

Omaha
Lincoln ★

DID YOU KNOW?
A favorite summer drink, Kool-Aid, was invented in Hastings.

NEVADA

ORIGIN OF NAME: From the Spanish, "snowcapped"

ENTERED UNION (RANK): October 31, 1864 (36)

MOTTO: All for our country

TREES: Single-leaf piñon and bristlecone pine

FLOWER: Sagebrush

BIRD: Mountain bluebird

OTHER: Metal: silver; reptile: desert tortoise

SONG: "Home Means Nevada"

NICKNAMES: Sagebrush State, Silver State and Battle Born State

RESIDENTS: Nevadan, Nevadian

LAND AREA: 109,806 square miles (284,397 sq km)

POPULATION (2006): 2,495,529

HOME OF: The Devil's Hole pupfish, found only in Devil's Hole, an underground pool near Death Valley

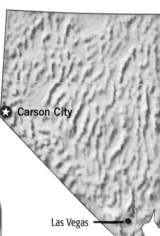

★ Carson City

Las Vegas ●

DID YOU KNOW?
Nevada is the driest state in the country, with about seven inches of rainfall each year.

NEW HAMPSHIRE

→ **CAPITAL: Concord**
→ **LARGEST CITY: Manchester**
→ **ABBREVIATION: N.H.**
→ **POSTAL CODE: NH**

ORIGIN OF NAME: From the English county of Hampshire
ENTERED UNION (RANK): June 21, 1788 (9)
MOTTO: Live free or die
TREE: White birch
FLOWER: Purple lilac
BIRD: Purple finch
OTHER: Amphibian: spotted newt; sport: skiing
SONGS: "Old New Hampshire" and "New Hampshire, My New Hampshire"
NICKNAME: Granite State
RESIDENTS: New Hampshirite
LAND AREA: 8,969 square miles (23,231 sq km)
POPULATION (2006): 1,314,895
HOME OF: Artificial rain, first used near Concord in 1947 to fight a forest fire

Concord
Manchester

DiD YOU KNOW?
The world's highest wind speed, 231 m.p.h., was recorded on top of Mount Washington.

NEW JERSEY

→ **CAPITAL: Trenton**
→ **LARGEST CITY: Newark**
→ **ABBREVIATION: N.J.**
→ **POSTAL CODE: NJ**

ORIGIN OF NAME: From the Isle of Jersey in the English Channel
ENTERED UNION (RANK): December 18, 1787 (3)
MOTTO: Liberty and prosperity
TREE: Red oak
FLOWER: Purple violet
BIRD: Eastern goldfinch
OTHER: Folk dance: square dance; shell: knobbed whelk
SONG: "I'm from New Jersey"
NICKNAME: Garden State
RESIDENTS: New Jerseyite, New Jerseyan
LAND AREA: 7,419 square miles (19,215 sq km)
POPULATION (2006): 8,724,560
HOME OF: The world's first drive-in movie theater, built in 1933 near Camden

Newark
Trenton

DiD YOU KNOW?
The street names in the game Monopoly were named after streets in Atlantic City.

NEW MEXICO

→ **CAPITAL:** Santa Fe
→ **LARGEST CITY:** Albuquerque
→ **ABBREVIATION:** N.M.
→ **POSTAL CODE:** NM

ORIGIN OF NAME: From Mexico

ENTERED UNION (RANK): January 6, 1912 (47)

MOTTO: *Crescit eundo* (It grows as it goes)

TREE: Piñon

FLOWER: Yucca

BIRD: Roadrunner

OTHER: Cookie: biscochito; vegetables: chilies and beans

SONG: "O Fair New Mexico"

NICKNAME: Land of Enchantment

RESIDENTS: New Mexican

LAND AREA: 121,365 square miles (314,334 sq km)

POPULATION (2006): 1,954,599

HOME OF: Smokey Bear, a cub orphaned by fire in 1950, buried in Smokey Bear Historical State Park in 1976

Santa Fe
Albuquerque

DiD YOU KNOW?
Each night thousands of bats swarm out of Carlsbad Caverns to eat insects.

NEW YORK

→ **CAPITAL:** Albany
→ **LARGEST CITY:** New York
→ **ABBREVIATION:** N.Y.
→ **POSTAL CODE:** NY

ORIGIN OF NAME: In honor of the Duke of York

ENTERED UNION (RANK): July 26, 1788 (11)

MOTTO: *Excelsior* (Ever upward)

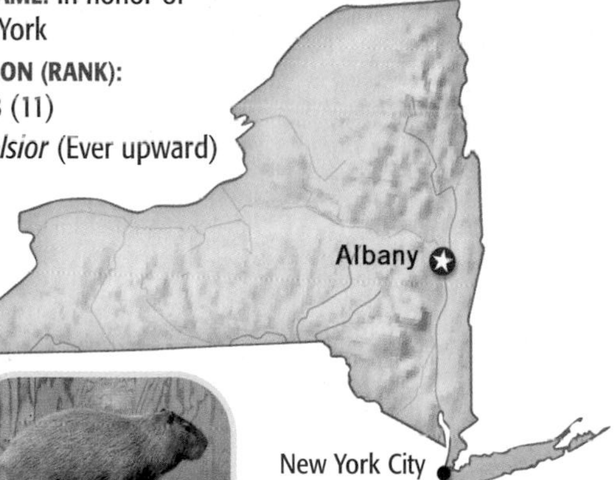

TREE: Sugar maple

FLOWER: Rose

BIRD: Bluebird

OTHER: Animal: beaver; muffin: apple

SONG: "I Love New York"

NICKNAME: Empire State

RESIDENTS: New Yorker

LAND AREA: 47,224 square miles (122,310 sq km)

POPULATION (2006): 19,306,183

HOME OF: The first presidential inauguration. George Washington took the oath of office in New York City on April 30, 1789.

Albany

New York City

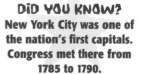

DiD YOU KNOW?
New York City was one of the nation's first capitals. Congress met there from 1785 to 1790.

NORTH CAROLINA

→ **CAPITAL: Raleigh**
→ **LARGEST CITY: Charlotte**
→ **ABBREVIATION: N.C.**
→ **POSTAL CODE: NC**

ORIGIN OF NAME: In honor of Charles I of England
ENTERED UNION (RANK): November 21, 1789 (12)
MOTTO: *Esse quam videri* (To be rather than to seem)
TREE: Pine
FLOWER: Dogwood
BIRD: Cardinal
OTHER: Dog: plott hound; historic boat: shad boat
SONG: "The Old North State"
NICKNAME: Tar Heel State
RESIDENTS: North Carolinian
LAND AREA: 48,718 square miles (126,180 sq km)
POPULATION (2006): 8,856,505
HOME OF: Virginia Dare, the first English child born in America, on Roanoke Island around 1587

DiD YOU KNOW?
Although the state was pro-Union and antislavery, it joined the Confederacy.

NORTH DAKOTA

→ **CAPITAL: Bismarck**
→ **LARGEST CITY: Fargo**
→ **ABBREVIATION: N.D.**
→ **POSTAL CODE: ND**

ORIGIN OF NAME: From the Sioux word, meaning "allies"
ENTERED UNION (RANK): November 2, 1889 (39)
MOTTO: Liberty and union, now and forever: one and inseparable
TREE: American elm
FLOWER: Wild prairie rose
BIRD: Western meadowlark
OTHER: Equine: Nokota horse; grass: western wheatgrass
SONG: "North Dakota Hymn"
NICKNAMES: Sioux State, Flickertail State, Peace Garden State and Rough Rider State
RESIDENTS: North Dakotan
LAND AREA: 70,704 square miles (183,123 sq km)
POPULATION (2006): 635,867
HOME OF: The "World's Largest Buffalo," a 26-foot-high, 60-ton concrete monument

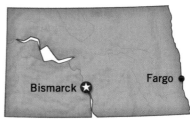

DiD YOU KNOW?
Farms cover more than 90% of North Dakota's land.

226

OHIO

ORIGIN OF NAME: From an Iroquoian word meaning "great river"

ENTERED UNION (RANK): March 1, 1803 (17)

MOTTO: With God all things are possible

TREE: Buckeye

FLOWER: Scarlet carnation

BIRD: Cardinal

OTHER: Beverage: tomato juice; fossil: trilobite

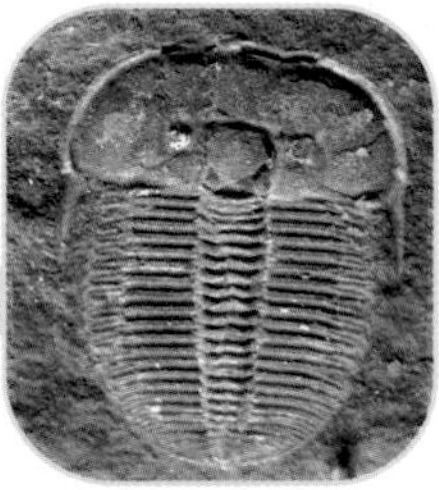

SONG: "Beautiful Ohio"

NICKNAME: Buckeye State

RESIDENTS: Ohioan

LAND AREA: 40,953 square miles (106,067 sq km)

POPULATION (2006): 11,478,006

HOME OF: The first electric traffic lights, invented and installed in Cleveland in 1914

Columbus

DID YOU KNOW?
The world's first professional baseball team was the Cincinnati Reds.

OKLAHOMA

ORIGIN OF NAME: From two Choctaw Indian words meaning "red people"

ENTERED UNION (RANK): November 16, 1907 (46)

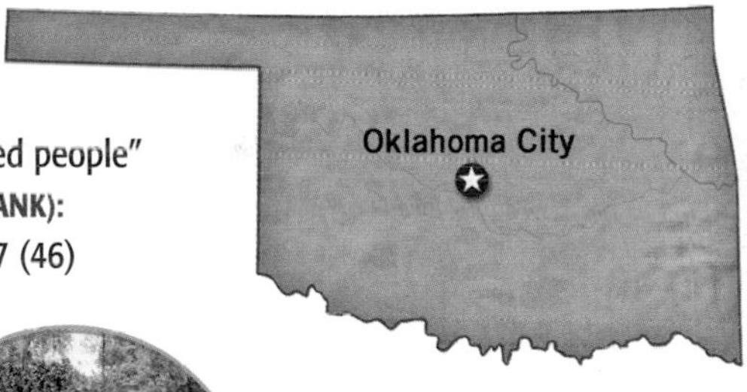

MOTTO: *Labor omnia vincit* (Labor conquers all things)

TREE: Redbud

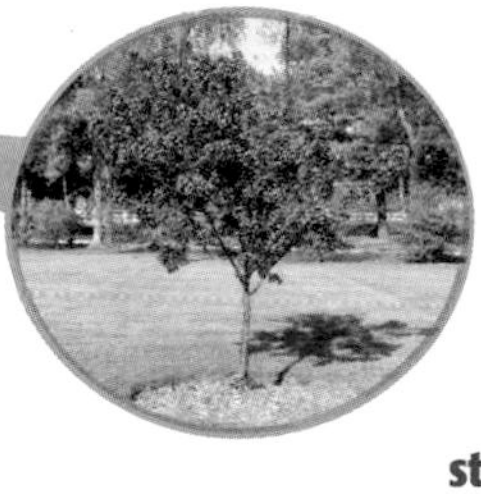

FLOWER: Oklahoma rose

BIRD: Scissor-tailed flycatcher

OTHER: Furbearer: raccoon; waltz: "Oklahoma Wind"

SONG: "Oklahoma!"

NICKNAME: Sooner State

RESIDENTS: Oklahoman

LAND AREA: 68,679 square miles (177,880 sq km)

POPULATION (2006): 3,579,212

HOME OF: The first parking meter, installed in Oklahoma City in 1935

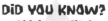

Oklahoma City

DID YOU KNOW?
Oklahoma City's state capitol building is the only capitol in the world with an oil well (it's dry) under it.

OREGON

→ **CAPITAL: Salem**
→ **LARGEST CITY: Portland**
→ **ABBREVIATION: Ore.**
→ **POSTAL CODE: OR**

STATE OF OREGON
1859

Portland

Salem

ORIGIN OF NAME:
Unknown

ENTERED UNION (RANK):
February 14, 1859 (33)

MOTTO: *Alis volat propriis*
(She flies with her own wings)

TREE: Douglas fir

FLOWER: Oregon grape

BIRD: Western meadowlark

OTHER: Fish: Chinook salmon; nut: hazelnut

SONG: "Oregon, My Oregon"

NICKNAME: Beaver State

RESIDENTS: Oregonian

LAND AREA: 96,003 square miles
(248,647 sq km)

POPULATION (2006): 3,700,758

HOME OF: The world's smallest park,
totaling 452 square inches, created in Portland in 1948
for snail races

DID YOU KNOW?
Oregon's state flag is
the only one with designs
on both sides.

PENNSYLVANIA

→ **CAPITAL: Harrisburg**
→ **LARGEST CITY: Philadelphia**
→ **ABBREVIATION: Pa.**
→ **POSTAL CODE: PA**

ORIGIN OF NAME: In honor of Sir William Penn, father of state
founder William Penn.
It means "Penn's
Woodland."

**ENTERED UNION
(RANK):** December
12, 1787 (2)

Harrisburg

Philadelphia

MOTTO: Virtue, liberty and independence

TREE: Hemlock

FLOWER: Mountain laurel

BIRD: Ruffed grouse

OTHER: Dog: Great Dane; insect: firefly

SONG: "Pennsylvania"

NICKNAME: Keystone State

RESIDENTS: Pennsylvanian

LAND AREA: 44,820 square miles (116,083 sq km)

POPULATION (2006): 12,440,621

HOME OF: The first magazine in America, *American Magazine*,
published in Philadelphia for three months in 1741

DID YOU KNOW?
The first baseball
stadium in the U.S.,
Pittsburgh's Forbes Field,
was built in 1909.

RHODE ISLAND

→ CAPITAL: **Providence**
→ LARGEST CITY: **Providence**
→ ABBREVIATION: **R.I.**
→ POSTAL CODE: **RI**

 Providence

ORIGIN OF NAME: From the Greek island of Rhodes
ENTERED UNION (RANK): May 29, 1790 (13)
MOTTO: Hope
TREE: Red maple
FLOWER: Violet
BIRD: Rhode Island Red hen
OTHER: Shellfish: quahog; stone: cumberlandite
SONG: "Rhode Island"
NICKNAME: Ocean State
RESIDENTS: Rhode Islander
LAND AREA: 1,045 square miles (2,706 sq km)
POPULATION (2006): 1,067,610
HOME OF: Rhode Island Red chickens, first bred in 1854; the start of poultry as a major American industry

DiD YOU KNOW?
Rhode Island is the smallest of the 50 U.S. states.

SOUTH CAROLINA

→ CAPITAL: **Columbia**
→ LARGEST CITY: **Columbia**
→ ABBREVIATION: **S.C.**
→ POSTAL CODE: **SC**

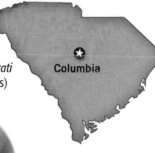
Columbia

ORIGIN OF NAME: In honor of Charles I of England
ENTERED UNION (RANK): May 23, 1788 (8)
MOTTOES: *Animis opibusque parati* (Prepared in mind and resources) and *Dum spiro spero* (While I breathe, I hope)
TREE: Palmetto
FLOWER: Yellow jessamine
BIRD: Carolina wren
OTHER: Hospitality beverage: tea; music: the spiritual
SONG: "Carolina"
NICKNAME: Palmetto State
RESIDENTS: South Carolinian
LAND AREA: 30,111 square miles (77,988 sq km)
POPULATION (2006): 4,321,249
HOME OF: The first tea farm in the U.S., created in 1890 near Summerville

DiD YOU KNOW?
South Carolina was the first state to secede from the Union. The Civil War started here.

United States

229

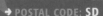

SOUTH DAKOTA

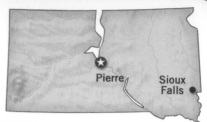

Pierre

Sioux Falls

ORIGIN OF NAME: From the Sioux word, meaning "allies"

ENTERED UNION (RANK): November 2, 1889 (40)

MOTTO: Under God the people rule

TREE: Black hills spruce

FLOWER: American pasqueflower

BIRD: Ring-necked pheasant

OTHER: Dessert: kuchen; jewelry: Black Hills gold

SONG: "Hail! South Dakota"

NICKNAMES: Mount Rushmore State and Coyote State

RESIDENTS: South Dakotan

LAND AREA: 75,898 square miles (196,575 sq km)

POPULATION (2006): 781,919

HOME OF: The world's largest natural indoor warm-water pool, Evans' Plunge, in Hot Springs

DID YOU KNOW?
It took Gutzon Borglum 14 years to carve Mount Rushmore.

TENNESSEE

Nashville

Memphis

ORIGIN OF NAME: Of Cherokee origin; the exact meaning is unknown

ENTERED UNION (RANK): June 1, 1796 (16)

MOTTO: Agriculture and commerce

TREE: Tulip poplar

FLOWER: Iris

BIRD: Mockingbird

OTHER: Amphibian: Tennessee cave salamander; animal: raccoon

SONGS: "Tennessee Waltz," "My Homeland, Tennessee," "When It's Iris Time in Tennessee" and "My Tennessee"

NICKNAME: Volunteer State

RESIDENTS: Tennessean, Tennesseean

LAND AREA: 41,220 square miles (106,759 sq km)

POPULATION (2006): 6,038,803

HOME OF: Graceland, the estate and gravesite of Elvis Presley

DID YOU KNOW?
Nashville, site of the Grand Ole Opry, is considered the country-music capital of the world.

TEXAS

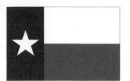

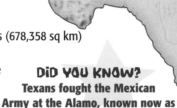

➔ **CAPITAL:** Austin
➔ **LARGEST CITY:** Houston
➔ **ABBREVIATION:** Tex.
➔ **POSTAL CODE:** TX

ORIGIN OF NAME: From a Native American word meaning "friends"
ENTERED UNION (RANK): December 29, 1845 (28)
MOTTO: Friendship

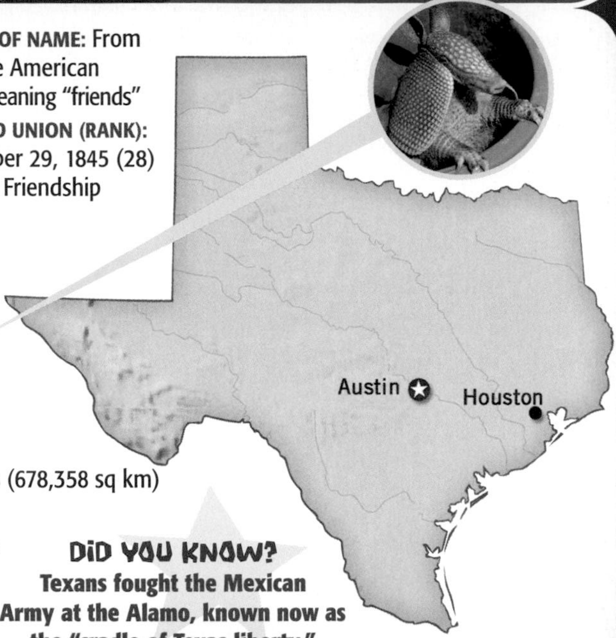

TREE: Pecan
FLOWER: Bluebonnet
BIRD: Mockingbird
OTHER: Fiber and fabric: cotton; small mammal: armadillo
SONG: "Texas, Our Texas"
NICKNAME: Lone Star State
RESIDENTS: Texan
LAND AREA: 261,914 square miles (678,358 sq km)
POPULATION (2006): 23,507,783
HOME OF: NASA, in Houston, the headquarters for all piloted U.S. space projects

DID YOU KNOW?

Texans fought the Mexican Army at the Alamo, known now as the "cradle of Texas liberty."

UTAH

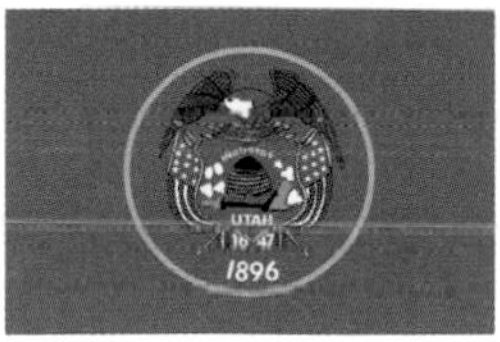

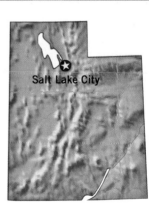

➔ **CAPITAL:** Salt Lake City
➔ **LARGEST CITY:** Salt Lake City
➔ **ABBREVIATION:** Utah
➔ **POSTAL CODE:** UT

ORIGIN OF NAME: From the Ute tribe, meaning "people of the mountains"
ENTERED UNION (RANK): January 4, 1896 (45)
MOTTO: Industry

TREE: Blue spruce
FLOWER: Sego lily
BIRD: California gull
OTHER: Cooking pot: Dutch oven; fruit: cherry
SONG: "Utah, We Love Thee"
NICKNAME: Beehive State
RESIDENTS: Utahn, Utahan
LAND AREA: 82,168 square miles (212,816 sq km)
POPULATION (2006): 2,550,063
HOME OF: Rainbow Bridge, the largest natural stone bridge in the world, 290 feet high, 275 feet across

DID YOU KNOW?

Driving the "golden spike" at Promontory Point in 1869 completed the transcontinental railroad.

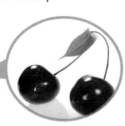

VERMONT

→ **CAPITAL:** Montpelier
→ **LARGEST CITY:** Burlington
→ **ABBREVIATION:** Vt.
→ **POSTAL CODE:** VT

ORIGIN OF NAME: From the French *vert mont,* meaning "green mountain"

ENTERED UNION (RANK): March 4, 1791 (14)

MOTTO: Vermont, freedom and unity

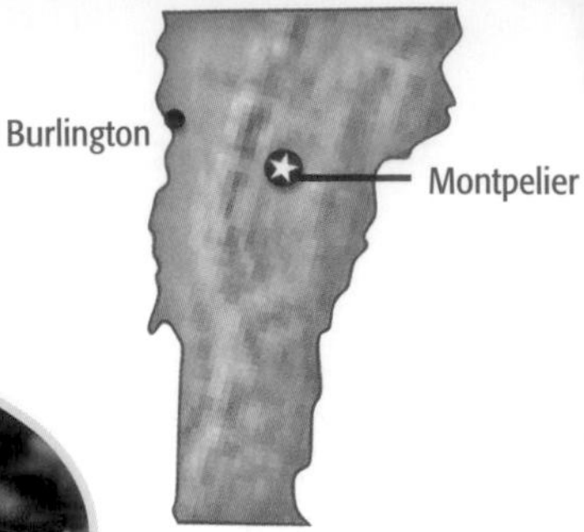

TREE: Sugar maple

FLOWER: Red clover

BIRD: Hermit thrush

OTHER: Animal: Morgan horse; insect: honeybee

SONG: "Hail, Vermont!"

NICKNAME: Green Mountain State

RESIDENTS: Vermonter

LAND AREA: 9,249 square miles (23,956 sq km)

POPULATION (2006): 623,908

HOME OF: The largest production of maple syrup in the U.S.

Burlington

Montpelier

DiD YOU KNOW?
Montpelier, with just over 8,000 residents, is the smallest state capital in the United States.

VIRGINIA

→ **CAPITAL:** Richmond
→ **LARGEST CITY:** Virginia Beach
→ **ABBREVIATION:** Va.
→ **POSTAL CODE:** VA

ORIGIN OF NAME: In honor of Elizabeth I, "Virgin Queen" of England

ENTERED UNION (RANK): June 25, 1788 (10)

MOTTO: *Sic semper tyrannis* (Thus always to tyrants)

TREE: Dogwood

FLOWER: American dogwood

BIRD: Cardinal

OTHER: Dog: American foxhound; shell: oyster shell

SONG: "Carry Me Back to Old Virginny"

NICKNAMES: The Old Dominion and Mother of Presidents

RESIDENTS: Virginian

LAND AREA: 39,598 square miles (102,558 sq km)

POPULATION (2006): 7,642,884

HOME OF: The only full-length statue of George Washington

Richmond

Virginia Beach

DiD YOU KNOW?
Jamestown was the first permanent English settlement in North America.

WASHINGTON

→ CAPITAL: **Olympia**
→ LARGEST CITY: **Seattle**
→ ABBREVIATION: **Wash.**
→ POSTAL CODE: **WA**

ORIGIN OF NAME: In honor of George Washington

ENTERED UNION (RANK): November 11, 1889 (42)

MOTTO: *Al-ki* (Indian word meaning "by and by")

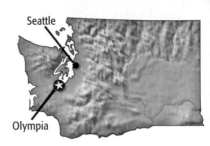

Seattle

Olympia

TREE: Western hemlock
FLOWER: Coast rhododendron
BIRD: Willow goldfinch
OTHER: Fossil: Columbian mammoth; fruit: apple
SONG: "Washington, My Home"
NICKNAME: Evergreen State
RESIDENTS: Washingtonian
LAND AREA: 66,582 square miles (17,447 sq km)
POPULATION (2006): 6,395,798
HOME OF: The Lunar Rover, the vehicle used by astronauts on the Moon in 1971. Boeing, in Seattle, makes aircraft and spacecraft.

DiD YOU KNOW?
The Grand Coulee dam, on the Columbia River, is the largest concrete structure in the U.S.

WEST VIRGINIA

→ CAPITAL: **Charleston**
→ LARGEST CITY: **Charleston**
→ ABBREVIATION: **W.Va.**
→ POSTAL CODE: **WV**

ORIGIN OF NAME: In honor of Elizabeth I, "Virgin Queen" of England

ENTERED UNION (RANK): June 20, 1863 (35)

MOTTO: *Montani semper liberi* (Mountaineers are always free)

Charleston

TREE: Sugar maple
FLOWER: Rhododendron
BIRD: Cardinal
OTHER: Animal: black bear; fruit: golden delicious apple
SONGS: "West Virginia," "My Home Sweet Home," "The West Virginia Hills" and "This Is My West Virginia"
NICKNAME: Mountain State
RESIDENTS: West Virginian
LAND AREA: 24,087 square miles (62,384 sq km)
POPULATION (2006): 1,818,470
HOME OF: Marbles. Most of the country's glass marbles are made around Parkersburg.

DiD YOU KNOW?
Mother's Day was first celebrated in Grafton in 1908.

WISCONSIN

→ CAPITAL: **Madison**
→ LARGEST CITY: **Milwaukee**
→ ABBREVIATION: **Wis.**
→ POSTAL CODE: **WI**

WISCONSIN
1848

Madison
Milwaukee

ORIGIN OF NAME: French corruption of an Indian word whose meaning is disputed
ENTERED UNION (RANK): May 29, 1848 (30)

MOTTO: Forward
TREE: Sugar maple
FLOWER: Wood violet
BIRD: Robin
OTHER: Dance: polka; symbol of peace: mourning dove

SONG: "On, Wisconsin"
NICKNAME: Badger State
RESIDENTS: Wisconsinite
LAND AREA: 54,314 square miles (140,673 sq km)
POPULATION (2006): 5,556,506
HOME OF: The typewriter, invented in Milwaukee in 1867

DiD YOU KNOW?
Wisconsin produced a 17-ton cheddar cheese for the 1964 New York World's Fair.

WYOMING

→ CAPITAL: **Cheyenne**
→ LARGEST CITY: **Cheyenne**
→ ABBREVIATION: **Wyo.**
→ POSTAL CODE: **WY**

Cheyenne

ORIGIN OF NAME: From a Delaware Indian word meaning "mountains and valleys alternating"
ENTERED UNION (RANK): July 10, 1890 (44)
MOTTO: Equal rights

TREE: Cottonwood
FLOWER: Indian paintbrush
BIRD: Meadowlark
OTHER: Dinosaur: *Triceratops;* gemstone: jade

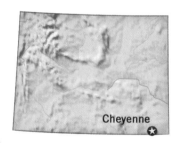

SONG: "Wyoming"
NICKNAME: Equality State
RESIDENTS: Wyomingite
LAND AREA: 97,105 square miles (251,501 sq km)
POPULATION (2006): 515,004
HOME OF: Independence Rock, a huge granite boulder that covers 27 acres and has the names of 5,000 early pioneers carved on it

DiD YOU KNOW?
Wyoming, with just over 500,000 people, ranks 50th in state population.

WASHINGTON, D.C.

THE DISTRICT OF COLUMBIA, which covers the same area as the city of Washington, is the capital of the United States. D.C. history began in 1790 when Congress took charge of organizing a new site for the capital. George Washington chose the spot, midway between the northern and southern states, on the Potomac River. The seat of government was transferred from Philadelphia, Pennsylvania, to Washington, D.C., on December 1, 1800, and President John Adams became the first resident of the White House.

MOTTO: *Justitia omnibus* (Justice to all)

FLOWER: American Beauty rose

TREE: Scarlet oak

LAND AREA: 68.25 square miles (177 sq km)

POPULATION (2006): 581,530

The Capitol

THE COMMONWEALTH OF PUERTO RICO

PUERTO RICO is located in the Caribbean Sea, about 1,000 miles east-southeast of Miami, Florida. A U.S. possession since 1898, it consists of the island of Puerto Rico plus the adjacent islets of Vieques, Culebra and Mona.

Vieques

CAPITAL: San Juan

LAND AREA: 3,459 square miles (8,959 sq km)

POPULATION ESTIMATE (2006): 3,927,776

LANGUAGES: Spanish and English

MOTTO: *Joannes Est Nomen Eius* (John is his name)

TREE: Silk-cotton

FLOWER: Puerto Rican hibiscus

BIRD: Stripe-headed tanager

NATIONAL ANTHEM: "La Borinqueña"

DID YOU KNOW?
The U.S. governs several other territories in addition to Puerto Rico. They include Guam, the Commonwealth of the Northern Mariana Islands, the U.S. Virgin Islands, American Samoa and Wake Island.

FROM TFK MAGAZINE

ADVENTURES AT THE NORTH POLE

TFK asks reporter and author Andrew Revkin about his new book, *The North Pole Was Here*

NORTH POLE AS WAS HERE

Andrew Revkin's love of nature began as a kid in Rhode Island. After graduating from Brown University, Revkin won a traveling fellowship that allowed him to study "man's relationship to the sea." He spent 17 months on a 60-foot sailboat, visiting 15 countries and covering 15,000 miles. In 2003, Revkin traveled with a crew of climate scientists to the sea ice around the North Pole. He wrote, photographed and videotaped on the shifting ice for three days, sending stories and pictures by satellite phone. The experience inspired his latest book, *The North Pole Was Here*.

TFK: You write that you 'never liked the cold much.' What was the average daily temperature during your trip?

Revkin: The air around the North Pole was typically around -15°F.

TFK: What were the hardships that you encountered reporting from the Arctic?

Revkin: Trying to take notes, pictures and video in such conditions was incredibly tough. The ink in pens freezes, so you use pencils. I wore two sets of gloves and had to take off the clunky outer ones to do anything with a camera or notepad. Within about 30 seconds my fingers were stinging. Batteries drained in minutes. Juice boxes and water bottles froze in my pockets.

The endless light made it nearly impossible to sleep. After a couple days, the warmth in the tents made the ice underneath the fabric floor melt, so we were camping on something like a cold water bed.

TFK: Did you see any signs of global warming?

Revkin: Evidence of global warming is not something that you can see in one visit to the Arctic. It only emerges if you study the region year after year and watch for changes that don't appear to be part of the natural cycles of melting and freezing that occur up there. That is what scientists feel they are seeing now.

TFK: You also write that the planet has seen great cycles of ice ages and warm periods. What would you say to those who believe that global warming is not caused by people?

Revkin: It is hard to find a scientist actively studying the climate these days who does not believe that people are contributing to the warming of the planet in ways that pose risks later in this century.

The basics are crystal clear. Certain gases released by burning coal, oil and similar fuels trap heat in the air and make the world warmer than it would otherwise be. If we keep burning those fuels the way we are now, growing economies and populations will guarantee a profound change in the global climate. No climate scientist with any credibility doubts this any more.

TFK: Is there anything that kids can do to slow the rate of warming?

Revkin: One of the most important things that needs to happen, I think, is that kids need to talk to the grownups around them and remind my generation that, right now, we are helping shape their climate in ways that will be nearly impossible to reverse. If you find an adult who doesn't understand the issues, show them books like mine; show them Web sites like realclimate.org, where scientists have posted clear explanations of what's going on; and do something every day to make a difference, even if it's as simple as turning out the lights when you leave a room.

– BY NELLIE GONZALEZ CUTLER

HIGHEST RECORDED TEMPERATURES

PLACE	DATE	°F*	°C**
WORLD:			
El Azizia, Libya	Sept. 13, 1922	136	58
UNITED STATES:			
Death Valley, California	July 10, 1913	134	57

LOWEST RECORDED TEMPERATURES

PLACE	DATE	°F*	°C**
WORLD:			
Vostok, Antarctica	July 21, 1983	−129	−89
UNITED STATES:			
Prospect Creek, Alaska	Jan. 23, 1971	−80	−62

*degrees Fahrenheit **degrees Celsius

GREATEST RAINFALLS IN THE WORLD

DURATION	PLACE	DATE	INCHES
1 minute	Unionville, Maryland	July 4, 1956	1.23
20 minutes	Curtea-de-Arges, Romania	July 7, 1889	8.1
12 hours	Grand Ilet, La Réunion	Jan. 26, 1980	46
24 hours	Foc-Foc, La Réunion	Jan. 7–8, 1966	72
12 months	Cherrapunji, India	Aug. 1860 –Aug. 1861	1,042

GREATEST SNOWFALLS IN THE UNITED STATES

DURATION	PLACE	DATE	INCHES
24 hours	Silver Lake, Colorado	Apr. 14–15, 1921	76
1 month	Tamarack, California	Jan. 1911	390
1 storm	Mt. Shasta Ski Bowl, California	Feb. 13–19, 1959	189
1 season	Mt. Baker, Washington	1998–1999	1,140

→ Droughts

Droughts are unusually long periods of insufficient rainfall that can ruin crops and dry up water supplies.

One of the worst droughts in history occurred in Egypt from 1200 to 1202 B.C. Every year, the flooding of the Nile River left rich soil that the ancient Egyptians used to grow crops. But after a shortage of rain, the Nile didn't rise. People were unable to grow food and began to starve to death. The final death toll was 110,000, from starvation and disease.

Many states in the U.S. experienced drought in the 1930s. About 80% of the population was affected by drought. An enormous Dust Bowl covered about 50 million acres of the Great Plains. During 1934, dry areas stretched from New York to the coast of California.

→ Avalanches

An avalanche is any fast movement of snow, ice, mud or rock down a mountainside or slope. Avalanches can reach speeds of more than 200 miles per hour. They are triggered by such events as earthquake tremors, human-made disturbances or excessive rainfall.

The worst snowslide in U.S. history occurred in 1910 in the Cascade Mountains in Wellington, Washington. Nearly 100 people were trapped when their train became snowbound. An avalanche then swept them to their deaths in a gorge 150 feet below the tracks.

The world's worst avalanche took place in Peru in 1962. About 4,000 people were killed when tons of ice and snow slid down Huascarán Peak in the Andes Mountains.

→ Floods

A flood happens when a body of water rises and overflows onto dry land. Floods are most often caused by heavy rain, melting ice and snow, or a combination of these. In 1889, a dam 74 miles upriver from Johnstown, Pennsylvania, broke after a rainstorm. Approximately 2,000 people were killed in less than an hour.

Weather

Weather Words

Air pressure Air has weight. Air pressure is the weight of the air, or atmosphere, pushing down on Earth. The closer you are to sea level, the greater is the air pressure because there's increasingly more air above you. The higher you are, the lower is the air pressure. Barometers measure air pressure.

Blizzard A major snowstorm with strong winds of 35 m.p.h. or more

Hail Pellets of ice and snow created within clouds that then fall to Earth. Hailstones can sometimes be quite large and can cause major damage.

Humidity The amount of water vapor in the air. Relative humidity is the amount of water in the air compared to the amount of water the air can hold at that temperature. When the relative humidity reaches 100%, the air has reached its dew point. Once the air reaches this point, water vapor turns back into water in the form of rain, snow, clouds or fog.

Hurricane Violent storms in the Atlantic Ocean with strong winds from 40 to 155 m.p.h. (or higher). They are called typhoons in the Pacific.

Sleet Small pellets of ice formed when rain or melted snow freezes while falling

Water cycle The process of water changing from one state to another and water's movement from one place to another. For example, when it rains, water drops fall to Earth. This water evaporates from the surface of Earth and enters the atmosphere as water vapor, which condenses into droplets that form clouds. The droplets grow heavier as they combine and fall to Earth as rain.

Wind chill The wind-chill temperature indicates how cold people feel when the wind blows during cold weather. Wind makes the temperature feel much colder than the thermometer reading.

Did You Know?

Did you ever wonder why we say, "It's raining cats and dogs," when it's raining very heavily? In Norse mythology, the dog is associated with wind and the cat with storms.

What's the Weather?

TEMPERATURE

Air temperature is often measured by a mercury thermometer. When the temperature rises, the mercury expands and rises in the thermometer tube. When the temperature falls, the mercury contracts and falls.

In the U.S., the **Fahrenheit** scale is used most often. On this scale, 32° is the freezing point of water, and 212° is the boiling point.

The **Celsius,** or centigrade, scale is used by the World Meteorological Organization and most countries in the world. On this scale, 0° is freezing, and 100° is boiling.

→ **To convert Fahrenheit to Celsius,** subtract 32, multiply by 5, and divide the result by 9.

EXAMPLE:
To convert 50°F to °C:
50 − 32 = 18;
18 x 5 = 90; 90 ÷ 9 = **10°C**

→ **To convert Celsius to Fahrenheit,** multiply by 9, divide by 5, and add 32.

EXAMPLE:
To convert 10°C to °F:
10 x 9 = 90; 90 ÷ 5 = 18;
18 + 32 = **50°F**

CELSIUS	FAHRENHEIT
−50	−58
−40	−40
−30	−22
−20	−4
−10	14
0	32
5	41
10	50
15	59
20	68
25	77
30	86
35	95
40	104
45	113
50	122

Clouds

Clouds are little drops of water that hang in the atmosphere. A ceilometer measures the height of clouds. When clouds become heavy with humidity, water falls from them. This is called precipitation. In warmer clouds, precipitation falls as rain. In colder clouds, precipitation falls as snow. Thunderstorm clouds can bring another kind of precipitation—hail. Here's a look at the different types of clouds.

CIRRUS

CIRROCUMULUS

CLOUD	NICKNAME	HEIGHT	APPEARANCE
CIRRUS	Mare's tails	4 miles or more	thin, feathery
CIRROCUMULUS	Mackerel sky	4 miles or more	small patches of white
CIRROSTRATUS	Bedsheet clouds	4 miles	thin, white sheets
STRATUS	High fogs	0 – 1 mile	low, gray blanket
CUMULUS	Cauliflowers	¼ – 4 miles	flat-bottomed, white puffy
CUMULONIMBUS	Thunderheads	¼ – 4 miles	mountains of heavy, dark clouds

CIRROSTRATUS

STRATUS

CUMULUS

CUMULONIMBUS

Wind

Wind is the movement of air. The surface of Earth, which is made up of different types of land and water, absorbs the Sun's heat unevenly. This uneven heating causes wind.

During the day, the air over land heats up faster than the air over the water. As the warm air over the land expands and rises, the heavier, cooler air rushes in to take its place. This movement creates winds. At night, the winds are reversed because the air cools more quickly over land than over water.

→ Hurricanes

A tropical storm is declared a hurricane when winds reach speeds of 74 miles per hour (m.p.h.). Wind speeds can exceed 190 m.p.h. in some hurricanes. The faster wind blows, the more destructive it gets. In the U.S., the official hurricane season is from June 1 to November 30, but hurricanes can happen any time of the year. Cyclones, typhoons and hurricanes are the same kind of tropical storm, but they are called different things in other parts of the world. Here's a look at how hurricanes are classified.

→ Tropical Storm: **Winds 40-73 m.p.h.**
→ Category 1 hurricane: **Winds 74–95 m.p.h.**
→ Category 2 hurricane: **Winds 96–110 m.p.h.**
→ Category 3 hurricane: **Winds 111–130 m.p.h.**
→ Category 4 hurricane: **Winds 131–155 m.p.h.**
→ Category 5 hurricane: **Winds greater than 155 m.p.h.**

Radar image of Hurricane Andrew hitting Florida

The devastation of Hurricane Katrina

What's in a Name?

Because several hurricanes can occur at the same time, officials assign short, distinctive names to the storms to avoid confusion among weather stations, coastal bases and ships at sea. A storm is given a name once its winds reach a speed of 40 m.p.h. These are the names that have been chosen by the National Hurricane Center for Atlantic storms in 2008 and 2009.

2008
Arthur
Bertha
Cristobal
Dolly
Edouard
Fay
Gustav
Hanna
Ike
Josephine
Kyle
Laura
Marco
Nana
Omar
Paloma
Rene
Sally
Teddy
Vicky
Wilfred

2009
Ana
Bill
Claudette
Danny
Erika
Fred
Grace
Henri
Ida
Joaquin
Kate
Larry
Mindy
Nicholas
Odette
Peter
Rose
Sam
Teresa
Victor
Wanda

TOP 5 TFK

Hurricanes that Caused the Most Damage

HURRICANE (YEAR)	LOCATION	CATEGORY	COST OF DAMAGE
1. Katrina (2005)	Louisiana, Mississippi	3	$96 billion
2. Andrew (1992)	Florida, Louisiana	5	$27 billion
3. Charley (2004)	Florida	4	$15 billion
4. Wilma (2005)	Florida	3	$14 billion
5. Ivan (2004)	Alabama, Florida	3	$14 billion

It's a Twister

A tornado is a dark, funnel-shaped cloud made up of violently churning winds that can reach speeds of up to 300 m.p.h. A tornado's width can measure from a few feet to a mile, and its track can extend from less than a mile to several hundred miles. Tornadoes generally travel in a northeast direction at speeds ranging from 20 to 60 m.p.h.

Tornadoes are most often caused by giant thunderstorms, called supercells. These highly powerful storms form when warm, moist air along the ground rushes upward, meeting cooler, drier air. As the rising warm air cools, the moisture it carries condenses, forming a massive thundercloud, sometimes growing to as much as 50,000 feet in height. Winds at different levels of the atmosphere feed the updraft and cause the formation of the tornado's characteristic funnel shape.

The Fujita scale classifies tornadoes according to the damage they cause.

Almost half of all tornadoes fall into the F1, or "moderate damage" category. These tornadoes reach speeds of 73 to 112 m.p.h. and can overturn automobiles and uproot trees.

Only about 1% of tornadoes are classified as F5, causing "incredible damage." With wind speeds in excess of 261 m.p.h., these storms can hurl houses and cars far and wide.

Most tornadoes form in the central and southern United States, where warm, humid air from the Gulf of Mexico collides with cool, dry air from the Rockies and Canada. This area, called tornado alley, extends from the Rocky Mountains to the Appalachians, and from Iowa and Nebraska to the Gulf of Mexico. Tornadoes can also take place in other places throughout the United States, Europe, Asia and Australia.

Did You Know?

The person who is believed to have been struck by lightning the most times is Roy C. Sullivan. This former park ranger survived seven different lightning strikes!

→ Thunderstorms

Nearly 1,800 thunderstorms are happening at any one moment around the world. That's 16 million a year!

You can estimate how many miles away a storm is by counting the number of seconds between the flash of lightning and the clap of thunder. Divide the number of seconds by five to get the distance in miles. The lightning is seen before the thunder is heard because light travels faster than sound.

Thunderstorms affect small areas when compared with hurricanes and winter storms. The typical thunderstorm is 15 miles in diameter and lasts an average of 30 minutes.

THUNDERSTORMS NEED THREE THINGS:

→ Moisture—to form clouds and rain

→ Unstable air—relatively warm air that can rise rapidly

→ Lift—fronts, sea breezes and mountains are capable of lifting air to help form thunderstorms

For information about lightning, see page 179.

? TFK MYSTERY PERSON

CLUE 1: I was born in Ireland in 1774. Today, my name is well known to meteorologists.

CLUE 2: As an admiral in the British Navy, I devised a scale to describe the force of the wind. The scale was based on the visible effects of wind on water and ships' sails.

CLUE 3: Used internationally, a slightly different version of this wind scale bears my name.

WHO AM I? (See Answer Key on page 242.)

Weather

241

ANSWERS

Page 23
MYSTERY PERSON: Maya Angelou

Page 27
MYSTERY PERSON: Emma Lazarus

Page 35
MYSTERY PERSON:
George Eastman

Page 91
MYSTERY PERSON:
Rachel Carson

Page 99
MYSTERY PERSON:
Amerigo Vespucci

Page 105 Secretary Elaine Chao could never be President. She was born in Taiwan.

Page 109
RIDING INTO HISTORY
1) 1964
2) False. Rosa Parks received the Presidential Medal of Freedom in 1996.
3) Rosa Parks challenged the seating laws in 1955. If you are reading this in 2007, that was 52 years ago. If you are reading this book in 2008, it was 53 years ago.

MYSTERY PERSON: Eleanor Roosevelt

Page 117
MYSTERY PERSON: Sir Roger Bannister

Page 119
MYSTERY PERSON: John Hancock

Page 134
MYSTERY PERSON: Venetia Burney

Page 141
LET YOUR FINGERS DO THE TALKING:
Stay cool this summer

MYSTERY PERSON: Anne Sullivan

Page 147
A MATH MESSAGE: "Early to bed and early to rise makes a man healthy, wealthy and wise"

MYSTERY PERSON: George Gallup

Page 151
MYSTERY PERSON: Julie Andrews

Page 157
MYSTERY PERSON: Fats Domino

Page 169
MYSTERY PERSON: President Dwight Eisenhower

Page 241
MYSTERY PERSON:
Sir Francis Beaufort

A

CREDITS

Front Cover: Associated Press, Paul Sakuma (iPhone); Columbia/Marvel/The Kobal Collection (Spider-Man); Bruce Fritz, U.S. Department of Agriculture/Agricultural Research Service (sunflower); U.S. Fish and Wildlife Service (polar bears); www.Shutterstock.com (chemist); Associated Press, Tammie Arroyo (*High School Musical* cast).

Back cover: www.Shutterstock.com (frog, Mt. Everest, boy, recycling bin); UN Photo/Andrea Brizzi (UN member flags); U.S. Department of Defense (Carrie Underwood).

Animals: 8: Associated Press, Iain Douglas Hamilton (elephant GPS collar); www.Shutterstock.com (elephants). 9: www.Shutterstock.com. 10: Associated Press, Roland Stoy (beefalo); www.Shutterstock.com (liger); Associated Press, Kamran Jebreili (cama). 11: U.S. Fish and Wildlife Service. 12: www.Shutterstock.com (crocodiles, sea urchin, tiger, jellyfish); U. S. Fish and Wildlife Service, Photo by John and Karen Hollingsworth (owl). 13: www.Shutterstock.com (hummingbird, mosquito, ostrich); Associated Press, Jessie Cohen/Photo Released by the National Zoo (cheetahs). 14: www.Shutterstock.com (starfish, hippopotamus); U.S. Fish and Wildlife Service (albatross). 15: Associated Press, Chen Fei (dinosaur exhibit); Associated Press, Renee Jean (*compsognathus*); Stan Osolinski/Oxford Scientific Collection/JupiterImages (*stegosaurus*); www.Shutterstock.com (T. rex bones, T. rex teeth).

Art: 16: iStockphoto.com (Versailles); SuperStock, Inc. (*Two Sisters on the Terrace*). 17: © 2008 Estate of Pablo Picasso/Artists Rights Society (ARS), New York (*The Three Musicians*; photo provided by SuperStock, Inc.); © 2008 Andy Warhol Foundation for the Visual Arts/ARS/SuperStock, Inc.); *Liz*; photo provided by New York Lowe Art Museum/SuperStock, Inc.). 18: Library of Congress, Prints and Photographs Division (basketmaker, Mathew Brady photograph); www.Shutterstock.com (mask, mosaic); New York Public Library, Humanities and Social Sciences Library, Art and Architecture Collection, Miriam and Ira D. Wallach Division of Art, Prints and Photographs, Astor, Lennox and Tilden Foundations (pottery); Christie's Images/SuperStock, Inc. (*The Thinker*). 19: Superstock, Inc. (Van Gogh's *Self Portrait in Grey Felt Hat*); Erich Lessing/Art Resource, NY (Klimt's *Adele Bloch-Bauer I*).

Books: 20: Associated Press, Ed Bailey (*Superman* covers); Associated Press, Koji Sasahara (*Yu-Gi-Oh*); *The Astonishing Life of Octavian Nothing, Traitor to the Nation, Volume 1: The Pox Party*, copyright © 2006 by M.T. Anderson. Reproduced by permission of the publisher, Candlewick Press, Inc., Cambridge, MA; *The Lady Grace Mysteries: Feud*, copyright © 2006 by Working Partners Ltd.; *Sammy Keyes and the Dead Giveaway* by Wendelin Van Draanen, illustration copyright © 2005 by Dan Yaccarino. 22: *The BFG* and *The Westing Game* covers reprinted by permission of Penguin Young Readers Group; *Eragon* by Christopher Paolini, jacket art copyright © 2003 by John Jude Palencar; *The Egypt Game*, copyright © 1967 by Zilpha Keatley Snyder; *Holes*, copyright © 1998 by Louis Sachar, Stepback cover illustration © 2000 by Bagram Ibatoulline; *Double Act*, copyright © 1995 by Jacqueline Wilson, illustrations ©1995 by Nick Sharratt and Sue Heap. 23: *Traitor* and *The Left Hand of Darkness* covers reprinted by permission of Penguin Young Readers Group; Associated Press, Nancy Robinson (Maya Angelou).

Buildings & Landmarks: 24–25: www.Shutterstock.com. 26: Library of Congress, Prints and Photographs Division (Golden Gate Bridge, Panama Canal); National Park Service (Lincoln Memorial, Washington Monument). 27: Library of Congress, Prints and Photographs Division (Disney Concert Hall, Falling Water, Emma Lazarus); National Park Service (Vietnam Memorial).

Calendars & Holidays: 28: www.Shutterstock.com. 29: Library of Congress, Prints and Photographs Division (Martin Luther King Jr., Christopher Columbus); www.Shutterstock.com (fireworks, turkey, pirate, Christmas tree). 30: www.Shutterstock.com. 31: www.Shutterstock.com (*hamantaschen*, Mardi Gras); Associated Press, Dexter Cruez (Esala Perahera).

Computers & the Internet: 32: U.S. Army photo (ENIAC); www.Shutterstock.com (Apple II, floppy disk, Bill Gates, laptop, iPod); Associated Press (Steve Jobs, MySpace founders); Al Luckow (Steve Wozniak); Google (Google office). 33: Associated Press, Greg Baker (China); Associated Press, Alexandre Meneghini (Brazil); www.Shutterstock.com (computer screen, child at computer, cell phone). 34: National Wildlife Federation (www.nwf.org/kids/); NASA (man on the moon); *Sports Illustrated Kids* (www.sikids.com); www.Shutterstock.com (computer screen). 35: Associated Press, Mark Avery (video games); Library of Congress, Prints and Photographs Division (George Eastman).

Countries of the World: 36: Associated Press, Boris Heger. 69: www.Shutterstock.com (Norway); UN Photo/Evan Schneider (Niger). 70–84: Maps by Joe Lertola. 85: UN Photo/Andrea Brizzi (UN member flags); www.Shutterstock.com (UN building).

Environment & Energy: 86: U.S. Fish and Wildlife Service, Photo by Dave Olsen. 87: www.Shutterstock.com (oil drum); DOE photo (wind farm, electric switchyard); U.S. Army Corps of Engineers (hydroelectric dam). 88: U.S. Fish and Wildlife Service (air pollution, garbage); Associated Press, Natacha Pisarenko (glacier); www.Shutterstock.com (L.A. smog). 89: Associated Press, Rainer Klostermeier (Chernobyl); www.Shutterstock.com (landfill). 90: www.Shutterstock.com (recycling bins); Associated Press, Steffen Schmidt (plastic recycling). 91: Associated Press, Michael Okoniewski (paper recycling); www.Shutterstock.com (faucet); U.S. Fish and Wildlife Service (Rachel Carson).

Fashion: 92: Library of Congress, Prints and Photographs Division (1900s–1930s); Associated Press (1940s, 1950s, 1960s, 1970s woman); National Archives and Records Administration (1970s students). 93: Associated Press, Michael Tweed (1980s Cyndi Lauper); Associated Press, Mark Elias (1980s Christie Brinkley); Associated Press, Kevork Djansezian (1990s); Associated Press, Jennifer Graylock (2000s); Library of Congress, Prints and Photographs Division (laborer); Warner Bros./The Kobal Collection (James Dean); Associated Press, Charles Bennett (Oprah Winfrey); Associated Press, Talaya Centeno (skinny jeans).

Geography: 94: www.Shutterstock.com. 95: The Granger Collection, New York (Lewis and Clark); www.Shutterstock.com (The Nile, Lake Baikal); Library of Congress, Prints and Photographs Division (Francisco Pizarro, Robert Peary). 96: FEMA/Adam Dubrowa (earthquake damage); www.Shutterstock.com (tsunami damage). 97: U.S. Department of the Interior, U.S. Geological Survey (Mauna Loa); www.Shutterstock.com (Krakatau). 98: www.Shutterstock.com (Mount Everest, time zone clocks); The Granger Collection, New York (Edmund Hillary and Tenzing Norgay). 99: www.Shutterstock.com (political map, road map); National Weather Service, NOAA (climate map); U.S. Central Intelligence Agency (economic map); U.S. Department of the Interior, U.S. Geological Survey (topographic map); U.S. Fish and Wildlife Service (physical map); Library of Congress, Prints and Photographs Division (Vespucci).

Government: 100: Library of Congress, Prints and Photographs Division (Continental Congress); National Archives and Records Administration (Constitution). 101: Library of Congress, Prints and Photographs Division (slavery, women's suffrage); Associated Press, Charles Tasnadi (flag burning). 102: Official Congressional Portraits. 103: U.S. Department of Defense (George W. Bush); U.S. Department of Defense (Dick Cheney); U.S. Department of Agriculture (Mike Johanns); U.S. Department of Commerce (Carlos Gutierrez); U.S. Department of Defense (Robert Gates); U.S. Department of Education (Margaret Spellings); U.S. Department of Energy (Samuel Bodman); U.S. Department of Health and Human Services (Michael Leavitt); Department of Homeland Security (Michael Chertoff); U.S. Department of Housing and Urban Development (Alphonso Jackson); U.S. Department of the Interior (Dirk Kempthorne); U.S. Department of Justice (Alberto Gonzales); U.S. Department of Labor (Elaine Chao); U.S. Department of State (Condoleezza Rice); U.S. Department of Transportation (Mary Peters); U.S. Department of the Treasury (Henry Paulson, Jr.); U.S. Department of Veteran's Affairs (Jim Nicholson). 104: Official Supreme Court Photo/SupremeCourtHistory.org (Supreme Court); Library of Congress, Prints and Photographs Division (Supreme Court building, Dred Scott); Associated Press, Rick Bowmer (protest). 105: National Archives and Records Administration (Truman); William J. Clinton Presidential Library (Clinton). 106–107: Library of Congress, Prints and Photographs Division. 108: U.S. Department of Defense (John Warner); Library of Congress, Prints and Photographs Division (Hiram Revels, Jeannette Rankin, Sandra Day O'Conner); Associated Press, Greg Gibson (Clinton); Associated Press, Haraz N. Ghanbari (Keith Ellison). 109: Associated Press, Gene Herrick (Rosa Parks's arrest); Time & Life Picture/Getty Images (bus boycott); LBJ Library photo by Cecil Stoughton (Johnson); William J. Clinton Presidential Library (Clinton and Parks); Library of Congress, Prints and Photographs Division (John Henry Eaton, Eleanor Roosevelt).

Health: 110: Dr. Brian Orr (Courtesy of Dr. Orr); www.Shutterstock.com (thermometer, boy). 111–113: www.Shutterstock.com. 114: U.S. Department of Agriculture. 115: Digital Stock. 116: www.Shutterstock.com. 117: www.Shutterstock.com (basketball, inline skating, karate, football); Associated Press (Roger Bannister).

History: 118: Associated Press, Kevin Wolf (Martin Luther King Jr. memorial); Library of Congress, Prints and Photographs Division (King and Malcom X); LBJ Library photo by Yoichi R. Okamoto (King and Johnson). 119: Library of Congress, Prints and Photographs Division (Douglas, Lincoln, Ford, Model T, Hancock); Associated Press (Ricky Nelson); www.Shutterstock.com (records). 120: www.Shutterstock.com (Sphinx, Stonehenge); The Granger Collection, New York (Confucius).

121: The Granger Collection, New York. 122–123: Library of Congress, Prints and Photographs Division. 124: Library of Congress, Prints and Photographs Division (Henson, Titanic); UN Photo (apartheid). 125: Associated Press, Mark Avery (Tiananmmen Square); Associated Press, Lionel Cironneau (Berlin Wall); U.S. Army, Staff Sgt. Samuel Bendet (Iraq). 126–127: Library of Congress, Prints and Photographs Division. 128: Library of Congress, Prints and Photographs Division (suffragette, Rosa Parks); NASA (moonwalk). 129: White House photo by Eric Draper (inauguration); FEMA (Ground Zero; Katrina flooding).

Inventions: 130: Themeaddicts, Inc. (mirror); UGOBE (Pleo); Koichi Kamoshida/Getty Images (Murata Boy). 131: Robert Visser/Photopress Washington (Aqua Sciences); Julie Chytrowksky (hypoallergenic kittens); www.Shutterstock.com (popsicle, cookies, potato chips); Structured Solutions II LLC (Wovel). 132: Library of Congress, Prints and Photographs Division (Braille, phonograph, bicycle, x-ray); New York Public Library, Humanities and Social Sciences Library, Photography Collection, Miriam and Ira D. Wallach Division of Art, Prints and Photographs, Astor, Lennox and Tilden Foundations (plane). 133: Library of Congress, Prints and Photographs Division (toaster); www.Shutterstock.com (helicopter, rollerblades, space shuttle, CD, camera phone).

Kids of the World: 134: Salma Siddique/Unicef (Dolly Akter); Ami Vitale/Getty Images (Kishan); New York Public Library, Humanities and Social Sciences Library, Art and Architecture Collection, Miriam and Ira D. Wallach Division of Art, Prints and Photographs, Astor, Lennox and Tilden Foundations (Venetia Burney). 135: www.Shutterstock.com. 136: Associated Press, Kent Gilbert (Costa Rica photos); www.Shutterstock.com (French children). 137: www.Shutterstock.com.

Language: 138: www.Shutterstock.com (signs); Associated Press (spelling bee). 139: www.Shutterstock.com (Santa, scuba diver); Digital Stock (orange). 140: www.Shutterstock.com. 141: Library of Congress, Prints and Photographs Division (Anne Sullivan); www.Shutterstock.com (teddy bear).

Math: 142–146: www.Shutterstock.com. 147: www.Shutterstock.com (unicorn); Associated Press (George Gallup).

Money: 148: www.Shutterstock.com. 149: www.Shutterstock.com (Cambodia); Digital Stock (milk).

Movies & Television: 150: Associated Press, Tammie Arroyo (*High School Musical* cast); NBC-TV/The Kobal Collection (*The Office*). 151: Associated Press, Lawrence Jackson (Julie Andrews); www.Shutterstock.com (remote control, television). 152: *Shrek 2* ® & © 2004 DreamWorks Animation LLC, used with permission of DreamWorks Animation LLC (*Shrek 2*); 20th Century Fox/The Kobal Collection (*Night at the Museum*); Universal/The Kobal Collection (*E.T.*); Walt Disney/The Kobal Collection (*Pirates of the Caribbean*); Touchstone/The Kobal Collection/Ron Batzdorff (*Flightplan*); 153: Associated Press, Mark J. Terrill (Jennifer Hudson); New Zealand Film Comm./The Kobal Collection (Keisha Castle-Hughes); The Kobal Collection (Katharine Hepburn); United Artists/The Kobal Collection (John Wayne).

Music: 154: Associated Press, Danny Moloshok (top); Associated Press, Tammie Arroyo (bottom). 155: Associated Press, Jennifer Graylock (Daniel Radcliffe); Associated Press, Tammie Arroyo (Jon Heder); Associated Press, Steve C. Wilson (Hannah Teter); Associated Press, Mark Avery (Jojo); The Kobal Collection (Michael Jackson); Associated Press (Elvis); Associated Press, Mark Lennihan (Gwen Stefani). 156: Associated Press, Richard Drew (Mary J. Blige); Associated Press (The Beatles). 157: Associated Press, Jennifer Graylock (Chamillionaire); Associated Press, Reed Saxon (Black Eyed Peas); Associated Press, Matt Sayles (Kelly Clarkson); U.S. Department of Defense (Carrie Underwood); Associated Press (Fats Domino).

Mythology: 158: The Granger Collection, New York. 159: The Granger Collection, New York (Athena); Peter Willi/SuperStock, Inc. (Hermes). 160: The Granger Collection, New York (Medusa, Hydra); Bridgeman Art Library, London/SuperStock, Inc. (Cerberus); Alinari/Art Resource, NY (Cyclops).

Presidents: 162: www.Shutterstock.com (White House); Library of Congress, Prints and Photographs Division (presidential portraits). 163–169: Library of Congress, Prints and Photographs Division.

Religion: 170–171: www.Shutterstock.com. 172: www.Shutterstock.com (Nativity scene, dreidel, Buddhist monks, Amish family); Associated Press (Ramadan); Associated Press, Anjum Naveed (Hijab dress); Associated Press, Bob Child (Orthodox Jew). 173: Library of Congress, Prints and Photographs Division (Mary Baker Eddy); Associated Press, Haraz N. Ghanbari (Bishop Schori); www.Shutterstock.com (Ganesh).

Science: 174: Stephanie Abramowicz ("terror bird" drawing); Associated Press, Jeff Gage (Richard Webber); www.Shutterstock.com (fossil). 175: U.S. Fish and Wildlife Service (botanist); www.Shutterstock.com (chemist, DNA); U.S. Department of Agriculture, Agricultural Research Service (microbiologist). 176: U.S. Department of Agriculture, Agricultural Research Service (bacteria, E. coli, algae, fungi, poinsettia, chicken); NASA (amoeba); U. S. Fish and Wildlife Service, Photo by Charles H. Smith (toad). 177: www.Shutterstock.com (atom, hydrogen peroxide, salt shaker); iStockphoto.com (sapphire). 178: Library of Congress, Prints and Photographs Division (Isaac Newton, Albert Einstein); New York Public Library, Humanities and Social Sciences Library, Manuscripts and Archives Division, Astor, Lennox and Tilden Foundations (Louis Pasteur); NASA (Hubble telescope). 179–181: www.Shutterstock.com.

Space: 182–186: NASA. 187: NASA (surface of the moon); Associated Press (Edwin Hubble); Library of Congress, Prints and Photographs Division (Galileo). 188: NASA (constellation photographs); Library of Congress, Prints and Photographs Division (Hercules and Gemini illustrations); The Granger Collection, New York (Orion and Aquarius illustrations). 189: The Granger Collection, New York.

Sports: 190: Associated Press, Ronen Zilberman. 191: Associated Press, Amy Sancetta (Peyton Manning); Associated Press, Ross D. Franklin (Chris Leak). 192: Associated Press, Steve Mitchell (Ryan Howard); Associated Press, Paul Battaglia (Johan Santana); Associated Press, Amy Sancetta (World Series 2006); Associated Press, Gene J. Puskar (Cody Walker). 193: Associated Press, Tom Hood (Diana Taurasi); Associated Press, Tom Mihalek (Allen Iverson); Associated Press, Eric Gay (Miami Heat); Associated Press, Rick Bowmer (Josh Shipp). 194: Associated Press, Michael Probst (World Cup final); Associated Press, Kevork Djansezian (U.S.A. vs. Mexico); Associated Press, Paul Chiasson (Rod Brind'Amour). 195: Associated Press, Kevork Djansezian (Li Ya); Associated Press, Lionel Cironneau (Cecile Alzina); Associated Press, Amy Sancetta (figure skating medalists); Associated Press, Rusty Kennedy (Monique Hennagan); Associated Press, Matt Dunham (Shani Davis); Associated Press, David Guttenfelder (Andreas Ditter and Martin Marinov). 196: Associated Press, Ross D. Franklin (auto racing); Associated Press, Don Petersen (Jimmie Johnson); Associated Press, Srdjan Ilic (Fernando Alonso). 197: Associated Press, Gautam Singh (kite fighting); Associated Press, Peter Dejong (Floyd Landis); www.Shutterstock.com (golf ball, ice skate). 198: Associated Press, Claudio Scaccini (Renate Götschi); Associated Press, Andreas Schaad (Jasey Jay Anderson). 199: Associated Press, Mark J. Terrill (Laura Perkins); Associated Press, Nathan Bilow (Chris Burandt); Associated Press, Dave Caulkin (Amelie Mauresmo); Associated Press, Peter Brenneken (Roger Federer). 200: Associated Press (Alexander Artemev); Associated Press, Matt Dunham (Alicia Sacramone, Sherri Steinhauer). 201: Associated Press, Al Grillo (Iditarod); Associated Press, Al Behrman (Preakness).

United States: 202: www.Shutterstock.com. 203: U.S. Census Bureau. 204: Library of Congress, Prints and Photographs Division (Great Seal, Uncle Sam); www.Shutterstock.com (American flag, bald eagle, Liberty Bell). 205: www.Shutterstock.com. 206: Library of Congress, Prints and Photographs Division (Boston Light); www.Shutterstock.com (Harvard). 207: www.Shutterstock.com. 209: Joe Lertola. 210: iStockphoto.com (yellowhammer); www.Shutterstock.com (dog sled). 211–212: www.Shutterstock.com. 213: www.Shutterstock.com (ladybug); Library of Congress, Prints and Photographs Division (Prudence Crandall). 214–217: www.Shutterstock.com. 218: www.Shutterstock.com (goldenrod); U. S. Fish and Wildlife Service, Photo by Gary M. Stolz (pelican). 219: www.Shutterstock.com. 220: www.Shutterstock.com (chickadee); U. S. Fish and Wildlife Service, Photo by Gary M. Stolz (turtle). 221–222: www.Shutterstock.com. 223: U. S. Fish and Wildlife Service, Photo by John and Karen Hollingsworth (western meadowlark); U. S. Fish and Wildlife Service, Photo by Beth Jackson (desert tortoise). 224–225: www.Shutterstock.com. 226: U. S. Fish and Wildlife Service, Photo by Ginger Corbin (dogwood); Public domain (buffalo sculpture). 227–231: www.Shutterstock.com. 232: U. S. Fish and Wildlife Service, Photo by Lee Karney (hermit thrush); www.Shutterstock.com (oyster shell). 233–235: www.Shutterstock.com.

Weather: 236: Peter West, National Science Foundation. 237: www.Shutterstock.com (drought); FEMA (flood); National Oceanic & Atmospheric Administration (avalanche). 238: www.Shutterstock.com (thermometer). 239: National Oceanic & Atmospheric Administration (hail); National Oceanic & Atmospheric Administration. 240: National Oceanic & Atmospheric Administration (hurricane over Florida); FEMA (hurricane aftermath); Operational Significant Event Imagery, NOAA (radar image). 241: National Oceanic & Atmospheric Administration (tornado, lightning); New York Public Library, Humanities and Social Sciences Library, Art and Architecture Collection, Miriam and Ira D. Wallach Division of Art, Prints and Photographs, Astor, Lennox and Tilden Foundations (Beaufort).

TIME FOR KIDS
online

Check out go timeforkids.com, your online news, homework helper and exploration destination!

Look for news, polls, interactive features and games.

Go Around the World with **Time For Kids** and learn about different cultures, languages and more.

Search the best kid-recommended websites to help you with your homework.

Use our step-by-step guides, idea organizers, checklists and more to help you write winning nonfiction papers.

Millions of kids each week go to **FACTMONSTER.COM** for tons of facts, puzzles and games, cool features and homework help!

Get the facts on animals, the planets, presidents, movies and more.

Tips and ideas for creating a spectacular science project.

How smart are you? Take a quiz on flags, ice cream, Harry Potter or Lemony Snicket.

Your opinion counts! Vote in our fun polls and see what other kids think.

 Webby Award Winner for Best Kids' Site

www.FactMonster.com
a Pearson Education Company